I0791588

# NEXT

# 2020

## Avoiding Reality
### Choosing the Wrong One
Read it, Accept It, Leave It, but Read It

# NEXT
## TRUMP 2020
## Avoiding Reality
### Choosing the Wrong One
### Read it, Accept It, Leave It, but Read It

\- \-



*Books may be purchased at www.Amazon.com*

---

*AMAZON Kindle eBook Title ID:* ASIN: B083136GV2
https://www.amazon.com/dp/B083136GV2
*AMAZON Paperback Title ID:* ASIN: 1672476917
www.amazon.com/dp/1672476917

*Jacked Design & Illustrations © Guebres Studios*

*ISBN-13:* 9781672476911 *(sc)*
*ISBN-10:* 1672476917 (ebk)

Printed in the United States of America
By AMAZON – date: 12/22/2019

*It is said, you know people by their deeds,*
*so their words mean very little.*
*It is the actions of people, not their words,*
*which most clearly define reality.*

*"Az ikh vel zayn vi yener,*
*ver vet zayn vi ikh?"*
**"If I am to be like someone else,**
**who will be like me?"**
**"If I am not for myself,**
**who will be for me?**
**"If I am only for myself,**
**what am I?**
**"And if not now, when?""**
~ Hillel

*"Suppose you were an idiot,*
*and suppose you were a member of Congress;*
*but I repeat myself."*
~ Mark Twain

*"Constantly choosing the lesser of two evils*
*is still choosing evil."*
~ Jerry Garcia

*"The cleverest lies are those*
*we are already inclined to believe."*

*"When the whole world is running towards a cliff, he who*
*is running in the opposite direction appears to have lost his*
*mind."* ~ C. S. Lewis

# CHAPTERS


| | | | |
|---|---|---|---|
| 1 | CHAPTER 01 | .... | *Americans* |
| 17 | CHAPTER 02 | .... | *Demographics* |
| 31 | CHAPTER 03 | .... | *Think Kosher* |
| 43 | CHAPTER 04 | .... | *Trump Opposition* |
| 57 | CHAPTER 05 | .... | *ICE* |
| 73 | CHAPTER 06 | .... | *THE Elephant* |
| 89 | CHAPTER 07 | .... | *Crisis Time* |
| 105 | CHAPTER 08 | .... | *Reality* |
| 123 | CHAPTER 09 | .... | *Greta Thunberg* |
| 137 | CHAPTER 10 | .... | *Climate Migrants* |
| 151 | CHAPTER 11 | .... | *Ukraine* |
| 177 | CHAPTER 12 | .... | *Joseph Biden* |
| 191 | CHAPTER 13 | .... | *19 & 57* |
| 207 | CHAPTER 14 | .... | *Consider* |

# CHAPTER ONE – Americans

*"[Democrats] seemed to be hoping for a national crisis for the sake of their own politics."*
**~ Senator Mitch McConnell, May 2019**

Be neutral, be objective, speak in the third person and then you an avoid responsibility.  But, what happens when a third party is the first-person because life interjects itself into that narrative?

On 28 Feb 2015, in Season1: Episode6 of *"The Good Witch,"* a principle character casually mentions how another character – the female town mayor – *"is going all Donald Trump on me with"* a newly found obsession for real estate development.  When if the history of the nation, or any nation, was its future leader the basis of a symbolic summary of behavior or economic renovation?  Has any nation ever had a leader whose very name was symbolic of the drive for economic development in a political context, when they, themselves were not politically active?

In another episode of *"The Good Witch,"* we hear a warning that befits those who promote impeachment over the power of democratic voting – {S1:E9} from *Sun Tzu, The Art of War, "who wishes to fight must first count the cost"*.  A common problem for those who seek impeachment – the Stock Market and economy frown on the destabilizing effect; as much as he deserved it when Nixon was investigated, until his resignation, the stock market lost 45-percent of its value.

Those familiar with the first six volumes of this book series are aware that TRUMP CARD book series focuses on explaining how Trump is turning the "stampeding herd"; how he managed to take charge of the Republican Party; how he managed to keep the Obama rally going and thus create the longest economic recovery in American history – the last time the economy experienced a 120 month expansion began March 1991, as a recovery from the global recession which had begun in July 1990.

It was an ascension of Vice President George H. W. Bush to the Oval Office, with his dutiful continuation of what, as the candidate opposing Reagan, he called *"Voodoo Economics,"* then came to accept as Reagan's political partner cum successor, quickly set the stage for America to be sucked into the global economic problems – problems like those created in Britain by the voters determining they wanted a Russian sponsored BREXIT. Of course, GHW was voted out after one term, and Bill Clinton showed the nation could prosper, have a balanced budget that produced record surpluses.

But then the voters determined they wanted another Bush – one who gained office by Florida hanging chads (counted by his brother) and a slim one-vote electoral victory of 271 electoral votes to Al Gore's 266 (with one elector abstaining). Of course, in 2016, the legitimacy of Trump's 304 electoral vote victory over Hillary Clinton (with 2 abstaining) resulted in yells of a rigged election, even though it gave Trump a 34 vote margin to the one vote that gave us Bush, a never-ending war and the Great Recession.

Maybe both elections were rigged – they have something in common. Neither conform to the requirements necessary to be considered among *Jonathon's POTUS Cousins* {JPC}; moreover, except for President Marin Van Buren, for whom even '*Burkes Presidential Families of the United States of America*' lacks the confirming data – every POTUS is a descendant of five daughters of Hugh De Kevelioc of Cyfeiliog, the 5th Earl of Chester; most are descendant from two or more of them.

Many shake their heads and reject a reality common to all animal species – a weird reality associated with Biblical Marriage Laws, and the science of "*eugenics*" which many associated with the Nazi "*Master Race*", but in really it refers animal husbandry as a science whose goal is the improvement of the population through a focus on increasing the occurrence of desirable hereditary traits while reducing detrimental ones. Since this could mean selective abortion, Right-wing Republicans use opposition to abortion as an excuse that masks their opposition to anything that will improve the population or the quality of life of an individual. Counterparts of the Right-wing are the Reagan-Democrats, who also oppose improving the human condition.

The cognitive dissonance, which swept the globe in 2016, is likely to fill history books when historians can finally get a grip on Trump's trade and immigration programs within the historical context. Bush produced the environment that allowed destruction of the World Trade Center, an ongoing Middle East War, the rise Jihadist power, and finalized his Administration with the Great Recession he worked so diligently to create – will GW be outdone by

Trump, or will the longest economic rally in American history continue, despite all who wish to see it end?

We should note, historically, exception for Trump, Republicans love recessions and cause them whenever possible; with the rise of Trump, it seems there is an element among the Democrats who wish to assume the mantel of responsibility for economic collapse – we call them The Reagan-Democrats and they are, like Reagan, proponents of open borders and full amnesty for those of Hispanic Origin who chose to violate Immigration Laws.

Naturally, the Reagan-Democrats expressed opposition to having "Citizenship Status" asked on the 2020 Census. The basis for reinserting that question into the census was in 26 March 2018 memo by Secretary Wilbur Ross to Under Secretary for Economic Affairs Karen Dunn Kelley, stating: *"As you know, on December 12, 2017, the Department of Justice ("DOJ") requested that the Census Bureau reinstate a citizenship question on the decennial census to provide census block level citizenship voting age population ("CVAP") data that are not currently available from government survey data ("DOJ request"). DOJ and the courts use CVAP data for determining violations of Section 2 of the Voting Rights Act ("VRA"), and having these data at the census block level will permit more effective enforcement of the Act. Section 2 protects minority population voting rights."*

Thus, the actual intent or purpose of the objection appears to be to deprive the Courts of *"data for determining violations of Section 2 of the Voting Rights Act."*

They lie by telling the truth, and assert that a lower count affects Constitutionally Representation – and they lie with truth by saying illegals will not respond to any Census which asks about citizenship. But that ignores the reality that other questions, and the very act of self-identification to a government agency, are also in play and will prevent illegals from Red Flagging themselves.

The "Citizenship Status" question serves to determine the number of eligible voters in a district. The form also asks about the language spoken in the home, phone number, exact date of birth and name. Note, within the Government computer network, and without violating privacy, the government can verify if the named individual has a Social Security Number. That is sufficient to Red Flag illegals and, given we are dealing with Latin American Border violations, the standard question about "Language spoken" provide another Red Flag – one that would be negated if there was a "Citizenship Status" question response of either "Legal Resident" or "Citizen".

There will be a variation in the population count, caused by illegals playing it safe and avoiding Red Flagging themselves or their families by responding to any format Census. The Citizenship Question is necessary for Court enforcement of *"VRA"*, and since this was known to both President Trump and Census authorities, on 11 July 2019, Trump adopted the alternative that had been suggested by the Census Bureau. By so doing, President Trump set the Reagan-Democrats up for exposure of their illegal intentions, while also getting the required Citizenship data via an Executive Order directing Federal agencies to share Citizenship related data with the Census Bureau.

Interestingly, given the Census requires name, address, and exact date of birth, the Social Security Administration can verify the existence of a Social Security Number – without disclosing the actual number, but with the added ability to state if the person is alive or dead, and so reveal any fraudulent use their identity.

So it is that those who are in the United States illegally and undocumented are unlikely to knowingly allow themselves to be included in the Census; those using someone else's documentation will risk exposure of any fraudulent use of documentation. None of which will alter the apportionment – since the illegals will likely be removed via deportation.

In making his announcement, Trump stated, *"It is essential that we have a clear breakdown of the number of citizens and non-citizens that make up the U.S. populations."* Naturally, those who seek to engage in violations of Voters Rights or outright voter fraud, and those, as has been alleged about the Russians, seeking to interfere with the election process, have, and will continue to, oppose the Citizenship Question or anything that will establish the number of lawful voters.

When the House passed the Permanent Apportionment Act of 1929 and fixed the number of Representatives at 435, it fixed the level of dilution any significant changes in population would have on Representation. Almost exactly 90-years to the day before the Census query became a Trump controversy, on 18 June 1929, the Permanent Apportionment Act became law – any apportionment issues were resolved in 1941 when it was determined that each state would "*have a minimum of one member in the U.S. House of Representatives, and then the apportionment calculation divides the remaining 385 seats among the 50 states.*"

The mathematical game is then played, which excludes any living in the District of Columbia, and progressively allocates 50-seats at a time among various populations within the states. But this hides the mathematical reality that the more the population grows, the more diluted the individual voices – with smaller states having the greatest voice.

Excluding citizenship status means not knowing how many eligible voters there are; which means the non-voter immigrant districts take on the quality of a low population state, but with the benefit of receiving greater monetary Federal benefits per legal voter – because the allocation of funds is based on population. It is also a nice way to create a voter fraud environment – if you do not know how many eligible voters there are, you have no way of knowing when there are fraudulent voter registrations or votes.

The Constitution not only dictates an allocation of seats in the House of Representatives based on the census and, by extension, also determines the Electoral College votes. Allocation formulas are the basis for drafting district lines for congressional and state legislative seats – allegedly it should ensure that various communities are fairly represented, but it provides a neat form of Gerrymandering by placing foreign-born non-voting individuals into districts where the lower number of legal voters allows easier manipulation of control by the Party controlling those legal voters. You object to a citizenship status question so you can both distort the vote and receive more federal funds for distribution among the legal voters.

In June 2019, the Bureau of Labor Statistics reported that the unemployment rate was at 3.6 percent, with analysis by Steve Rattner, a Bloomberg L.P. money manager, pointing out, if Americans were more willing to relocate for jobs, it would be even lower. There are also indications of problems yet to come – the long-term vs short-term interest rate yield curve is inverted, which means there is a home buyer opportunity because all interest rates have fallen and a 30-year mortgage is cheaper than a 15-year loan; which also means home equity loans are a bargain.

What happens when your opponents behave like you, echo your

actions and actively use the tactics you had previously used against them?

It is what Mitch McConnell was complaining about with the Mueller Report aftermath with its return to the Russian puppets phishing for justifications for impeachment, and Mueller himself breaking his silence to infer criminal behavior which he could not identify and enumerate in his report. So long as the President can be attacked, the government can be paralyzed and the outcome of the 2020 election manipulated.

Impeach the President and/or the Attorney General. Pass legislation in the House or Senate – let it rot in the other branch.

As has been stated throughout the Trump Card series, and, then repeated by McConnell on 7 May 2019: *"Russia sought out to sow discord. But on that front, given the left's total fixation on delegitimizing the president ... I'm afraid the Russians hardly need to lift a finger."*

Based on CIA memos dating as far back as the Kennedy Era, the Russians have been perfecting their propaganda system to the point where they have now organized their *"Circular Firing Squad"* puppets into a functional formation composed of social media, conventional media, and politicians.

The beauty of a *"Circular Firing Squad"* is found in the fact that every miss is a potential hit that will wound or kill a member of the firing squad. One characteristic of the modern American political scene emerges from the simplicity by which the media is manipulated into convincing political leaders to kill each other off – when they are not actively working to undermine the nation.

One aspect of the firing squad is the use of algorithms to define what "information" is distributed to users as "newsworthy." Instead of providing objective information, viewers are provided with data based on either "what they want to see" based on users' viewing habits or on high "hit rates" achieved by stories clicked on by either large numbers of individuals, or robot-clicks that inflate the viewership to promote influence – propaganda driven by the idea that others are interested.

Algorithm-based presentations are, by design, not tainted by such trivial concepts as Truth and Honesty, they promote fake news stories, provide misinformation, serve as clickbait, and are fully consistent with the tabloid journalistic idea *"if it bleeds it leads."* Sensationalistic stories are preferable to factual news, or things which are otherwise well known.

For those who do not grasp the reality, we have the New York Times article of 8 May 2019: *"Decade in the Red: Trump Tax Figures Show Over $1 Billion in Business Losses."* This shocking revelation was presented as a new discovery. Trump had boasted of the loss – it was an example of Graduate School Level, Master's degree, Tax Accounting. Comically, it was mentioned on page 66 of Book One of this series – published 8 April 2017, which means 25-months before the Times "revelation":

> *"Those same debt-based policies financed a global military and underwrote a tax code which allowed their billionaire President to boast he hadn't paid Federal taxes for at least a decade – all because he had taken a 'paper loss' of one billion dollars when he was negotiating and disputing a divorce settlement with his first wife."*

Of course, Trump addressed the issue with a pair of Tweets on Twitter:

> *"Real estate developers in the 1980's & 1990's, more than 30 years ago, were entitled to massive write-offs and depreciation which would, if one was actively building, show losses and tax losses in almost all cases. Much was non- monetary. Sometimes considered 'tax shelter,' ...*

> *"... you would get it by building, or even buying. You always wanted to show losses for tax purposes....almost all real estate developers did - and often re-negotiate with banks, it was sport. Additionally, the very old information put out is a highly inaccurate Fake News hit job!"*

Unlike the Reaganomics which has proved so popular with professional politicians seeking "PAC money" and NYT reporters, Trump understands there is a real difference between paper loses and negative cash flow. Politicians and their pet reporters do not think about the future or the consequences of irrational spending. They are the Shakespearean characters of Antonio and  Bassanio – who routinely borrow money for business or pleasure, and often cheat the lender who charges interest.

These fools have no concept of a secure cash flow and paper

losses. They are politicians who run up the National Debt with the idea that inflation will erase it, will, in the Reagan era explanation, "monetized the debt" – cheat the lender by paying back money of lesser purchasing power than that borrowed.

Of course, introduce someone like Trump, someone who keeps inflation in check, and thinks in terms of cash flow (so will speak of Trade War Tariffs as bringing billions into the treasury to offset tax reductions) and the crooks get screwed; they get angry, want him removed and replaced with an incompetent individual.

They must impeach him, and restore the algorithmic basis of their short-term political thinking; they must restore the long-term detrimental objectives which increased the National Debt while undermining Social Security and other programs designed to help the citizens they are supposed to represent – and might if they were not lining their own pockets in the certain knowledge that they will be dead before the fruits of their evil are manifested.

The basis of algorithmic engineering is a technology designed to promote commercial business models based on user preference or bias. This reduces propaganda to a simple formula that can be reused. In previous books in the series, I mentioned that Trump's #MAGA slogan had its origins in Ronald Reagan's successful use of the exact same slogan in 1980.

Retasking successful campaigns is a longstanding practice in advertising. In the age of algorithmically filtered data bubbles, the ability to use misinformation propaganda for profit has taken on a dual role by exploiting users' limited attention spans to enhance advertising revenues, while disseminating misinformation based on the dictum: "*The greatest Liar has his Believers; and it often happens, that if a Lie be believed only for an Hour, it has done its Work, and there is no farther occasion for it.*" [Jonathan Swift, November 1710]

Of course, as every journalist knows, that hour is symbolic of a news cycle. Of course, Swift was speaking 300-years ago and in that time the expression evolved and roughly 200-years later we find a similar concept attributed to Mark Twain: "*A lie travels around the globe while the truth is putting on its shoes.*"

To which is added the basis all social media propaganda: "*Falsehood flies, and the Truth comes limping after it; so that when Men come to be undeceived, it is too late; the Jest is over, and the Tale has had its Effect...*"

To see this effect, we can look to page 4 of the Mueller Report to learn the names of those responsible for the discord which has Congress happily attacking Trump while ignoring their responsibilities to those who place them in power:

*"The Internet Research Agency (IRA) carried out the earliest Russian interference operations identified by the investigation – a social media campaign designed to provoke and amplify political and social discord in the United States. The IRA was based in St. Petersburg, Russia, and received funding from Russian oligarch Yevgeniy Prigozhin and companies he controlled."*

In looking at the *"Jest"* or the provocation of *"political and social discord"*, we can see Trump avoids using broad-brushes and prefers a narrow focus to deliver the message that will trigger the foolishness of his opponents. He intentionally encourages and/or allows, his opponents to broaden it and, by so doing, splatter the paint on themselves.

On 14 July, Trump vaguely attacked one member of the four-member female group labeling themselves *"The Squad"* and the other three immediately made themselves the intended target. It is an action or reaction which weakens the group because they are prone to personalize.

Interestingly, Trump predicted the reaction with a 14 July {8:02 AM} tweet saying: *"Whenever confronted, they call their adversaries, including Nancy Pelosi, "RACIST." Their disgusting language....."*

Then, twenty-five minutes later, having dutifully given the proper notice that he knew what was to come, he posted the tweet that triggered The Squad and claimed control of the news cycle: *"So interesting to see "Progressive" Democrat Congresswomen, who originally came from countries whose governments are a complete and total catastrophe, the worst, most corrupt and inept anywhere in the world (if they even have a functioning government at all), now loudly......"*

Think about the events or comments surrounding the June passage of a $4.6 BILLION administration-friendly bill intended to provide both "border security" and "humanitarian relief" at the southern border. The acting director of Immigration and Customs Enforcement, Mark Morgan, had said, *"I'm here as ICE begging for this. We need that to get the families out of the Border Patrol detention facilities and into better facilities."*

Supporting the expenditure, Alabama's Republican Senator Richard C. Shelby, said, *"Our border security professionals and the children and families in their care cannot afford further delay. I'm hopeful that a strong bipartisan vote will provide the momentum needed to assist our folks on the front lines."*

However, when the votes were tallied, 91 Democrats, lead by "The Squad" – Reps. Alexandria Ocasio-Cortez, Ilhan Omar, Ayanna Pressley, Rashida Tlaib – voted against funding border facilities, even with the knowledge that the Department of Health and Human Services said existing funding would not last through the end of the month (or less than a week from the vote).

Subsequently, we saw The Squad, and specifically, Ocasio-Cortez {AOC}, were eager to grab tearful photo-ops at the facilities and exhibit similar displays before news cameras on the House floor. But, that did not prevent passage of *H.R. 3401: Emergency Supplemental Appropriations for Humanitarian Assistance and Security at the Southern Border Act, 2019*, or it being enacted — Signed by President Trump – on 1 July 2019.

We should note, the $4.6BILLION single year expenditure was necessitated by the 2017 refusal to provide the $3BILLION for the Fence/Wall which would have prevented the entry of most of the migrants in ICE care and custody. In effect, The Squad – who entered the House with the 2018 mid-term election – were continuing the work begun by Pelosi and the Reagan-Democrats in 2017.

Of course, having made themselves easy targets, Trump directly attacked them with a focus on Ilhan Omar – not because of anything other than she is their weakest link. When asked about President Trump's comment, which had said:

*"...look at Omar, I don't know, I never met her. I hear the way she talks about al-Qaida. Al-Qaida has killed many Americans. She said you could hold your chest out. When I think of America, huh. When I think of al-Qaida, I can hold my chest out. When she talked about the World Trade Center being knocked down, some people, you remember the famous, some people."*

Representative Ilhan Omar responded, *"I will not dignify it with an answer, because I know that every single Islamophobe, every single person who is hateful, who is driven by an ideology of 'othering' as this president is, rejoices in us responding to that and us defending ourselves."*

Of course, the problem is one of interpretation of the Omar comment. Trump utilized the technique which has been used against him – he spun a comment to mean something other than what was being said. As cited in previous Trump Card books, he made use of the technique in the Jack Sparrow line, *"You lied to me by telling me the truth."*

Think about a different hearing of the statement: *"When I think of America — uhh. When I think of al-Qaeda, I can hold my chest out."* Think in terms of her starting to praise America, and then inserting al-Qaeda as an example of what makes her proud to be American. That America I NOT al-Qaeda, but thinking of al-Qaeda triggers her pride in America.

Is Trump's reading of her statement false? Or is he simply following the Golden Rule and doing to others as they routinely do to him?

On 16 July {9:59 AM} Trump effectively tweeted that his gambit worked: *".....Congresswomen, who I truly believe, based on their actions, hate our Country. Get a list of the HORRIBLE things they have said. Omar is polling at 8%, Cortez at 21%. Nancy Pelosi tried to push them away, but now they are forever wedded to the Democrat Party. See you in 2020!"*

What few, outside readers of the Trump Card book series, seem to realize is that Trump is taking a mainstream Democratic approach with a spin that appeals to the Republican base. The fact he has taken to attacking, and setting up for attack, The Squad has the effect of echoing the internal war between Pelosi and The Squad. And defeating the Squad has the effect of defeating any of the Progressive goals promoted by Bernie Sanders. After all, AOC is Sanders' protegee.

Pelosi effectively dismissed The Squad with the comment: *"All these people have their public whatever and their Twitter world. But they didn't have any following. They're four people and that's how many votes they got."*

Behind the comment is the reality of the voter constituency each member of the Squad represents. Yes, they are only four votes in the House, but they represent districts, each of whom has more voters in their district than are in Wyoming, or Vermont, or Alaska, and either North or South Dakota. Combined The Squad represents a total of 2.9 million people.

In terms of the 2020 election, Senator Bernie Sanders told Pelosi, he warned Pelosi, *"You cannot ignore the young people of this country who are passionate about economic and racial and social and environmental justice. You gotta bring them in, not alienate them."* In response, AOC played a dual gender-race card saying: *"But the persistent singling out ... it got to a point where it was just outright disrespectful ... the explicit singling out of newly elected women of color."*

We hear variations on the same rhetorical nonsense as the basis for the attacks on Trump – inject that, regardless of reality, he becomes a misogynistic xenophobe. Of course, when AOC was challenged on her Pelosi comment, she immediately backtracked on whether House Speaker Pelosi was racist, and had no option but to assert: *"No, no, absolutely not, absolutely not."* Though, it is clear that if her comment had been aimed at Trump, she would have said she was calling him a misogynistic-racist.

The reliability of their strategy and responses is what gives Trump confidence. So long as he promotes a Democratic Agenda of the type Reagan ranted against, he has the subliminal memory of older Democratic voters working for him. As many known, the use of the term "Socialist" will have the effect of triggering the very same subliminal response among those raised in a "Cold War Era" environment.

Even here, the older generation Democrats are invoking the knee-jerk response to "Draft Dodging" and the mixed emotions it has for the Baby-Boomer generation.

It doesn't matter that, from the time he was 18, Trump was 1A-status, and unlike Biden or Sanders – who were Draft Dodgers – his reclassification didn't come until the Vietnam War was at an end, and the nation was shifting to a volunteer army. Nor does it matter reached the age of automatic exemption – except in event of a Congressionally declared war. Trump detractors will raise the specter of Draft Dodger while turning a blind eye to both Biden and Sanders.

Note Trump's use of *'"Progressive" Democrat'* to describe the subject of his broadside, and how it differs from the 15 July Tweet {5:08 PM} tweet which said:

*"We will never be a Socialist or Communist Country. IF YOU ARE NOT HAPPY HERE, YOU CAN LEAVE! It is your choice, and your choice alone. This is about love for America. Certain people HATE our Country.... / ....They are anti-Israel, pro Al-Qaeda, and comment on the 9/11 attack, "some people did something." Radical Left Democrats want Open Borders, which means drugs, crime, human trafficking, and much more.... / ....Detention facilities are not Concentration Camps! America has never been stronger than it is now – rebuilt Military, highest Stock Market EVER, lowest unemployment and more people working than ever before. Keep America Great!".*

He begins with the "Cold War-era" rendering of Socialist being analogous to Communism, then proceeds to the dire warnings which the Democrats made about "Open Borders" before Reagan and then after 9/11 when a 2006 Secure Fence Act was promoted by Obama, Clinton, and Schumer – people who "did something" though Schumer, now a Reagan-Democrat, seeks to undo what he promoted throughout the Obama Administration.

Trump ends by invoking the fruits of a properly run Capitalist government – Capitalist gains for retired Baby-Boomers and low unemployment among the generations rising to replace them.

Trump can invoke *"Keep America Great!"* without invoking the Minimum Wage issue as Sanders had done, or immediately confronting the 18 July, Democrat House vote passing the *Raise The Wage Act* – opposed by only 6 Democrats, and supported by only 3 Republicans. That 30 states had already passed laws which would raise their minimum wage by 2025 meant the vote was safe in 60% of States – the new Act used the same 2025 target.

There is something about the year 2025 – which is also the year when China requires all new vehicles to be electric, and the year the Iran Nuclear agreement was set to expire.

Doubling the Minimum Wage needed to phased-in. As Pelosi mentioned, the last increase happened under Bush's Administration – inferring Obama had used the government wage subsidy of welfare rather than sound economics.

Ronald Reagan introduced *"Workfare"* – *"welfare system that requires those receiving benefits to perform some work or be a volunteer, or participate in job training."* On one level, they can be counted as 'employed', on another, they are Minimum Wage workers whose welfare subsidy increases those on welfare and facilitates accusations of welfare fraud and '*welfare queens*' milking the system.

We find a similar game being played with Social Security, which they yelled was going to run out of money, but, rather than remove the cap on income subject to contributions, they raised the retirement age and suppressed benefits.  Again, their long-term goal was to increase the numbers receiving welfare – a statistic used in the 2018 election. That political propaganda tool logic is still being used – though Bernie Sanders has been attacking it and offering some viable economically sound solutions.

With Trump's victory, Reaganites quickly became Reagan-Democrats.  Those wishing to inflict 'The Most Harm to the Most People' {@MHMP} began the anti-Trump propaganda campaigns.

The result was one where traditional Democrats faced a Sophie's Choice the choice between what is morally correct and that which is either economically wise or politically expedient in the approach to securing the border.  It was easy when they backed President Barack Obama, who stated: "*Our message, absolutely, is don't send your children unaccompanied, on trains or through a bunch of smugglers...that is our direct message to the families in Central America. Do not send your children to the borders. If they do make it, they'll get sent back. More importantly, they may not make it.*" {June 2014}

Concurrent with Obama's statement, polls revealed that 41-percent of all Americans favored a decrease in immigration – for Republicans, it was 50-percent, for Democrats 32-percent.  Trump is following his political base, *The Squad* is targeting the majority among the Democrats – the 68-percent favoring either consistent levels or increased ones.

In 2014, Obama asserted the position that: "*the issue is not that people are evading our enforcement officials. The issue is that we're apprehending them in large numbers. And we're working to make sure that we have sufficient facilities to detain, house, and process them appropriately, while attending to unaccompanied children with the care and compassion that they deserve while they're in our custody.*"

In 2017 Reagan-Democrats, lead by Nancy Pelosi opposed securing the border and offered nothing in the way of improved facilities.  If we look at their record, they made no effort to ensure *"sufficient facilities to detain, house, and process"* those they are so anxious to see admitted.  Exactly 5-years passed after Obama's statement, and 95 Reagan-Democrats voted to deny funding of the facilities necessary to house and process the people they invited to both violate American border laws and the International Asylum Rules.

They are opposing Obama, as defined in the official White House statement of 1 August 2014, which begins: *"The influx of children being apprehended trying to cross the southwest border shows that our immigration system is broken and Congress needs to advance comprehensive immigration reform so we can fix the system now."*

As we, the 2014 Obama assertion, when Trump says the system is broken and it needs to be fixed, he asserting Democratic Positions, which, in 2014 held that the *"Republicans have had more than a year to comprehensively fix the Nation's broken immigration system. In the absence of Congressional action, the President mounted a significant effort to deal with this urgent humanitarian situation...."*

In 2018, Democrats who took control of the House and so, by July 2019, had over a year to deal with the issue – and in June 2019, 95 Reagan-Democrats decided they'd vote to either keep it the same or make things worse.  In 2020, Americans will have the opportunity to replace the Reagan-Democrats with Democrats or Republicans dedicated to addressing the growing border problem – one you know will become even worse, if you accept Climate Change.

On 16 July 2019, Newsweek published an article asserting: *"Climate Change will expose millions of people in U.S. to off-the-charts extreme heat."*

If the U.S. anticipates heat *"surpassing 105 degrees,"* what temperature levels will Central American Nations achieve?  What northern migration will it trigger?  What is *The Squad* doing to prepare the nation for an influx of refugees and the destruction of farmland – which were beginning to be seen with the increased rain, flooding, and record heat which marked June 2019 and continued throughout the summer?  These weather and migration patterns will reach critical proportions sometime around 2030.

Reality is upon them, but Reagan-Democrats and members of *The Squad* prefer to rant about an allegedly amoral bigot in the White House, those two things are not always the same, the false morality dominates and you get what you were told, you see; *THE EMPEROR'S NEW CLOTHES* mentality define Democrats who see what they have, since the 2016 election, been told what they should see.

Under Obama, the border crisis was real, it is more real in 2019, and will get worse as Climate Change reaches full force. One aspect is that the U.S. needs to decentralize the power grid and get ready for more black-outs of the kind that hit Times Square on 13 July 2019. Electric cooling, not oil or gas heating, will become the focus of energy needs – modern renewables allow electricity to be generated on-site, with a broader grid serving as a counterbalance for any surplus or transient shortfall.

Congress seemed focused on impeaching the POTUS who created the longest economic expansion in history by maintaining Obama's recovery. They branded xenophobic and Misogynistic – ignoring global migration patterns he was addressing. Reality dictates that, by definition, affected populations, cultures, and races are equatorial, therefore, not of European origin – they are a product of Climate Change they prefer to ignore.

# CHAPTER TWO – DEMOGRAPHICS

*"Always be yourself, express yourself,*
*have faith in yourself,*
*do not go out and look for a successful personality and*
*duplicate it."*
**~ Bruce Lee**

Climate Change and Minimum Wage are two factors that shall shape the world in 2030 – a third is the Baby-Boom defined as those born in the twenty years from December 1945 to January 1965, and during which time 75.8 million Americans were born.

The biggest one-year birthrate, 4.3 million, was in 1957 and marked the year, the majority of Boomers came into existence – meaning the majority of surviving Boomers will be at least 70-years-old by December 2027; the last vestige of them will exceed age 70 in 2035. Give the American life-expectancy, effectively, the Baby-Boom generation will be dead soon after 2040. If we apply the global Boomer births to the peak global population, by 2050, a third of human life will have died, with climate change killing of about a third of other life forms. It's a point of consideration for the few who grasp the relevance of these facts – everyone else will simply experience it.

Demographically, a of January 2019, there were roughly 72 million Boomers with an American population of 329 million – or about a fifth of the population in a world where America is about 4.25% of the global population and constitutes the prime example of the Elite or, if we consider only adults, they are the One-Percent that everyone loves to rail against.

America appears to be composed of people who take pride in hating themselves for being Great, and hate Trump for wanting us to be who we really are – a historic global elite everyone else would love to be a part of, and failing that, chooses to hate. Just as the Founders envisioned, Americans are the new global "Jews".

It is said we learn all that will define us within the first 7- years of our lives. The Hippy Generation were the Boomers raised during the bigotry era of McCarthyism (1950/54) and taught by parents who understood the fight against the Nazis; they learned to rebel against these images or anything resembling them.

The millennial generation is defined as those born January 1981 to December 1996; Alexandria Ocasio-Cortez was born {13 October 1989}, which means attitudes toward Ronald Reagan shaped the first of the millennials and then they were influenced by attitudes toward George H. W. Bush.  GHWB would also have defined the first four years of AOC's life, followed by Bill Clinton, whose daughter Chelsea was ideal as a young girl's role model.

Note that AOC came from a rather hi-IQ family – her father was a graduate of the Prestigious and selective Brooklyn Technical High School, Bill Clinton was a Rhodes Scholar, while Chelsea was a 1997 National Merit Scholarship semifinalist and received more news coverage that any previous or subsequent Presidential child – it was even suggested she'd grow to be the first female president.

On many levels, AOC has lived up to the expectations of an individual from an intellectually elite Puerto Rican family who, in college, became an intern to U.S. Senator Ted Kennedy, and later worked with Senator Bernie Sanders.

AOC is said to be an environmental hard-liner whose 2018 Platform stated:*"Climate change is the single biggest national security threat for the United States and the single biggest threat to worldwide industrialized civilization, and the effects of warming can be hard to predict and self-reinforcing.  We need to avoid a worldwide refugee crisis by waging a war for climate justice through the mobilization of our population and our government.  This starts with the United States being a leader on the actions we take both globally and locally."*

Yet, she opposes the establishment of the border processing systems necessary to address what will soon become the growing number of climate refugees.  On the contrary, she accuses Trump of racism becomes he focuses on the orderly processing of those escaping the very regions which are and will be most devastated by the heatwave effects of Climate Change.

In her 2018 Platform, she asserted: *"It's time to abolish ICE {Immigration and Customs Enforcement agency}, clear the path to citizenship, and protect the rights of families to remain together."* But she did not explain how the immigrants were to be processed – she presents no "Ellis Island" port of entry alternative to the rampant disregard for America's Borders or as a means of documenting those who wish to enter as undocumented. Without proper documentation, there is no right to vote or citizenship.

Scanning the internet discussion groups reveals many are questioning the intelligence of both Trump and AOC, yet both defeated candidates with far more political experience.

Trump offered and promoted Democratic approaches of the type embodied in the *2006 Secure Fence Act* and, while he had proposed extending protections for DACA children, Nancy Pelosi and other Reagan-Democrats reproached him because he failed to perform their job and provide legislation that would give DACA the path to citizenship mentioned in AOC's Platform – legislation that should have followed on the heel of the Obamas Executive Order which created DACA status.

As we know, AOC made a point to avoid the issue – because she gets more mileage out of crying in front of cages built under the Obama Administration than she possibly could from attempts to make immigrant children lawful citizens.

This is all about Demographics. Trump's record economy represents his willingness to allow and assist the Demographics of the Boomer Era as reflected in a Negative Population Growth era in which Artificial intelligence and Automation are assisting the NPG to negate an old form of economics based on putting to work and ever-expanding population.

We hear that doubling the Minimum Wage will cost jobs, but they are jobs which, because of a lack of new births, will be unfilled and replaced by automation or AI. Rather than being a bad thing, raising the wage will remove the embarrassment they often feel in using welfare subsidies – that embarrassment comes in two forms, the personal sense of failure that accompanies the inability to meet one's own survival needs, and the derogation we see imposed by those immoral Far Right-wing bigots who build their own egos by attacking recipients of those biblical mandates which, when followed, define the blessed who bestow assistance and the cursed who oppose it.

In the 2017/18 period, America's population growth of 0.62 percent was the lowest rate in 80-years. During the 2007/9 Great Recession, the rate had fallen to 0.80 percent and then remained below that level throughout the Obama Administration.

Note that immigration accounts for over 42% of annual population growth between 1991 and 2018. Therefore, America remains a nation of immigrants.

That immigrant reality is being manipulated by Reagan-Democrats as the basis for "lawful" Gerrymandering.

Gerrymandering is a manipulation of an electoral boundary so that it will favor one party or class of individuals so as to grant them more power, and takes its name from Elbridge Gerry, the Governor of Massachusetts in 1812, who created a Boston voting district that was said to resemble the shape of a mythological salamander, the practice obviously goes back to the early days of the nation.

Originally, city populations grew in relationship to their proximity to travel routes such as rivers or seaports. Immigrants tend to go where they are familiar. When they arrived in America, farmers established farms, explorers explored, and the educated established Colleges, while merchants established those industries which allowed for shipping and long-distance trade.

Economic changes and increased efficiencies reduced the need for farmers and created new, city-centered occupations. This enhanced the need for bookkeepers and lawyers – "white collar" jobs where brains were more important than brawn evolved to the point where the traditional work of the Dickensian Age of the Civil War era have either ceased to exist or been marginalized to Third World economies.

Those Third World economies are now both the source of most major migrant populations and the focal point of the worst effects of Climate Change. When Trump says his version of this reality – the version acceptable to those who comprise his political base demographic – he is attacked as a racist. And, consistent with the attitudes or intentional ignorance of his attackers, he is also classified as a climate denier. But, whether or not he accepts the delusion of humans fixing Climate Change before it takes full effect over the next decade, when, the effects will be mitigated by the decline in population and move to renewable energy – much of which will be point-of-use generated – really doesn't matter.

If we are talking about Gerrymandering or manipulation of elections, the only thing of importance is immigration. Before any immigrant can become a voter, they must first become a citizen, and before they can become a citizen, they must be documented.

But, when it comes to counting bodies – a Census – nobody

cares if they are documented, so long as they get counted. In the Hippy Era, the University of California at Berkeley took on some focus, but it was to the south of Alameda County, in Los Angeles County, that we find the reality of population Gerrymandering in a context which could be behind the open border movement lead by Nancy Pelosi.

In the 1960s, 40 percent of California's population lived in Los Angeles County, but the voting rules that gave every county the same representation. As a result, 40 percent of the population received only 2.5 percent of the state's Senate seats.

In Reynolds v. Sims, 377 U.S. 533, {15 June 1964} we see a Supreme ruling which holds the *"Equal Protection Clause of the 14th Amendment includes a "one-person, one-vote" principle."*

But the *"one-vote"* goes to the representation and not the actual right to vote by one specific person. As a result, population count, rather than voter count, dictates the lawful district. As was expressed by Chief Justice Earl Warren, anything having the effect of diluting the strength of a vote was something to *"be carefully and meticulously scrutinized."*

The explicit focus of the Alabama case was population, not citizenship, and Warren wrote *"legislators represent people, not trees or acres"* and *"legislators are elected by voters, not farms or cities or economic interests."* The mention of voters infers that the number of voters per legislative district was a consideration; but nothing in the decision specifies voter count superseded head-count – nor could it, if children are represented in the body count. But the ruling is interpreted to hold that population must always be the "controlling consideration" in state redistricting, with that interpretation we have the beauty of having massive influxes of immigrants – especially statistically enumerated undocumented ones.

In 2016, the Supreme Court affirmed the irrelevance of the actual citizen voters, when it ruled in *Evenwel v. Abbott, Gov of Texas* that Under the one-person, one-vote principle, jurisdictions must design legislative districts with equal populations. The case had been brought by those who realized apportionment on total population, dilutes the votes of actual voters relative to districts of an equal population but fewer actual voters.

Justice Ruth B. Ginsburg delivered the majority opinion:

*Texas, like all other States, draws its legislative districts on the basis of total population. Plaintiffs-appellants are Texas voters; they challenge this uniform method of districting on the ground that it produces un-equal districts when measured by voter-eligible population. Voter-eligible population, not total population, they urge, must be used to ensure that their votes will not be devalued in relation to citizens' votes in other districts. We hold, based on constitutional history, this Court's decisions, and longstanding practice, that a State may draw its legislative districts based on total population.*

Thus we have a definitive affirmation that the number of actual voters and, by extension, lawful citizens, is of less important than body count. Thus we have the basis for what could become the ultimate Gerrymander – districts built around or defined by their immigrant populations.

To understand this, we must first recognize and accept that a similar population tends to self-segregate. When the Chinese came to America, we saw China Towns, Italian arrival created places like New York's "Little Italy", Southern Blacks moved north to redefine New York's Harlem, the Puerto Ricans created Spanish Harlem, then there are the German and Jewish neighborhoods With the influx from Central and South American countries, we can expect the emergence densely populated migrant communities that are based on their language and culture.

With a rapid influx, the effect will be a handful of citizens will determine the district representation – without a connection or relationship to the actual population.

We've seen the effect of "Gentrification" and those who are old enough might remember what was called "White Flight" in the 1960s and into the early 1970s.

Consider this simplistic model of what Reagan-Democrats want to create.

You have two districts of equal population, where there are only nuclear families – a husband, wife, two children. Consider these designated as District One and Two, and are started with a one Representative and one family in each district – all the other families are equally distributed between two groups designated A and B. Under the Supreme Court model, for every family from Group A added to District One, there is a family from Group B added to District Two.

If the husband and wife are citizens, we have equal voting with an equal population.

But what happens when we add 'nuclear' migrant families and they all go into Group B – but, for every two migrant families that go into Group B, one Citizen family moves into Group A?  The count of families would remain equal, but the demographics now reflect those which created *Evenwel v. Abbott* – where the voter family in District Two gains more power with every two migrant families that enter Group Two.

We can play the game until there are no citizen voters in B and only the Husband and wife in District Two are determining the Representative, and that Representative only represents the interests of that one family – if the Elected Representative were foolish enough to support interests of the migrants over that of the family, the family would vote them out.

Ultimately, this is the Gerrymandering that is created by a Reagan-Democratic open border agenda.  And it is supported by the SCOTUS decisions.  The effect is to have a handful of voters are the determining voice of the majority of residents.   Immigrant neighborhoods have few citizens -- thus few voters -- a hundred people could determine who represents tens of thousands ... This is the ultimate power grab and assures the power for a generation.

Only when legislative districts have voter parity, in parallel with population parity, can the one-person-one-vote ideal be met.

Again, consider our model, but add a District Three with a Group C of equal size to Groups A & B, but with the demographics of B – non-citizen immigrants.  And we have a symbolic repeat of Los Angeles in the 1960s – the actual citizens have only one-third the State Senate representation, but exceed 90 percent of citizens and voters. As for population-based representation in the state's House, relative to the 1960s situation, they lost ground and have only a third of the House seats.

Pelosi's California had an estimated 2018 population of 39 million; the 2019 apprehended migrant population annualizes to over a million people a year, meaning, in a decade, they would increase the California population by 25% and effectively replace the *"trees or acres"*; since they are only suited to rural agricultural work, we would see *"legislators represent people"* who serve as the legal compliance stand-ins for *"farms or cities or economic interests,"* the SCOTUS decision was to protect against.

Understand, due to the heat waves that will accompany Climate Change – heat waves that were experienced all across the United States during the summer of 2019 – the migrant numbers will approach a significant percentage of the Central American population which, in July 2019 was estimated to be 181 million people. Only 20 percent of them need to head north to escape heat levels in excess of 120 degrees Fahrenheit and the population of California doubles without adding a single voter.

Central America represents 2.4 percent of the total global population. Mexico and the United States will be receiving them and people from South America – adding another 6 percent. This potential problem is complicated by the October 2018 declaration of Brazil's newly elected president, Jair Bolsonaro, to reinstate Amazon Rainforest deforestation. That would accelerate Climate Change and increase the forces driving the Northern Migration.

By 2035, the United States should be feeling the full effect of Gerrymandering being set in motion by Reagan-Democrats.

At the same time, we have Bernie Sanders seeking to add to the potential problems with an attack on the Constitution.

When the Constitution was originally drafted, slaves were the ones representing counted non-voters whose existence could distort representation. If uncounted, Northern Free States would gain the representative advantage; if fully counted, it would be the Southern States that gained the advantage. To keep a balance, it was determined that slaves would be two-thirds of a person.

They also created an additional balance which allowed each state a voice – regardless of its population, but which reflected the population in the same way they were represented in both the House and Senate. This was called the Electoral College and, on 19 July 2019, Bernie Sanders responded to the prospect of Trump winning a second term by calling for the abolition of the electoral college – an act that would require a Constitutional Amendment be initiated, passed, and ratified in less than fourteen months.

From day it was proposed to final ratification, the disaster known as Prohibition took a full year – 18 December 1917 to 16 January 1919 – and went into effect a year later. Consider that, for it to have an affect the 2020 election, Sanders is proposing changing a critical aspect of the Constitution and a major change in the Democratic Process, with no time for rational discussion or consideration – and that it take immediate effect.

This raises an issue about Sanders. He appears willing to undermine the check-and-balances of the Constitution based upon a long-shot possibility he would be the 2020 Nominee – if not him, then he wants to shift the voting process in a way that would invest control into the hands of a ten-percent of the states. This is the ideal election interference – it will place control into the hands of those states which Russia showed it could easily reach via the internet.

Note that abolishing or circumventing the electoral college also emerged as part of the agenda put forth by Senator Elizabeth Warren and Washington Governor Jay Inslee, who also suggested a method that would circumvent the electoral college rendering it functionally irrelevant.

In an era of election interference, we see the move toward open borders as a means of distorting the population in districts in a way that alters the balance of legislative power; this is then combined with an attack on the electoral process that would vest power in California and Texas – the nation's two most populous states and the major beneficiaries of the migrant Gerrymandering.

It's all about a manipulation of demographics to influence elections. But demographics are a powerful tool especially if they can be weaponized in the way Social Security was when politicians promoted the assumption that population growth was perpetual. Using that assumption, Republicans initiated an economic time bomb designed to justify reducing worker purchased benefits to below poverty levels – the average benefit for 2019 was $1,461 per month, which is $160 above poverty for an individual and $300 below poverty for a couple.

With the current cap on base wages subject to the contribution, the year 2035 marks a point when average benefits will need to be reduced by 20 percent ($292).

Assuming no inflation, individual income will fall $130 below poverty – which would then trigger a welfare subsidy. Based on Social Security Administration figures, for a quarter of recipients, Social Security is at least 90 percent of their retirement income and, for at least half of recipients, it is half their income. Seeking to address the emerging problem, Senator Elizabeth Warren and Senator Bernie

Sanders are leading a group of 19 Senators and 150 Representatives to explore ways to finance the cost of additional benefits. Designated as the "Expand Social Security Caucus," part of their solution is a fiscally rational raise in the Base Wage subject to contributions.

Consider the ramifications of bringing the Obama-Trump economic expansion to an abrupt end – as would happen if the Reagan-Democrats were able to initiate an impeachment which had the same effect as the Nixon one. The Stock Market provides the additional or supplemental income for retirees and, following the Nixonian pattern, would lose 45 percent of its value. Add the economic drain of millions of migrants, and the Great Recession becomes a minor economic blip.

The accusations against Clinton began in June 1998 and on 17 July the market peaked at 9418; by 1 September it had dropped to a low of 7360 or about 21.8 percent. A mild recovery followed, but when formal impeachment was initiated on 8 October 1998, the market registered a low of 7500. Realizing the nonsensical nature of the "*Oral in the Oval*" related perjury charges, which the Market ignored, then moved to recovery; on 12 February 1999, the Senate returned a Not Guilty verdict, while the Market moved to a high of 11405 on 24 August, then, after a 10 percent correction, on 30 December 1999, finished the year with a high of 11,685.

On 17 July 2019, by a vote of  332-95 the House tabled the impeachment resolution by Texas Democrat Rep. Al Green, which effectively declared alleged racist comments against The Squad to qualify as either a "High Crime or Misdemeanor."

Cinco De Mayo 2019, allowed the nation to see the fruits of Donald Trump allowing Demographics to control the economy. The GOP Chairwoman, Ronna McDaniel, tweeted the fact that April's economic report indicated 263,000 jobs were created and beat expectations to bring the Trump Administration job creation total to 5.4 Million. At the same time, unemployment marked a 49-year low of 3.6% – which held stable into the summer.

With the Democratic House voting to incrementally raise the Minimum Wage to 15/hour, they effectively endorsed Bernie Sanders, who has calling for a raise commensurate with inflation – one that, based on 1968 Vietnam Era levels, should, in 2019, be over $18/hour; if productivity is factored in with the inflation, the wage would be closer to $27/hour. As is, the *Raise The Wage Act* is designed to address wage issues, but still keeps wages depressed as the majority of Baby-Boomers attain age seventy and approach the end of the average lifespan.

Note, this means migrant children the Reagan-Democrats want admitted now will be entering the workforce at wages well below those received by Baby-Boomers when they were between 18 and 23 – a time when the purchasing power of a dollar was the same as ten dollars in 2019.

Senators Warren and Sanders have the opportunity to show unifying leadership – on 18 July 2019 the House passed the 2019 *Raise The Wage Act* and sent it to the Senate. Had the Senate voted and passed *The Wage Act*, Trump could sign it and become the POTUS who allowed working Americans to escape the welfare subsidies that underwrite low wage full-time employment. Its passage House bestows a mantel of leadership upon Sanders and befits his decades-long struggle for a living Minimum Wage. The Senate Republicans had the opportunity to gain benefits as those who want to share prosperity and encourage economic growth not seen since the Boomers were children.

However, "*Most Harm to the Most People*" types desire to keep people on public assistance, they seek to bankrupt the Social Security system and, for their own destructive reasons, they want the economy to crash. This is why they pursue impeachment.

Concurrent with the House passage of the *Raise The Wage Act*, there were three other news items of significance to the view America would have of The Squad and others who oppose Trump. First, the Environmental Protection Agency {EPA} decline placing a ban on chlorpyrifos, a pesticide used for killing insects, which has been linked to harming children of women who are exposed to the pesticide when pregnant; a study was released which showed that, in areas of intense oil or gas well production, women were more likely to have children with heart defects; Elizabeth Warren began echoing the idea of an 11-year recession cycle and then warned of crippling economic crisis similar to 2008 — which she held would be fueled by rising household and corporate debt.

According to Warren, "*Whether it's this year or next year, the odds of another economic downturn are high—and growing.*"

The 11-year cycle would have the crash in late 2019 or early 2020. With the election of the American born Boris Johnson as the new Prime Minister of Great Britain, the global economy is faced with a man who promised: "*We are going to get Brexit done on 31 October and take advantage of all the opportunities it will bring with a new spirit of can do. We are once again going to believe in ourselves, and like some slumbering giant we are going to rise and ping off the guy ropes of self-doubt and negativity.*"

BREXIT is an economic separation, an end to 1978 treaty which formed the European Union {EU} and then helped foster European markets.  During the period which followed the 2016 leave vote, Britain has experienced numerous negative economic effects. The Trade War between the United States and China has also had a negative effect – most visible in Germany.  To that, we can add the North African migrants who have flooded Europe and are creating an economic situation across the EU – one which the Democratic Secure Fence Act, and now Trump's persistent call for a border wall, was intended to prevent happening in the U.S.

Warren could place blame, or ascribe as the basis for her prediction, whatever she wants, but the same forces are at work in America as are being displayed in Europe.  And if either falls, the other will feel it and react – in 2019, the economy was dependent on BREXIT.  There is a longer and more defined economic cycle, known as the K-WAVE, due to impact Europe in 2027.

America and/or the EU will have experienced a Recession whose aftershock could become a Great Depression which occurs 98-years after the famed 1929 one.  If America prepares it will have both balanced its economic relations with Asia and created an immigration system designed to integrate waves of Equatorial Climate Change migrants who soon will be flooding Guatemala, Mexico, and the United States.  These are the same immigrants who will add to the horrors defining 2027.

The current border crisis is the "elephant in the room" that will only be accepted as a crisis when the elephant "poops" – now it's just farting a bit.

Warren is deliberately ignoring the long-term reality for a shot at the short-term possibility that she could become the first female POTUS.  In the process, she is preparing the foundational basis for Trump to blame her for any recession.  She asserted there is a problem, she's an elected Senator, what is she doing to avert it?  The Party she wishes to head is the one controlling the House and therefore responsible for initiating financial legislation. What is she doing to demonstrate leadership? What is she doing in the Senate to advance the *Raise The Wage Act* and get it to Trump's desk?

Reagan-Republicans promoting the nonsense that the *Raise The Wage Act* would cost jobs, hurt the economy – they're playing an 11-year recession cycle card. Warren and Sanders need to convince the Senate Republicans that legally promising a $15 wage in 2025 will help Republican Senators get reelected. They need to sell the idea that it will please Trump – he can boast of the higher wages and decrease in welfare costs. That way, if things go back, they get the blame, and under any other conditions, Sanders would have achieved his long-term goal, while Warren would have demonstrated bipartisan leadership skills befitting someone who could become a functional POTUS.

As the Bruce Lee quote indicates, be yourself, do not try to be someone else or anyone that you are not. Those who lie about who they are tend to be upset by people like Trump – those who are who they are, and are not ashamed of who they are; thereby showing they are much more.

In many ways, it is comical to think that Trump is the person Mark Twain was describing when he said: "*All you need in this life is ignorance and confidence, and then success is sure.*"

Of course, that assumes that Trump suffers the ignorance his opponents routinely ascribe to him. But, if he were ignorant, could he have amassed enough wealth to make it worth the effort to obtain his tax returns? And what can Congress find that the trained IRS auditors routinely failed to detect or discover?

Mueller effectively declared the rules that apply to Trump – *Guilty until proved innocent.* It was stated with reference to the original 448-page report – despite the lack of evidence to infer guilt, they couldn't declare him innocent because they lack clear evidence of that innocence.

This *Guilty until proved innocent* approach was affirmed when, on 24 July 2019, Rep. John Ratcliffe (R-TX) asked Mueller the point-blank question: "*Can you give me an example other than Donald Trump where the Justice Department determined that an investigated person was not exonerated because their innocence was not conclusively determined?*" Robert Mueller replied: "*I cannot.*"

All the attacks on Trump are not about trump.  These are global attacks on the leadership in multiple nations taking various forms. They mark the nature of the era which, in part, is defined in the United States by the beginning of the second 57-Presidential Election Cycle. But, as we have seen in the 2016 BREXIT vote and the July 2019 election of Boris Johnson as Prime Minister, change is a reality of the times.

When change occurs -- be it Good or Bad – people have an obligation to examine the nature of that change and place it in the correct context.  In 2019, change is a factor of demographics and communication – without the internet and instantaneous visual communication, and a population which is enormous, very little to none of what we see today could happen.

In the 1960s, a poster on a New York City subway declared: *"Half of all the people who ever lived are alive today."*

That stuck with me because it could also mean that all the human souls who ever existed have reincarnated and are on earth today.  Of course, the population has grown even more in the 57-years since that Hippy Era poster, but the reality of it would seem to still hold – and they can communicate in real-time.

Is change good or bad?  Population demographics has set the stage for declaring Judgment Day – exactly on schedule.  That doesn't mean the religious types of two millennia ago were right, it just means facts can be spun any way we want.

# CHAPTER THREE – THINK KOSHER

*"If you do not think about your future,*
*you cannot have one."*
**~ John Galsworthy**

By May 2019, it was clear that Alexandria Ocasio-Cortez [AOC] and Bernie Sanders comprised political tag-team whose agenda included the *Green New Deal*. One element was seen in Sanders' assertion: "*In the last decade alone, the oil and gas industry has pumped more than 700 million dollars' worth of campaign contributions into federal, state and local elections. In that same period, they spent more than $1.5 billion lobbying Washington. This is what we are up against.*"

AOC took the tact: "*Let me tell you what's too much for me. What's too much for me is politicians looking and allowing babies' blood to get poisoned in Flint, Michigan, for corporate profits. What's too much for me is coal barons coming up to Washington, D.C., and demanding bailout after tax breaks, after bailout themselves, and then not even paying their own miners' pensions.*"

In both cases, they were dealing with something that is not "Kosher." And it isn't "Kosher" is the truest sense and usage of the term – because to be Kosher is to care about others, to care about the environment and to care about health. Of course, most people don't realize that – especially those who wave the Bible and then use it to justify the harm they inflict upon their neighbor.

Are we going to be KOSHER?

It's said, we should not 'seethe' [boil] a calf in its mother's milk and, from that, Orthodox Hasidic Jews allowed the rule to evolve into one saying they should not have milk and meat at the same meal. A consistent rule regarding "being Kosher" – or doing things properly – is that you should "play it safe" and achieve the objective with the least risk. In terms of milk and meat, they often go so far as to have different dishes and utensils for dietary meat and dairy products.

Chefs braise meat – brown it in oil before applying a boiling related technique – which destroys the protein that all humans are allergic to, and which is the scientific justification for prohibiting the double use of the same cattle based DNA protein in preparing the calf for consumption. It also relates to Lactose intolerance – a reaction to the milk carbohydrate, lactose.

In life, being Kosher is recognizing the various dangers that are common to all people, but affect a few to a greater extent than the average member of the population.  Rather than attempt to single out the few who are susceptible to the problem – usually by letting them first be harmed – the act of being Kosher is to avoid discrimination and ensure the safety of all.

With the advent of the Internet, Social Media, and instant Global Communication, the need to become Kosher has increased significantly.  An example is Climate Change, another Healthcare.

As observed, Climate Change affects everyone to a different extent.  For some, it might even prove beneficial; for others, it will be deadly.  We have groups like THE SQUAD who follow the old, pre-internet, habit of "playing the Race Card" – making everything a racial issue when, in fact, it is geographic and, because it has a geographical origin, therefore cultural or culturally specific to the geographic region.  To the extent that the origins of religion are geographically specific, this also means it is religious.

When speaking of Climate Change, as I showed in religion-based books, we are speaking of something that, along with the Baby Boom or population growth reaching environmental limits, might well have been the basis for the Book of Revelation – which explicitly places the death of a third of life in this century.  And we need to acknowledge that, every day we see news reports which mention the effects of Climate Change.

On 26 July 2019, the summer heatwave was the basis of a Reuters story on record temperature in Europe which pointed out that, normal records are marked by a fraction of a degree, but recent records are measured in increase units of three and four degrees.  It was also mentioned that the heatwave was melting the Greenland Glacier, and, should it melt completely, sea levels would rise by as much as seven meters {7.6 yards, about 23 feet}.  On a realistic basis, such a rise would, even at low tide, place the State of Florida underwater.  Conversely, many in Maine would welcome year-round warm weather, while many old fishing and shipbuilding towns would be lost, many inland properties would become coastal resorts.

On the same day, a day after Trump yelled at them for their failure to sign, it was announced that Guatemala finally signed the immigrant asylum agreement.  Note that, even though there were court challenges in his country, the Guatemalan President went ahead with a signing – even though his Supreme Court had said it required Congressional approval, an action that, if the American model is followed, can come after signing as a formal ratification.

As much as THE SQUAD and others would like to make the border issue about race, it is, in reality, actually about addressing Climate Change. Those who cannot understand this, or refuse to understand, should read John Steinbeck, *The Grapes of Wrath*, a story set during the 1930's decade when the economic hardships of *The Great Depression* were accompanied by a period of climate disruption which consumed Midwestern High Plains State farm-land with droughts severe enough to turn the topsoil to fine dust – the result was dust storms which blanketed portions of the five-state region centered on the Oklahoma panhandle, an area which became known as *The Dust Bowl.*

Being Oklahoma centric, the poverty-driven population of "Climate migrant" families that emerged in the region were given the name "*Okies.*" Having taken Office on 4 March 1929 as the 31st POTUS, Herbert Clark Hoover had the distinction of marking his first seven months with the 1929 Stock Market crash and then beginning his second year with the *Dust Bowl* and related migrant crisis which resonated as the "Border Crisis" that Trump repeatedly mentioned.

Interestingly, Hoover became a one-term President for the very reason that he ignored a growing migrant crisis, and Trump is being threatened with impeachment because he has sought to address one – in both cases, poverty and climate are the common elements, and California a common destination.

There are differences.

The overcrowded camps of the 1930s – which were known by the derogatory designation of "Hoovervilles" – were defined by starving migrants, who were taking their frustration and anger out on each other; with Obama, and now Trump, migrant detention centers are still overcrowded, but the Hispanic migrants are well behaved, and the shortages are centered around soap, showers, and toothpaste. In the 1940s, Hitler turned the Hooverville model into concentration camps, while America improved them slightly and they became Japanese Internment Camps.

In both cases, individuals from local communities attacked ad belittled their fellow citizens – in the 1930s, they were fearful of the influx of newcomers, the "Okies"; in 2019, they attacked the border agents who were charged for control and processing of the influx of individuals illegally infiltrating America's borders – places to hold natural-born American citizens of Japanese ancestry and their immigrant relatives.

Then as now, there is no work for the newly arrived, and, even when Latino migrants can obtain work permits, the best they can hope for is a meager paycheck which is insufficient to support themselves and any children. In the 1930s, at least the migrants could speak, read, and write English. Today language creates an additional barrier to self-sufficiency – but, as previously pointed out, their bodies serve to replace the "*trees or acres*" which had served to deprive voters of their lawful voice and representation. Using taxpayer money to pay welfare benefits to illiterates is thus the cost of acquiring disproportionate gerrymandered power at taxpayer expense – the expense of those being deprived of power.

In the short-term, on 29 July, California Governor Gavin Newsom signed a law requiring disclosure of five-years tax returns before a presidential candidate being listed on the Election Ballot. But the State does not care if the candidate boasted of impeachable legal or ethical violations.

This is a form of legal gerrymandering believed to target but targets numerous candidates. Because it denies voters the right to chose an incumbent or any other candidate, it is unconstitutional; it is illogical, because it does not make the same requirement for a Vice President who is the lawful successor and, as in the case of the death of William Henry Harrison, might be the actual POTUS within a month of the inauguration. The law serves to manipulate the Electoral College and popular vote in a way that exceeds anything the Russians allegedly attempted – inferring a legislature and Governor under Russian control.

That criminality and election manipulation aside, there is the economic reality associated with the Reaganesque open border and anti-fence migrant policy which Pelosi and THE SQUAD have been shown to advocate.

In the Hoover era, there were no Food stamps, there was no minimum wage, there was no Medicaid – that would only come after 4 March 1933, when Roosevelt took office and created *The New Deal*. Now we know, by the show of hands seen at the first nomination debate, that the Democrats all favor giving the illegal migrants free healthcare – care denied their average constituent.

Then as now, the economic system was structured to keep the migrants poor and dependent. In 1929, it was because the Depression had triggered high poverty and everything was farm-based, and climate-dependent while yielding low returns. Today it is a matter of technological skills – migrants who have them have no problem entering the country legally, those who don't will spend their lives dependent upon public assistance, even if they are working full-time, because the Federal Minimum Wage they would likely receive is a below poverty wage.

As we know, the push for impeachment is one intended to crash the economy. As stated, the Clinton effort cost 21.8-percent of Stock Market value; and the process terminated with Nixon's resignation cost 45-percent.

The obvious difference between then and now was the age and economic strength of the Baby-Boomer generation. In 1973, when the move to impeach Nixon for documented crime-related involvement, the boomers had yet to turn thirty, and most of them were still working on their educations. They were not involved in the Stock Market, and, if their parents were in the market, it was in the old and reliable Blue Chip Stocks.

In October 1998, when the "Oral in the Oval" impeachment of Clinton began, the Boomers were just turning fifty, tech stocks were still new – shares in Apple were a dollar – and the downturn was seen as a retirement fund buying opportunity.

If impeachment were initiated concurrent with a Hard-Exit BREXIT, the combination could be expected to depress the stock market, end the Obama-Trump recovery, and trigger the serious economic downturn Warren predicted on 22 July 2019 – a wise prediction that would, if she were to become President, cover her from responsibility, and, if it occurred before the election, yield economic knowledge credit she otherwise showed she lacked.

Of course, the comedy of the Trump impeachment is that he allegedly is working with Russia. But the Russians want, and need, to see the American economy crash, and Trump is devoutly devoted to strengthening it – to repatriating lost industries, and strengthening America's trading partners {Mexico and Canada}.

Russia would want America's border open to the migrants

from the South and Central American regions. They would be a drain on the economy and disrupt the social/cultural structure in much the same way that the 1957 Broadway Musical, *West Side Story*, depicted the disruption Puerto Ricans brought to New York City. Granted, it was based on Shakespeare's *Romeo and Juliet*, with the Capulets and Montagues depicted opposing street gangs with different ethnic backgrounds.

The lyrics of *"Gee, Officer Krupke"* could be straight from 2019 political media: *"My Daddy beats my Mommy/ My Mommy clobbers me/ My Grandpa is a Commie/ My Grandma pushes tea/ My sister wears a mustache/ My brother wears a dress/ Goodness Gracious, that's why I'm a mess!"*

Consider those 75-year-old words. Their family defined by parents who are a spouse and child abusers; grandparents who are socialists and marijuana user-sellers; a LGBTQ sister and brother; no mention or allusion to traits that emphasize being productive or educated individuals – just those things people complain about or demonstrate against, things which society uses to justify its close-minded bigotry.

And yes, the abuse must be viewed that way too. There was a time when corporal punishment was common in schools, and a time when the traditional saying, *"Beat your wife every day, if you don't know why she will,"* was deemed wisdom, while the converse image, mama taking a rolling pin to her husband's head was the subject of gossip and song – as in the Ella Fitzgerald jazz lyric *"Stone Cold Dead in the Market"*: *"Last night I went out drinking /When I came home I gave her a beating /So she catch up the rolling pin and went to work on my head /Until she bash it in."*

Cultural norms, acceptance, even items or actions of pride and entertainment, change with time – though bigotry and social views they are often connected with often do not. That which is occasionally proved true can be called bigoted – if it only serves an agenda of the one doing the calling. When you need a distraction, Play the Race Card and avoid having your true agenda discovered. But, play it too well and you become a Nazi, a Grand Inquisitor, or someone else worthy of becoming a historic role model.

We have classic stuff tied to Latino-White conflicts that are as old as the Mexican-American War, and older if we look at the Spanish Inquisitions and 1492 expulsion which had brought the first

Jews to the New World aboard Columbus' ships. In July 2019 we saw the demonstrations which resulted in the removal of the Puerto Rican governor and to similar disruptions throughout Latin America. There is an apparent disorder associated with the  Latino culture – one which Russia would love to see be both real and inflicted upon prosperous states such as California, New York, and Texas.

Those who oppose the wall, border security, and the orderly introduction and assimilation of Latin migrants, are actually in the process of engaging in Climate Change denial.  The Dust Bowl experience – which caused countless deaths and the relocation of over 200,000 Okies to California – is minor in comparison to the heat which will engulf equatorial regions between Honduras and Brazil.  If we view Climate Change Denial in terms of the way the Second Debate Democratic nominees address it, it's obvious they don't care about something which will be shaping the nation by the 2028 election.

There is one exception – Congresswoman Tulsi Gabbard, who is a JPC and, therefore, is traditionally compatible with other Presidents.  In a 31 July Tweet {10:47PM} Gabbard said, *"This is personal.  I grew up in Hawaii which is the most remote island chain in the world.  Protecting our environment is not a political issue, it's a way of life.  This is why I introduced OFF Act to transition to 100% renewable energy."*

The OFF Act is formally designated the *"Off Fossil Fuels for a Better Future Act, H.R. 3671"*.  Some might view it as simply a green imitative and lump it in with other things the Republicans have found is to lie about.  But, Gabbard is a Hawaiian National Guard Major who has served in combat zones and understands the realities of the Bush initiated 18-years war, and the realities of National Security.

Keeping what oil we have in the ground, while also freeing us from the need for oil in civilian life, makes America free from the Arab Oil.  By June 1944, the had Germans seen their access to lost a significant portion of their access to Middle Eastern Oil, and that significantly contributed to the defeat of the Nazis.  America is now engaged in Fracking – scraping the bottom of the oil barrel before its reserves are completely depleted.  Knowing this, and the strategic threat represented by the loss of Arab oil, while other reserves are controlled by Russia, the military initiated multiple programs for the development of electric vehicles and the onsite generation of necessary energy.

As noted, China is already promoting Green Energy. What is not widely discussed is the reality that Middle Eastern powers, like Saudi Arabia, The United Arab Emirates, Morocco and Egypt are becoming leaders in the development of renewable energy.

The current behavior displayed and engaged in by Reagan-Democrats is not Kosher. It protects neither nation nor planet – it only furthers the agenda of those seeking to topple the king so they can become both king and despot. It was what history shows followed the French Revolution and then the Russian one.

America avoided being one of those later models when its elites chose to separate from, rather than overthrow, their parents and family.

We tend to see that truth hidden by the history books – the fact that those who were the leaders in America were all the sons, grandsons, and cousins of the very nobility whose power they were seeking to bring to an end – or restructure – in portion of the New World now known as the United States of America, or simply by the abbreviation America.

The Nazis, Russians, French, and, in 1492, the Spanish, all based their power grabs on attacks against those they alleged to be the "Elite." But, when we look at the history in *Jonathon's POTUS Cousins* {JPC}, we see there is an elected class of individuals who are all related by common ancestors – a genetic class, Biblical Levites or "British Gentry", who actually constitute the truly elite class that has always provided American leaders in all fields – be it politics, the arts, or business.

If we stretch the connection back further that the founding of the colonies – the cutoff date used in JPC was 1575 – we find a genetic link which extends William the Conqueror and further to his ancestor, Charlemagne.

Naturally, naysayers would be quick to dismiss a reality based on "thoroughbred" generics, those which the lowest intellect would even confuse it with Hitler's Master race – which attacked and belittled members of the educated elites based expressly upon their educational, cultural, and economic achievements. It seems a bit comical that, when speaking of Hitler, it is seldom-if-ever in the context of him having used the classical attacks to amass huge wealth.

His book *"Mein Kampf"* was an enormous bestseller that earned him millions only a year before western society fell into the Great Depression. Soon after coming to power, he promoted his book – by giving it away to newly married couples, but having it paid for by their local community – and then failed to pay taxes on proceeds from book sales; when caught, he played the good politician and made himself tax-exempt. Seeking an American model for what Hitler did in terms of evading taxes, we need only look at Evangelical preachers and the vast tax-free wealth they acquire.

On 8 August 2002, the New York Times ran an article that expressly stated: *"In all the continuing fascination with Hitler since his suicide on April 30, 1945, in his Berlin bunker as the Soviet Army closed in, little attention has been paid, until now, to his personal finances."*

Based on known sales of *"Mein Kampf,"* it is estimated that during the Great Depression Hitler amassed the equivalent of $64 million in terms of today's purchasing power or value of a dollar.

If we think in terms of the post-political office earnings of a modern politician, it is worth noting another point in the Times article: *"From the time he became chancellor until his death in 1945, Hitler received some 700 million reichsmarks in corporate payments, ... -- well over $3 billion. In return, the businessmen made millions more on their investments and their war work."*

Those wishing to draw parallels to Hitler really should have their attention focused on his connection to the Military-Industrial complex or Big Business. But that might mean people would focus on their activities in that same context – much easier to rant about the Holocaust or Racism.

Yet, if we think *Kosher*, we see an American Swamp filled with *Economic Hitlers* who bend to the political breeze – so long as they can line their pockets, and, in the process, exempt both themselves and their Party benefactors from taxes.

When we look at Trump in these terms, we see a man who entered office wealthy and is the poorer for it – but the economy is richer. Under POTUS-45 the United States achieved the lowest unemployment rate since 1969, yielding the highest employment among minorities in the nation's history and the longest period of economic expansion with a GDP growth rate deemed impossible during the Obama era – which invites a parallel to Britain.

In Britain, media portrayals of Prime Minister Johnson as their Trump are, in part, based on prior characterizations of him as a person "*polarizing opinions to the extreme*", and include the idea he is "*variously evil, a clown, a racist and a bigot.*"  Since he also happens to have Trump's hair coloring and styling, but also a well-documented history as a philanderer that easily exceeds anything associated with Trump.

The only major difference in media representations is that BREXIT – which British voters approved in 2016. Johnson said, with or without a divorce agreement, Britain exits the European Union in October 2019.  British economists noted the result would be falling home prices, a 25-percent increase in the cost of many canned goods, and the value the pound falling to parity with both the dollar and the euro.  Which means, by popular vote and under the leadership of the British Trump, we have the expectation of an economic crash in Europe, while in America, 101 Democrats have said they want to move for impeachment and a 22-45 percent fall in the Stock Market that would represent the American equivalent of BREXIT.

Something is not Kosher.  And we can see it if we look back to October 2016, in the context of 2019 claims that Russia rigged the election – which means the Electoral College – overturning a popular vote majority in a handful of states.

One state was California, where we saw representation was, in Los Angeles, 40-percent of voters were effectively denied their rightful voice.  Fast forward sixty years, and we see the Governor of California sign into law denying the Presidential Candidate of a Major Political Party – or any candidate – a place on the State Ballot unless they first provide their tax returns for the previous five years.

In October 2016, President Obama commented on Trump asserting the election was rigged:  *"There is no serious person out there who would suggest somehow that you could even rig America's elections, in part because they're so decentralized and the numbers of votes involved.  There's no evidence that that has happened in the past or that there are instances in which that will happen this time. And so, I'd advise Mr. Trump to stop whining and go try to make his case to get votes. ... I have never seen in my lifetime or in modern political history any presidential candidate trying to discredit the elections and the election process before votes have even taken place."*

Yet three years later, the Democrats are saying Trump was correct, but he was the one colluding with those who were rigging the election. In effect, the Democrats are systematically attacking Obama – but they need to keep those attacks covert.

In terms of election manipulation, the previously mentioned California legislation requiring all candidates for either President or Governor to provide the California secretary of state with copies of the previous five years tax returns – not less than three months before the state's primary – demonstrates an attempt to exclude candidates. This was tried in 2017 but was vetoed by Governor Jerry Brown as both unconstitutional and as a gateway to requiring other documents – such as certified copies of birth certificates and medical records.

There was no secret made of the fact that this was explicitly attacking Trump. As described by Governor Gavin Newsom, *"The disclosure required by this bill will shed light on conflicts of interest, self-dealing, or influence from domestic and foreign business interest."*

However, no such data is actually on the Tex Return forms. If it were to exist at all, it would be buried within the corporate records of those entities from which income and loses are derived. Those firms would, by law, only need have to provide a single page form disclosing total income paid and any taxes withheld.

Given that the Constitution specifies the requirements for eligibility, any restrictions imposed by states are illegal; plus there is a First Amendment right of association issue which appears to cover political party selection of candidates who otherwise meet the eligibility requirements. Effectively, California is dictating which candidates citizens can vote for in a primary and thus effectively dictate the candidates in a National General Election.

It is clear that Newsom, in conjunction with the California Legislature, is criminally bent on attracting the Constitution and Democracy and therefore should be recalled along with all who voted to pass the legislation.

The second Democratic Debate occurred on 30 July, and so corresponded to the news of the California Tax Return disclosure law. This would have prevented any intelligent discussion of the issue by the candidates – including how they felt about releasing their taxes to detailed scrutiny before they officially became the Party nominee. Neither the law nor its timing appears Kosher.

Place that into the context of the use of migrants to replace trees as a basis for gerrymandering representation, and California appears to be at the epicenter of any attempts to "rig" the 2020 election. By extension, the law would allow the State to require that its electors only vote for a candidate who has provided their tax returns before the primary – this then manipulates Electoral College Vote and possibly, without regard for the popular vote, the election outcome.

We already know the intent was to target Trump – if they were to repeal the law after the 2020 election, that action would provide clear proof of criminal intent to manipulate an election outcome. As is, there is the legal issue of the law not covering the Vice President, who, though unknown at the time of the primary, would, as the lawful successor to the President, still need have to be vetted using the Newsom excuse for the law.

## CHAPTER FOUR – Trump Opposition

*"Why waste your money looking up your family tree?*
*Just go into politics and your opponents will do it for*
*you." ~* Mark Twain
*"If you don't know history, you don't know anything.*
*You are a leaf that doesn't know it is part of a tree."*
— Michael Crichton

Clearly, there are numerous things which aren't Kosher, and many of them point to intentional election manipulation centered on California and its history of – to paraphrase Justice Warren – having *"legislators who represent trees or acres rather than its voters and citizens."*

Trump can face attacks because he adhered to the wisdom of Martin Luther King Jr.: *"In the end, we will remember not the words of our enemies, but the silence of our friends."* Trump has a record of supporting his friends or those who do not oppose him – he allows his opposition to destroy themselves, and the best way to do that is to have them oppose their own best interests or that which was their agenda.

As previously mentioned in this book series, Trump often plays a Willy Wonka style character. To explain, look at a letter Gene Wilder wrote describing how he intended to play the Wonka character, and its entrance:

*"When I make my first entrance, I'd like to come out of the door carrying a cane and then walk toward the crowd with a limp. After the crowd sees Willy Wonka is a cripple, they all whisper to themselves and then become deathly quiet. As I walk toward them, my cane sinks into one of the cobblestones I'm walking on and stands straight up, by itself; but I keep on walking, until I realize that I no longer have my cane. I start to fall forward, and just before I hit the ground, I do a beautiful forward somersault and bounce back up, to great applause.*

*"From that time on, no one will know if I'm lying or telling the truth"*

As we see from how the pundits describe Trump, were they speaking of Wonka, the bit with the limp would forever rank him as a devout liar. They tend to bask in the fact they miss the wisdom Wilder has revealed in at various times in his career, and the tactics Trump applies to his business persona.

This point was brought home on 5 August 2019, by Boston Globe columnist Joan Vennochi: *"When Trump condemns racism and bigotry, no one takes him seriously."* But, as is repeatedly demonstrated, they also infer racism where none exists.

Ronald Reagan showed his racism quite clearly in a private recording in which he states very clearly states: *"To see those... monkeys from those African countries — damn them, they're still uncomfortable wearing shoes!"* Had Reagan said *"in Africa,"* the meaning would have been less inclusive than *"from Africa,"* since the former would be specific to Africa, while the latter includes all whose ancestry is tied to that continent. If the statement is placed in context, it related to UN African delegates, clearly would incorporate African Americans and be consistent with Nixon (to whom he said it) and the Reagan-Republicans.

Nixon would later relate how the California Governor had cited, *"these...cannibals on television last night. Christ, they weren't even wearing shoes, and here the United States is going to submit its fate to that."* And it's a matter of record that, in the 1970s, Reagan publicly defended the apartheid states of Rhodesia and South Africa. Reagan's policy record was sufficiently clear to allow him to run for governor, in 1966, on a platform aimed at an elimination of the FAIR HOUSING ACT. After all, he asserted, *"If an individual wants to discriminate against Negroes or others in selling or renting his house, he has a right to do so."*

Comically, we have moved so far from the accepted Reagan mentality that it becomes racist to believe "good people" can see a in monuments to Southern Civil War Heros, or that "Love It, or Leave It" is a racist assertion. Worse, it is presented that way at a time when the nation needs to be brought together, rather than torn asunder by fantasy interpretations or rational alternatives.

As we know, on 9 September 2016, Hillary Clinton chose to label half of Trump's supporters – the majority of those occupying the majority of states – people who occupy what she deemed to be a *"Basket of Deplorables."* It's a group she defined as people who were *"racist, sexist, homophobic, xenophobic, Obamaphobic and whatever."* With the one characterization, which she repeated in several venues, Clinton attacked a quarter of American voters.

Clinton showed she hated most of the nation – something that works in California, New York, and even Texas. Then we have the issue Trump ran on – the Border Wall. That was the *2006 Secure Fence Act* that Hillary sponsored with Barack Obama, it was a Democratic program that Reagan's Republican base opposed in 1980.

Now along comes Trump, a former Democrat, who realized he could use Democratic programs to win Republican votes – if he phrased it correctly. By the way, that's an application of a classic psychologist explanation of how a Hypnotist can get people to do things they are morally opposed to doing – *"You can get anyone to do anything if you phrase it properly."*

Deeply religious Jihadists are told to commit suicide while committing mass murder by telling them they are killing infidels and the act will get them a guaranteed place in Paradise. Does it matter if they are murdering women, children, and innocents (acts expressly forbidden by the Koran), or that they were killing people who are making a pilgrimage to Mecca, none of it matters, their action will erase their sins and give them a free ticket to paradise.

You sell your point by making it personal – by stimulating natural tendencies toward various reactions (some would be called bigoted, or self-preservation, and even be 'selfless' as when we risk our lives and kill a to save another).

You cannot attack a person's beliefs and expect them to comply with yours. But you can phrase your belief in a manner that complies with or conforms to theirs. As I pointed out in *The GENESIS OF GENESIS*, the Biblical authors used this 'conversion' technique.

The use of the woman, serpent, and tree at the opening of the Garden of Eden story was not an accident, it invoked images and connections documented in neolithic cave art  – the three symbols are were all accepted traditional references to knowledge, with the wise serpent being the oldest and most universal of all symbols. Adam was the blindly obedient dummy who had to be given or led into accepting, knowledge before evolution occurred.

In *GRANDPA WAS A DEITY* we have the same tribe spread to all the places where civilization would evolve. And a common element of their travels – apart from their use of the three symbols for wisdom – was that they claimed, via a divine son, to have been directly descended from the creator.  We see this in the preamble to the Flood Story as the origin of the "Men of Renown" and, of course, when the mythology was transferred to Jesus, the sons were removed from the story and he becomes the only begotten Creator's son who has a human mother.

*"You can get anyone to believe anything if you phrase it properly."*  We see this as the basis for the story, *"The Emperor's New Clothes,"* in which the rumor is spread that only fools cannot see the wondrous garments created for the Emperor.  Phrase it in the correct ego attacking manner, and propaganda can get people to see what does not exist.

When Hillary decided to make her *"Basket of Deplorables"* a routine talking point, she was attempting to make those who backed her feel superior, but, because Trump had already usurped wat had, for decades, been key elements of Democratic agenda, it turned out that Hillary actually drove away Democratic voters – but might have captured California's Reagan-Democrats.

Looking back, we saw how Trump reacted.  He felt sorry for her and played it down – indicating Hillary made a self-sustaining gaff.  The following month (October 2016), Trump was at a roast – which Hillary attended – where Trump said it was *"dinner with friends,"* but for Hillary, her *"largest crowd of the season."*  Since it was an Archdiocese related event, Trump played with the idea of celebrating a guy who started as a carpenter working for his father – pointing out that, for several months he had worked as a carpenter for his father.  The line received sold laughter.  He then pointed out that the heads of the major media were her campaign staff.

However, if we again look to Gene Wilder, this time at what was an ad-lib line in the film *"Blazing Saddles"*, we might gain insight into where Hillary obtained her Middle America strategy:

As the Waco Kid, Wilder says, *"You've got to remember that these are just simple farmers. These are people of the land. The common clay of the new West... You know... morons."*

Shall we upset the deplorables? Or, just simply point to the reality that brought a racist Ronald Reagan into the Oval Office so that he could practice his Voodoo Economics on the nation?

In 1980, 50.7 percent of the popular vote, it was distributed across the nation in a state-by-state majority which yielded 489 electoral votes to only 49 for non-racist, God-serving, incumbent

Jimmy Carter.  Have we learned, or are we going to continue the Reagan programs – while inventing derogatory things to say about Trump?

Reagan gave us what promises to become a bankrupt Social Security.  He did it by implementing cutbacks on social programs, cutting taxes beyond the income/expense balance point, making sure military spending was increased, then engaging in activities designed to utilize the killing power.  Of course, Reagan gave us the Socialist idea called trickle-down economics – the idea that, if you make the Rich super-rich, they will generously permit the overflow to drip down upon the starving masses. But only after their businesses were deregulated and we engage outsourcing of a type which has *Made China Great Again*.

Had Reagan not proclaimed "*Let's make America great again*," would we have engaged in regime change, Iran Contra, or have seen the *Gulf War* (August 1990-February 1991) and then an "*Operation Desert Storm*" (January 1991-February 1991), which set the stage for an anniversary retaliation on 26 February 1993 – the destruction of the World Trade Center accompanied by an attack on the Pentagon.

Bill Clinton gained the Oval and gave America eight years of budget surpluses; an impeachment for obstructing justice of the definition of "Sexual Relations" following that bout of "Oral in the Oval" with an intern.  But, the Jihadists were kind enough to await Bush-43 before their infamous second attack, which yielded a "War on Terror" that terrorize the Middle East for eighteen years, which allowing the architect of the attack to live comfortably in a villa overlooking the troops who were supposedly looking for him.

As was done with Clinton, with a record settling growing economy and stocks making record highs, once again, the public – or the opposing Congress – is calling for impeachment while we see, as a result of Trump's efforts, North and South Korea meeting for the first time in the seventy years since the beginning of the Korean War. Trump is branded a racist – and all because he has raised incomes and lowered unemployment for minorities, while also applying the Democratic Border Security concept which will address the threat of mass Climate Change migrations that have already begun in other parts of the world.

He's in office because *"These are people of the land...You know…morons,*" whose Electoral Votes refuted Reaganite policies, turned away from "Open Borders" and blanket amnesty for those who enter the nation illegally. Trump got them to accept and cheer both the Obama Democratic hard-line and seek to improve upon Obama's Secure Fence Act. So, how were they rewarded for "seeing the light"?

Hillary demonstrated she considered the residents of 40 of the 50 states to be morons, a "*Basket of Deplorables.*" The issue before the nation is which of the possible Democratic Candidates will think of them in the same way. When I began to layout this book, I was thinking in terms of the traditional family connection – the fact that every POTUS and significant American has been in the line that goes back to Charlemagne. Moreover, that line is one routed through William the Conqueror, and from him, the line is passed through five sisters whose descendants intermarried along with an interval averaging about every seven generations.

Probably a third of the nation is in that family line. While they might not be directly descended, they would be some level of JPC – one of the commercials for Ancestry.com features a woman who discovers she is a cousin to George Washington, so is a JPC but we are not told that she is also related to another Washington cousin, Barack Obama.

Throughout the history of the nation, only those who are descended from the five sisters have led the colonies, and only those I now refer to as POTUS Cousins have held the Oval Office. As with most things, the exception that marks or proves the rule – for POTUS Cousins, Martin Van Buren, whose known ancestry is insufficient to affirm the connection, is that exception. He still has a cousin who married into the established lineage and so he is a cousin within the 1575 criteria.

With JPC membership vetting the opposition or candidates for the 2020 election, of the broad field of Democratic Candidates, all but 8 are eliminated as those who, in historic terms, cannot be elected. As a cross-reference, we can look at Hillary Clinton's loss. Bill Clinton is descended from two of the sisters, making Hillary a relative. But Hillary is not a descendant and lost in the Electoral College vote. But so did Al Gore, who also is unrelated to the JPC lineage. For some inexplicable reason, the Electoral College vote will reject non-JPC candidates.

As popular as he is, Bernie Sanders is not a JPC – nor is he married to one.  A thousand years of history decrees Sanders could not win the election and the nation expects to survive.  But that is not to say he cannot be a powerful Senator and excellent guide for Presidential policy.

We do not have details on Warren's first husband, but he might well be a JPC.  Not that it matters.  Bruce Mann, her current husband, is descended from three of the sisters, and Warren herself comes from two of them.  Joe Biden also comes from two of them.

But the strongest connect is that presented by Major Tulsi Gabbard, a Congresswoman with a lineage that includes four of the sisters.  By contrast, Donald Trump has only two present in his ancestry, while Tiffany, his daughter with Marla Maples, has four – because, like her mother, she is a product of a marriage between descendants.

Considering the historical connection pattern, and taking into account her presentation and military experience, Gabbard is the logical Democratic nominee.  She need not be the nominee for 2020 – there is too much trivial-garbage going on – but she would be the type of leader America needs to properly position itself in the Climate Change world which will emerge after 2024.  But all that means is that, in 2024, she can be running as an incumbent or successor.  Either way, given the ages of those who comprise the likely candidates – Trump vs Bidden, Warren, or Sanders – it is clear 2024 will be an open race defined by either a term-limited incumbent or an individual whose age exceeds the lifespan of an American.  In the case of Sanders and Biden, either man would have a POTUS age record as the first octogenarian in the Oval.

For now, the opposition generated garbage and the related messes represent a far greater issue than the factual reality that whoever wins in 2020 will likely be a one-term POTUS or die in office and elevate their Vice President to occupancy of the Oval.

As they continue to promote an agenda that has not been thought through, Democrats are engaging in the hate speech that they are accusing Trump of. They are being as counterproductive as Hillary Clinton was when she used the "Deplorables" approach.

It's the reality behind the con presented in *The Emperor's New Clothes*: Morons don't like to be called Morons; Deplorable people don't like being called Deplorable.  And good people who are acting rationally do not like to be lumped in with either of those groups. People like to be praised, they like to hear positives, they want solutions and defeatist assertions of negativity.

The adage says, "*You catch more flies with honey than with vinegar.*" But, as we saw, during the Obama era, Far-Right types became rabble-rousers by being negative, without suggesting any positive alternative. Now we see that the Far-Left has adopted that same approach. They want people to turn-off their minds and see the clothes that aren't there. And worse, they want people to focus on those clothes, on the immediate false reality, rather than consider the long-term reality of having a naked Emperor.

The Naked Emperor is the fact that, six months before the anticipated February 2020 contest, a Suffolk University/Boston Globe poll disclosed that the 76-year-old former vice president Joe Biden had the support of 21 percent of likely Democratic primary voters. In second place, with 17 percent support, was 77-year-old Senator Bernie Sanders of Vermont; in third place, 70-year-old Senator Elizabeth Warren of Massachusetts with 14 percent.

Consider, that was baby born in 2016 could expect to live 78.6 years. Those living in Hawaii or California can expect to live almost 82-years, which means fourth place Senator Kamala Harris (54) and sixth place Representative Tulsi Gabbard (38) can easily make it through two terms. Of course, as a JPC – which Harris is not – National Guard Major Tulsi Gabbard is the historic ideal to be the first Female POTUS and would replace Theodore Roosevelt as the youngest person to Occupy the Oval.

However, determining which candidate should run against Trump is a rather academic exercise. If we look at the focus on trying to invent a reason to impeach – a process that began with the announcement of the 2016 election outcome – the Democrats' focus on impeachment indicates that those currently in the House of Representatives do not doubt they cannot defeat Trump in the 2020 election.

Working with the knowledge Senate Republicans would not vote for removal, 100 Congressman decided they would strive to manipulate the 2020 Senate election by first creating propaganda to convince the masses the Emperor is fully dressed, and then turn voting masses against any who said he wasn't.

Ideally, that would result in the Democrats taking control of the House and Senate, which would then allow the Reagan-Democrats to promote an agenda that is contrary to the historic pattern of the Democratic Party – which has already been seen by their strong opposition to the expansion of the 2006 Secure Fence Act and Border Control  which the nation will need as Climate Change worsens and causes Climate Migration to increase.

For those who don't understand, under Reagan' amnesty, illegal border crossings began to increase and in FY2000 Border Patrol agents on the Southwestern border had apprehended a total of 1,643,679 individuals.  In the same period, a total of 32,759 were caught illegally crossing the other three borders.  Even with a 9/11 effect, for the next six years apprehensions easily exceeded an average of over 1.1 million per year.

But that ended with passage of the 2006 Secure Fence Act, sponsored by Senators Clinton, Schumer, and Obama.  Thereafter the border saw a steady decline until the 2017 low of 303,916 was achieved; at that point, Reagan-Democrats were expressing their opposition to Trump improving and completing the  Secure Fence, Obama's legacy – which Trump was now referring to as a "Wall".

There are members of the media who have realized that the Reagan-Democrats – though not referred to by that term – are in the process of attacking and undermining the Obama Legacy.

A popular technique, utilized by THE SQUAD, has been to grab the media and social media microphone, then describe the president with a range of profanity, while invoking their various hateful canards, their defamatory false allegations, and unfounded rumors.  When called on their actions, they quickly hide behind an ancestry of choice or appearance and claim the mantel of being the victims of racism.

Copying the example of Elizabeth Warren's claim of being an "American Indian," Alexandria Ocasio-Cortez made the family claim that *"One of the things that we discovered about ourselves is that a very, very long time ago, generations and generations ago, my family consisted of Sephardic Jews."*

That December 2018 assertion exerted a political effect that was purely psychological – it gave her soon-to-be constituents of Jewish faith and heritage to identify her as *"Converso"* – one of the numerous Spanish Jews forced to become Catholics.

She then claimed a later symbolic connection to the Jew who

sailed with Columbus to the Gulf of Mexico, or from Portugal to Brazil, to become founding citizens of the Western Hemisphere – bru, with the arrival of Spanish Inquisitors, those same Spanish Jews headed North, into what is now New Mexico and California, to be absorbed by the indigenous Native American population.

In a way, AOC's claim allows her leeway to oppose the usual Democratic position toward Israel that is so important to many in her district; it also provides a bit of cover when she sides with Muslim Squad members against Israel.  It seems Progressive Jews accepted the stunt, but for Orthodox and Conservative but, as with Evangelicals or others who accept Biblical Prophecy, her positions are very divisive in an era when the objective should be increasing Middle Eastern stability.

It is a pattern of intentionally created divisiveness that helps define the approach to the Southern Border.  In April 2019, AOC made it clear she could understand the effect of Climate Change in the next decade.  Granted, she was focused on the climate effect associated with fossil fuels and carbon dioxide, but it seems ridiculous to assume a woman of proven intelligence and the daughter proud to say her father attended Brooklyn Tech – a high school whose students are vetted for admission based on IQ – that such a woman is ignorant of the temperature levels that will define the region between Honduras and northern Brazil.

It is to some extent equally ridiculous that she would be ignorant of deadly heat-waves that have already begun in various equatorial regions.  Granted, she was speaking before heat-waves struck the American Midwest and setting records in Europe.

Look at the 2000 apprehension numbers, and look at the overcrowding in border detention facilities. Look at AOC's display of crocodile tears as she avails herself of a classic media capturing political photo-op as she views those in a detention center.  Kie so many Reagan-Democrats, she seeks a return to the apprehension numbers of 2000.  Though she would be happier to simply allow them to enter and impose their effect on the American economy.

Imagine the negative economic effect – America attempting to absorb 1.6 million Latin American Climate Change refugees as defined by illiterate women skilled only in unskilled manual work and children, who are likely to comprise 60% of asylum seekers.

Over a decade, that means 16 million added to the current

American population of 328 million – that would be a five percent growth above normal population growth.  And that's 9.6 million children in addition to the 76.3 million between the ages of 1 and 17 that the census projects for 2030.  Phrased another way, that's about a 12.5-percent in educational costs, and property taxes to cover them.  It also means more educators in all grade levels – many of whom would need to be bilingual.

If they were concentrated along in southern border states, it would be the equivalent of an eightfold increase population in  New Mexico – if they were all to reside there.  They also represent a lot of "Trees", a lot of non-voting entities, bodies that will shift the allocation of representatives toward those states that decide to take them in.  That could also shift the Electoral College votes to those states, granting enormous power to a handful of citizens.

But hey!  Why not panic over the possibility of a three-cent change in the cost of a China-related product.  Can a trade war, which might repatriate outsourced jobs that, due to the record low unemployment, would provide the jobs for Latino immigrants, be that bad?  Or does rational thought dictate that we can support New Mexico if its population suddenly was nine times larger after a decade of Climate Change refugee arrivals?

Consider the current reality which sees the average annual temperatures in equatorial lowlands around 31°C (88°F) during the afternoon and 23°C (73°F) at sunrise.  Heading north, we have an average summer temperature in Mexico City in the area of 72°F to 75°F – the same as the equatorial sunrise.  During the summer, temperatures along the southern border of the United States are a bit higher and average between 75°F to 80°F – midpoint being about 78°F or ten degrees below equatorial temperatures.  If we look at Honduras, the average winter temperature is the same as the sunrise temperature at the equator and within many southern border states.

On 18 July 2019, we saw a report that *"Amid widespread US heatwave, experts predict dangerous extremes in summer temperatures will only get worse."*

In the story, we learned that the upper limit of the National Weather Service's heat-index scale, is 127°F, and toward the end of the century it will be exceeded in many areas of the U.S., and more than one-third of the population could experience a week or more in that temperature range.

If we assume Climate Change is real and the temperature variance holds, temperatures at the equator will exceed 137°F as their normal average.  This means those people who will be living in the nations between Honduras and northern Brazil are going to effectively be living in a sauna at temperatures.  That is, something between the 120-130°F for infrared saunas, and temperatures of 150-175°F found in traditional saunas.

Of course, if there is high humidity, we could compare it to living in a steam bath where the normal temperature is 110-115°F – which means, at 127-137°F, the temperature would exceed the safe setting on a convention bath or shower water heater.

However, the July 2019 heatwave which in the American Midwest and Europe has led to a timeline revision and many of the forecasts indicate major problems will be experienced before mid-century.  With that in mind, imagine that equatorial temperatures beyond normal endurance of average plant, animal, and human life are achieved much sooner.

The Squad and Reagan-Democrats don't seem to be able to make the connection between Climate Change and the reason for a crowd control wall along the southern border.  They like to yell it is racist, or racially motivated.  They certainly haven't shown any interest in redesigning American Immigration policies to deal with a reality where millions of Climate Change refugees head to the northern regions to escape the persistent deadly heat.

There are only about ten million people in Honduras.  And El Salvador, Nicaragua, and Costa Rica might add another twenty million. Once you get past Panama, and into the northern nations of South America, you should think in terms of adding about half the current United States population.

Then there are ever-present economic problems in both Venezuela and Argentina.

In August 2019, Argentina, which is  Latin America's third-largest economy, had roughly a third of its population living below poverty levels.  It is a nation that saw taxes raised and utility bills soar at a time when unemployment and inflation rates were also trending upward.  As with BREXIT, October has significance – it is when Argentina has its President Election and determines who will be held responsible for any new economic problems.

Venezuela has already entered unthinkable inflation rates –

but exactly the rates Reaganomics had assumed would befall the United States and thus monetize (make meaningless) the National Debt. The economic problems in Venezuela are sending its people west, into Columbia, and south, into Brazil. But Brazil is teetering on the brink of a recession and there had been no advancement in the economy since 2014.

Unlike Trump, Brazil's President Jair Bolsonaro can be seen as a business illiterate who delegated all the economic decisions to a "super-minister of the economy" – a businessman named Paulo Guedes. It appears to be an economic Bush-Cheney relationship which saw the country's economy contract by almost 7% in 2015 and 2016, only to be followed in 2017 and 2018, by a recovery of only 1.1% a year. Since 2012, unemployment has increased by 50% to about 13%, while in America the Obama-Trump rate has fallen from over 9% to under 3.7%.

There is the tradition, the horrible economic history, that defines South America. Naturally, stating this documentable fact is enough to get The Squad to yell racist. But their irrational need scream racism does not change the harsh reality. Moreover, it does not change the fact that, with more frequent heatwaves, and a scientific expectation these same equatorial region nations will be experiencing daily temperatures exceed the levels of human tolerance, either their populations will head south to a bankrupt Argentina or North to Mexico and the United States.

With the looming recessions in Hong Kong and throughout South America, plus the emerging indicators of a recession in both German and Britain as a result of BREXIT, the Reagan-Democrats seem delighted by economists projections that there could be a recession before the November 2020 election. Basically, because governments around the world have worked to undermine or even destroy their economies, Reagan-Democrats are basking in the prospect America will be sucked under so they can blame Trump.

Trump speaks of an invasion – he's a bit premature but is not wrong. At least not if we accept the reality of Climate Change and the heatwave it will cause across the equatorial regions. There is a real need for systems to deal with the migrant threat, and the massive culture shock they will impose on the nation.

But, as seen in the Summer of 2019, Reagan-Democrats have no interest in establishing policies and systems which will be needed to deal with the invasion of South Americans seeking a climate that allows for their survival. Instead, we see The Squad whine and moan about the use of terms like an invasion to describe the millions of Climate refugees that America will be absorbing.

Granted, just as they currently pass through Mexico, in the future, they will be ushered past the United States into Canada.

Canada is 3.855 million mi² and its population is only 37 million. So it is about the size of the United States but with only one-tenth the population. Do Canadians realize the realities of the pending Climate Refugee problem?

Those who neither want to see enforcement of and improve upon the 2006 Secure Fence Act are, even if they wish to lie about it, actively supporting Reagan's no fence open border policy. They are arguing that Climate Change is not real, and therefore that it will not spawn mass migrations. But, even setting aside the facts, they are also arguing against the economic and social realities that are driving the current wave of migrants.

Trump's opposition opposes reality. It offers no solutions because it denies there is a looming problem. Those who deny the reality of a massive climate caused migration are the worst form of Climate deniers; they show their position through their denial of a need for the border wall. They are Reaganites screaming for open borders – but are too cowardly to say the words.

# CHAPTER FIVE – ICE

**"We need to accept that we won't always make the right decisions, that we'll screw up royally sometimes – understanding that failure is not the opposite of success, it's part of success." — @ariannahuff"**

August 2019 saw two interesting events. After ramping up Trump's tough stance on illegal border crossings and instituting aggressive actions against those employing the undocumented, it was reported by U.S. Customs and Border Protection that illegal crossings had fallen for the second straight month.

Department of Homeland Security officials attributed the decline to several things, including Mexico's crackdown on Central American migration through a process of interception before they can reach the United States border. Another part of the process is to intercept them at Mexico's southern border.

In July 2019, apprehensions fell 21 percent and marked the first time in five months the total number fell below the 100,000. In may, apprehensions had reached 144,000, with the drop to 82,000, the result of Trump's policies yielded a 43% decline between May and July. Still, U.S. Customs and Border Protection Commissioner Mark Morgan termed was "in full-blown crisis" because of the economic situation in Central America.

After deploying almost 26,000 troops, relative to the same period in 2018, Mexico doubled the number of individuals it had apprehended. In addition, there was a tightening on the handling of asylum claims, whereby claimants were required to await their decision in Mexico. The agreement with Guatemala authorizes the U.S. to send asylum seekers there until their claim is resolved; in accordance with UN asylum protocols, it also requires that asylum seekers first apply to Guatemala for that status.

On 12 August, the results of the Guatemalan presidential election were announced; President-elect Alejandro Giammattei, then said, *"We will rebuild Guatemala. I have no words to say how grateful I am."* He might as well have promised he would be making Guatemala great again – as a Mesoamerican civilization or Mayan equivalent of ancient Egypt, the region was once truly great.

As with Joe Biden, Giammattei had failed in three previous

bids to secure the presidency, and, the conservative 63-year-old has shown that persistence can pay-off. In speaking of the asylum deal, called a new "safe third country" deal, he has said, as Trump has about various deals, it's "bad news", asserting that his nation was economically struggling nation was not ready to cope with the potential population bump – a sentiment apparently shared with eight out of 10 surveyed Guatemalans.

Under the new accord, asylum seekers from Honduras and El Salvador would apply for asylum in Guatemala rather than the US, and Guatemalan workers would gain an advantage in seeking US visas. How the deal could be improved is not clear; breaking or failing to honor it would expose Guatemala to high tariffs on its goods or US taxes on remittances.

Guatemala was struggling with widespread unemployment and crime with a 60% poverty rate, which has caused hundreds of thousands of its citizens to migrate north in the same way those Honduras and El Salvador were. To curb migration, Giammattei has promised to create what he termed to be a border "investment wall" between Guatemala and Mexico -- the true nature of "the wall" is unknown. But it would augment whatever Mexico initiated when it sent it's troops south. To address the crime problem, Giammattei also proposed reinstating the death penalty.

President-elect Giammattei said, "I don't think there are a lot of people from El Salvador and Honduras who want to seek asylum in Guatemala, especially if they are fleeing poverty. They are looking for asylum in the United States." He mused it unlikely asylum seekers would willing adhere to "safe third country" rules. Though he did hope those among the Guatemalan who had what it takes to contribute to the U.S. and that his "wall of investment" would encourage citizens to stay home and invest in the economic development of their own country.

But can it be done? United Nations Food and Agricultural Organization (FAO) describes the region as, *"The Dry Corridor in Central America."* In 2016, when border crossings under Obama were approaching their lowest point, FAO reported *"Guatemala, Honduras and El Salvador [were] experiencing one of the worst droughts of the last ten years with over 3.5 million in need of humanitarian assistance."*

By 2017, the droughts had caused an increase in the insect

population while destroying crops, eliminating drinking water and killing off a quarter of Honduran conifers.  In 2019, the water shortage was threatening 291,725 poor Guatemalan farm families.

Throughout the "Dry Corridor", Climate-related disasters have been intensifying and threatening the survival of subsistence farmers, who lack food to eat or sell and therefore lack a surplus to see them through the lean time between harvests.

These conditions, which, over the next decade, will become worse, are the driving force behind the "Border Crisis" that Trump referred to.  This is the "Border Crisis" that AOC and The Squad deny exists while also calling any reference to the people involved as simply being racist.

Where Reagan-Democrats sought to have open borders and flood the nation with migrants, Trump is establishing a processing system that will begin at the Honduran-Guatemalan border.  At the same time, the next Guatemalan President is seeking to secure his nation's survival.  Both men understand the need for an orderly system of integration of migrants into the existing social structures.  Whether or not either is thinking about the long-term nature of the problem doesn't really matter.  What we know is that the most visible Democrats – Reagan-Democrats – seem to be intentionally ignoring reality in a way that will ensure the economic collapse of the United States and those nations to the South.

On 7 August, while Joe Biden was in Iowa preparing for a Town Hall campaign stop, agents of the Immigration and Customs Enforcement Service {ICE} raided seven chicken processing plants in Mississippi – taking 680 individuals into custody.

Such raids were common under President George W. Bush, who signed Senator Obama's *Secure Fence Act* into law.  President Obama entered office with less need for such raids because work on the Border Fence/Wall had already begun and the Bush raids made it clear the government was serious about border security, and, as could be expected, as illegal border crossings declined, so did the need for such raids.

Court documents related to the August raid showed those individuals arrested lacked the authorization to work in the United States, and due to previous immigration violations, some workers were wearing electronic monitoring bracelets – moreover, those individuals were under explicit court order not to attempt to work.

This was the biggest raid in a decade and represented the culminated of an investigation into firms using illegal workers and possibly doing so to evade employment and other tax liabilities. In this instance, the year-long investigation focused on companies "*willfully and unlawfully*" engaged in the use of illegal workers – the migrants themselves were not the targets and roughly 40% of those detained were released within 24-hours.

Court papers established that two of the seven plants had a Chinese owner and that supervisors at other plants had turned a blind eye to evidence strongly suggesting job applicants were using fraudulent documents and bogus Social Security numbers.

The National Chicken Council - a poultry industry lobbying group – informed the White House the industry "*uses every tool available to verify the identity and legal immigration status of all prospective employees.*" But sought to assign blame for hiring the illegals on the government by asserting there was no system available to "*confirm with confidence that new hires are legally authorized to work in the United States.*"

However, a simple Google search reveals the existence of a Social Security Administration provided "*Social Security Number Verification Service*" – the SSNVS Overview:

*There are two Internet verification options you can use to verify that your employee names and Social Security numbers (SSN) match Social Security's records. You can:*

- *Verify up to 10 names and SSNs (per screen) online and receive immediate results. This option is ideal to verify new hires.*

- *Upload overnight files of up to 250,000 names and SSNs and usually receive results the next government business day. This option is ideal if you want to verify an entire payroll database or if you hire a large number of workers at a time.*

*While the service is available to all employers and third-party submitters, it can only be used to verify current or former employees and only for wage reporting (Form W-2) purposes.*

Knowing acceptance of fraudulent documents indicates one of several possibilities in which either the floor supervisors, plant managers of the owners were also engaged in tax fraud – no taxes or withholding can be paid based on fraudulent and invalid social security numbers. Neither the SSA or IRS has a means of properly crediting funds received in connection with a false number.

Employers often claim to have been fooled by fraudulent documents, when it would take only a few minutes to verify the documents. This raises an issue of whether the related tax money was submitted to the IRS, how was it booked without a valid taxpayer identification? Or, did the employer show the funds on the books, but not actually provide it to the government?

Or maybe they didn't even book the withheld taxes and employee Social Security contributions – but, knowing employees could not risk exposure by actually filing taxes, showed it on the pay-stubs but booked the money under another employee, who would then recover it as an overpayment of taxes.

It was noted that when applying for work, the illegal job-seeker will use their real names in conjunction with an invented Social Security number. In other instances workers, have been known to use legitimate document of someone else who is no longer working, and possibly no longer residing in the USA.

Investigators also found documentation that inferred one manager was embezzling money by adding fraudulent names and Social Security numbers to the payroll and keeping the proceeds. In those instances, there was no illegal immigrant involved and the matter was simply fraud against the employing company.

A Trump-owned construction company that does work on Trump's golf courses building fountains and waterfalls, apparently employees roving crews of Latino workers – which include illegal immigrants. And, according to the reports, a work supervisor had told an illegal he fake identity documents could be bought on any New York City street corner. It is also reported that, in 2000, a crew of 15 workers was hired to work six-day a week for $15/hour – at the time, the minimum wage was $5.15/hour, so there was no intent to take advantage of an individual's status, and, at the time, the SSA did not have the verification website.

It is interesting to note that news reports connected with the August raid made mention of children as young as 14-years old being illegally employed by firms targeted by ICE.

Ignoring child labor and tax evasion, NEWSWEEK went on record calling for the abolishment of ICE. But this is a song that has been sung on their pages since June of 2018, when Alexandria Ocasio-Cortez defeated 10-term Representative Joe Crowley with a campaign that was, in part, based on abolishing ICE, which had been established by Bush-43 in 2003.

In 2018, Senator Kirsten Gillibrand, who has since become a presidential hopeful, said, "*I don't think ICE today is working as intended. I believe that it has become a deportation force, and I think you should separate the criminal justice from the immigration issues.*"

However, separating criminal and immigration issues, when the immigration issues are criminal ones, seems irrational. If the FBI had to do this work, they would need to coordinate with the IRS, and immigration authorities. The FBI would also need to prioritize issues involved in the ICE raid against those associated with mass shootings of the kind that happened a few days earlier.

Keep in mind, abolishing ICE and hampering enforcement of immigration laws has been a campaign agenda issue for those politicians whose states would benefit from non-voter bodies. It means they have bodies to manipulate representation allocations and thus dilute the power of a citizen's vote.

As a presidential hopeful, Gillibrand stands no chance at the nomination, and, if nominated, cannot win. A victory for her would have the effect of destroying the ancestral continuity that has marked the occupants of the Oval Office since the founding of the nation. Neither Gillibrand nor her husband appears to have a JPC connection. But, more important than ancestral history, she doe not seem to have ideas which will enable America to survive the history now being created – her stance against ICE reflects her inability to deal with the reality of Climate Change migration.

The ICE raids came on the same day Trump visited El Paso – which was still reeling from mass murders committed by a man motivated or animated by racial hatred. Acting upon his delusional white supremacist based fixation, he authored a manifesto fixated on Hispanic immigrants – then shoot and killed 22 people literally in a matter of seconds.

Texas and Ohio are two states which allow Civilians to own military grand assault weapons with high capacity magazines. The same-day shooter in Dayton Ohio carried 250 rounds and killed nine people, injured 27, and did so in only 30 seconds. Had he not be killed by law enforcement it would have taken him less than 4.5 minutes to fire every bullet he had.

In a crowded area, that could mean any person wounded by one round would be killed by a subsequent one. In combat against an attacking force, this ability to kill isn't that bad. But, in terms of what the framers of the Constitution intended as their reason behind the words "*the right of the people to keep and bear Arms, shall not be infringed,*" we have a rational problem.

The 2<sup>nd</sup> Amendment was clearly stated to be "*necessary to the security of a free State,*" and was written to ensure all citizens could mount a door-to-door defense of their towns. Any military assault weapon whose use results in the shooter running out of ammunition in less than 5 minutes is not practical in the context of a community cut-off from outside supplies or in a real-world combat situation were full or semi-automatic firing capabilities have limited use.

Background checks and licensing have a practical place in a modern context, but, as we know from the record, nearly all the mass shootings in America are by people who pass background checks. It's controlling the weapon that is important. There is no reason for any civilian to have a weapon that can kill a person a second. If we argue America is invaded by a well-armed enemy, then an accurate single-shot rifle, selectively targeting an enemy whose weapon can be acquired when they are dead, is far better. Take their semi-automatic and their ammunition, and then, every enemy you kill provides you with ammunition with the weapon you are now using.

Fortunately, those who yell about 2nd Amendment rights seldom actually think about what was intended. America has this huge military budget that is forcing the National Debt to rise and is creating a far greater risk to the nation than any alleged enemy.

In Britain, there is an army recruitment crisis that has seen the operational strength of frontline combat units decline by 40%. And data released under the freedom of information laws show the Ministry of Defence records confirmed there has been a five-year steady decline of soldiers in the British army's infantry regiments. As of 1 January 2019, there was a 7.6% army personnel deficit – something of absolutely no concern for the average American.

Interestingly, the last two great wars all began with Britain in conflict with Europe, with the Middle East as a shadow problem or element. Predictions of the next great war also focus on  Europe and the Middle East, with the likelihood of war in 2033.

Russia was a "Johnny-come-lately" in both wars and when we look at Russia today, we see it teaming up with Iran and Iran both in a military-based conflict with Saudis Arabia and also on track to develop nuclear weapons just in time to deploy them after 2030.

How involved were Latin America Countries in any of the World Wars? Does it matter? Are Latin countries even prone to war – other than Civil war or internal revolutions?  How about their parent – Spain – a nation that was neutral in the First World War, and limited involvement in the Second War to allowing its citizens to volunteer to fight the Bolshevik alongside Nazi troops.  Will first-generation immigrants, still bathed in the traditions of ancestors, partake in a Third World War?  Does it matter?

Is there a connection between ICE, a possible war a decade from now – around the time Climate Change is locked in and with its effects being felt across central latitudes which correspond to the Middle East?

On 9 August, it was reported the Netherlands had suffered 400 more deaths related to the heatwave which began around 22 July – the total was 2940 – making the number comparable to the deaths associated with the World Trade Center.  Is it comparable, can we compare temperatures of a mere 40 degrees Celsius (104 Fahrenheit) to a planned terrorist attack?

We know those who follow current asylum seekers will be escaping poverty and heat above 52.5C (127F); how many of them will die on the journey?

Do those opposing or ignoring Trump's repeated calls for immigration reform even care.  After all, it will only have meaning two or three presidential election cycles from now.

As deaths in the Netherlands approached 3,000, Joe Biden was on the campaign trail in Iowa telling people "*it's absolutely bazaar*" that America, a nation of 300 million, can't take in two million. Of course, Joe was acting like that's all there would be – he's totally out of touch with the reality behind the Secure Fence Act; he cannot grasp he is speaking of two million A YEAR being admitted across the southern border – if he was elected President.

The United States currently admits about 1.2 million legal immigrants annually – people who are self-supporting and have skills that contribute or enrich the culture, society, and economy.

Pappa Joe seeks to double or triple that number – but with people who will be fully dependent on the State for their support. It's scary, it sounds like a socialist state in which the elite support the masses. Only in this case, the masses are non-citizens who will quickly outnumber the citizens. And when we talk of "Elite", it's not the "One Percent," but the average local taxpayer who will be providing the support.

Why local taxpayers and not those who pay Federal taxes? That's easy: a 1982 Supreme Court decision, mandated that all children, regardless of immigration status, be given the K through 12 education they are entitled to.

In 2018, Palm Beach County enrolled 4,555 Guatemalan in K-12. It was a 50 percent increase over the 2015/16 school year and many of the students were from came from remote highlands of Guatemala, where the speak neither Spanish nor English. This means finding teachers who speak their language, expand bilingual training for staff and also have specialists to handle traumatized students – traumatized either by the situation they were escaping, or the journey and being in a land where they cannot communicate and have a reference point to deal with the cultural differences.

If the numbers hold, 60 percent of Uncle Joe's two million, or 1.2 million, will be K to 12 or younger. In Palm Beach County they doubled the K through 5 elementary school enrollment.

Naturally, Trump Tweeted as fast as Uncle Joe said it:

*"ALERT: Joe Biden wants to almost triple immigration!*

    *2 million more EACH YEAR would:*

        *Crush wages for working class*

        *Kill blue-collar jobs*

        *Ravage Medicare & Social Security*

        *Drain federal treasury*

        *Crowd schools & hospitals"*

The gaffes Biden made on the campaign trail in Iowa were sufficient to gain Kamala Harris endorsement from the Iowa Asian and Latino Coalition – who represent minorities that account for ten percent of the Iowa population.

Ten percent doesn't sound like very much but considered in

terms of them being Democratic voters, and that 47.5 percent of the 2018 gubernatorial election vote was Democrat, it translates into 42 percent of the Iowa Democratic vote.

Consider Biden's racist gaffe:  *"Poor kids are just as bright and just as talented as white kids."*  Reacting to the reaction of others, Biden quickly caught himself and added, *"wealthy kids, black kids, Asian kids."*  The fact that he enumerated economic classes and racial groups in an attempt to mitigate the revelation does not change the reality that he believes the poor to be *"people of the land... You know... morons."*

Biden's gaffes are often Freudian Slip realities that reveal his inner beliefs.  Like a misogynistic or condescending choice to greet Kamala Harris with *"Take it easy on me, kid."*

New York Times reporter Maggie Haberman noted, *"Most grown women don't like being called 'kid' or 'kiddo' by, well, anyone but their parents."*  For that matter, most people, be they adults or children, don't like strangers calling them 'kid' or 'kiddo'.

Subconsciously, Joe Biden was reminding everyone of his age and that he was old enough to be her father.  And, give he was addressing someone who was past the half-century mark, we are talking seriously old – though not quite Bernie Sanders old, if we allow for gender differences, it is still Elizabeth Warren old.  That exposes a problem with the current front-running candidates, an ageist problem.  Will the average voter discriminate based on the candidate's age?  Should they?

Many of the things we are hearing reflect belief systems and ways of being that were the accepted norm when these candidates were in their twenties.  They were raised on the *"Red Scare"* and the *Korean War*, came into adulthood as Vietnam Draft Dodgers attending College, deciding upon or experiencing a relationship to Timothy Leary's admonition to *"Turn on, tune in, drop out"*.  They creating a based on the ideals of the counterculture-era.

On 19 September 1966, Leary introduced the dropout goal as a way of being reflecting rebellion against t existing conventions and societal hierarchies.  They were opposing mainstream-culture of a 1950's era that saw mom at home, in the kitchen and caring for the babies.  Dad went to work with the goal of obtaining a new car and suburban home with a garage to keep it in – maybe with a basketball net over the garage door.

Then there was owning a TV. Now Millennials have wi-fi and cellphones, but for the generation of Sanders, Biden, Trump, and Warren, growing up in the late 1940s, just having a ten-inch screen TV that receives one to three channels was a major step up the economic ladder. Back then, a 10-inch screen meant owning a piece of furniture which required two people to move it safely. Now we have the same screen on something thin and as light as a school notebook.

In the sixties, it was called the *"generation gap"* – young people latching on to new ideas and adopting ideas while the old remained hesitant. Today it has diverged to the extent that we no longer think of the ramifications, we have lost that conservative element often associated with caution.

Television replaced print as the mode of social influence and propaganda; as Marshall McLuhan phrased it, *"The medium is the message"*, and now, in the age of internet instant messaging, that medium gets the message out so fast that the saying, *"A lie travels around the globe while the truth is putting on its shoes."*

Truth requires many words, a line is an "elevator pitch" and takes root in the back of the brain as the next pitch is thrown. The pitch often invokes morality without concern for a consequence – is it moral to save the life of another? Is it moral to save the life of another, if it means your children or loved ones will die?

We look at the 2020 Campaign and hear Joe Biden claim a nation of 330 million can easily take in 2 million. But he fails to say that it, because of the economic collapse of their countries and the Climate Change heatwaves that will soon render those same countries barely inhabitable, he's asserting Americans can easily support adding the equivalent of a tenth of the population to the welfare rolls. And if we go by the immigration pattern that defined influx between 1880-1914, he's saying Americans could wait for a generation or two to see the children of those immigrants create the economic boom that began in the 1950s.

We have the Palm Beach County example. Those children will be highly productive; they will adopt the "American Dream" and they will grow with technological advances. But they will not be contributing to society for twenty-years – the time it will take to get from a first grade education to University Graduate.

If America adopts the Democratic Socialist programs, those

children will, for the next twenty years, be government-supported – and that will include the University Degree.

But, if we look at Trump, we see a nutcase who wants to admit only those who can afford to support themselves and who can immediately contribute to the economy.  He wants those who need a safe-haven to find it in a "safe third country" as they work their way North and, ideally, acquire both language and skills that would allow them to partake in the American Dream as soon as they or their children arrive.

Biden's logic reflects the idea that there is a moral obligation to '*Help Beautify Junkyards.  Throw Something Lovely Away Today.*'  What he, and those who argue variations on his case, are prone to advocate are those things which will destroy an economy.

Consider this: those who think they '*Beautify Junkyards*', by removing things of beauty from their homes, are working to make their home less '*Lovely*' – and possibly the nation as well.

In May 2019, 36 million Americans were on food stamps or SNAP – the Supplemental Nutrition Assistance Program – as part of 18 million households.  Relative to May 2018, and as a result of the record employment levels achieved by Trump, those numbers had declined by over 2 million individuals – the same number we heard Biden said he wants to add to the SNAP rolls.  The total cost of the SNAP program for May 2019 was about $4.38 Billion – meaning we add about $122 per month per individual; if we added Biden's 2 million people, we are adding $244 million a month or about $3 billion a year, which is close to what Trump wanted for the Wall which would have finalized a border security process which began with Barack Obama's 2006 Secure Fence Act.

Neither Biden or anyone else – other than President Trump – seems interested in finalizing major elements of Obama's Legacy of Border Security. As both Senator and President, Obama was a strong and vocal opponent of illegal entry into the nation. With the election of Trump, Democrats effectively turned on Obama – they renounced border security, what to eliminate ICE, and, as we saw with Joe Biden, have no problem allowing millions to enter a nation without any preparation or system for handling the influx.

There was once a time when we would have expected Right-wing Evangelical zealots to be screaming invocations of a "moral" responsibility to bring these people in, it is now the non-religious

Left-wing that yells it.

But the issue is not one welcoming migrants – we decided that by accepting the words of the Jewish poetess Emma Lazarus. Her words focused on the new Statue of Liberty which would, on 28 October 1886 be dedicated and henceforth stand to welcome those entering New York Harbor. Her words were speaking to her Eastern European kinsmen – Jews finally able to escape "The Pale of Settlement" place of exile created by Russia, a territory bounded on the west by the anti-Semitism of the German Lutherans who would, four decades later, be the backbone of the Nazis Party. It was also an invitation to escape the Cossacks whose bigotry had resulted in the creation of the ultra-orthodox Hasidic movement in the 1600s.

Her words were entitled "The New Colossus" {2 November 1883}, and are a sonnet deemed to be a universal invitation:

> ...
>
> *Here at our sea-washed, sunset gates shall stand*
> *A mighty woman with a torch, whose flame*
> *Is the imprisoned lightning, and her name*
> *Mother of Exiles.*
>
> ...
>
> *Keep, ancient lands, your storied pomp!" cries she*
> *With silent lips. "Give me your tired, your poor,*
> *Your huddled masses yearning to breathe free,*
> *The wretched refuse of your teeming shore.*
> *Send these, the homeless, tempest-tost to me,*
> *I lift my lamp beside the golden door!"*

How interesting is the cognitive dissonance which ignores the fact that the year before, on 6 May 1882, President Chester A. Arthur signed into Federal law *The Chinese Exclusion Act*, which prohibited all immigration of Chinese laborers?

Chinese were excluded, but, from 1891 to 1910, Liberty's light welcomed roughly 12.5 million Eastern Europeans, roughly 6 million had ancestry connected to the Jewish occupied regions of Austria-Hungary, Poland, and Russia. Deemed *"You know... morons"* when they arrived – an evaluation supported or verified by the newly introduced IQ Test – yet, by 1909, the children of Jewish immigrants comprised 6% of the incoming enrollment at Harvard University.

By 1912, Eastern European children had displaced the "Ivy League" elite at the best Universities in the nation.  It was also the first year a United States President {Taft} attended a Seder in celebration of Passover – it at the home of a Russian born American citizen who was a colonel in the Rhode Island National Guard. {Eight days later, the Titanic sunk.)

The year 1912 was when Republican Theodore Roosevelt proposed his National Health Insurance program and gained the backing of Progressive healthcare reformers.  Of course, it would be 98-years before Obamacare would be achieved by a Democrat.

Why is this century-old immigrant trivia relevant?

First, those seeking to invoke Emma Lazarus would ignore the reality of the times and who she was speaking of.  Yet, we need to welcome those who are in need, but this is now simply a matter of taking in socially oppressed seeking freedom. Yes, they are poor, but they had lived that way since the time of Columbus or the fall of the Mayan Empire.   Today we are seeing the first of the Climate Refugees – we are not talking only the 2 million Joe Biden asserted Eventually we will be looking at the bulk of the population of affected nations.

Those who scream we should throw open the 'golden gates' are ignoring reality – they are saying 'take shelter from the storm', but pointing to empty fields that may or may not have tents, but the tents that are there are rolled up and of no use.

We need to revise our immigration laws to include plans for the resettlement of tens of millions of Climate Refugees.  Those who wish to deny that reality are, in fact, in total denial of what Climate Change means to the future of the planet.

In Iowa, Joe Biden attacked Trump's moral character, yet it is Biden who revealed his racism and regularity bias by saying poor children are *"just as bright and just as talented as white kids*," and then saying "*wealthy kids*" because, as we know, poor kids are never white and wealthy kids are never non-white.

But this is a man who will "chose facts over truth" – as we know, the truth can never be factual.  And we have the fact that Obama did not endorse his own Vice President, and then there is the Truth of Obama both sponsoring the Secure Fence Act and, as President, being proud to have completed the authorized portion.

Obama was tough on illegals, and Biden has now advocated accepting 2 million migrants a year, or 25% more than the highest on record – those lower levels justified the fence/wall.

Biden is clearly anti-Obama, and Trump is pro-Obama. Is that 'truth' or 'fact' – both or neither?

Then we have the ageist issue and the parallels being drawn between Ronald Reagan and Joseph Biden – after he left office we learned Reagan was senile, there are signs Biden is already senile.

Biographer, Lou Cannon, characterized Reagan's behavior as President: *"inattentive, unfocused and incurious"*; he fell asleep during meetings and was known to recount movie plots as real-life events – which is a sign his senility was already evident while he was in office.

Where Joe Biden to become the nation's 46th President, he would be the oldest person to occupy that office, and his routine gaffes, combined with a clear lack of understanding of the threat of Climate Change – in terms of population displacement – show he would quickly destroy the economy and the nation.  His staff knew his mental condition and curtailed campaign schedule.

After Hillary was defeated, a segment of the nation suffered a mental breakdown which led to calling for an end to the Electoral College.  But that required a Constitutional Amendment whereas the ability of states to allocate their Electoral College votes rested with the individual states and gave rise to a legalistic workaround.

*"The National Popular Vote Interstate Compact (NPVIC) is an agreement among a group of U.S. states and the District of Columbia to award all their electoral votes to whichever presidential candidate wins the overall popular vote in the 50 states and the District of Columbia."* – Wikipedia definition

By the summer of 2019, California, Colorado, Connecticut, Delaware, Hawaii, Maryland, Massachusetts, New Jersey, New Mexico, New York, Oregon, Rhode Island, Vermont, Washington, and the District of Columbia had all enacted NPVIC legislation.

The practical effect of NPVIC is to negate the state vote so that a state which overwhelmingly voted for one candidate would give all its Electoral College votes to the loser – because that person managed to gain a majority of the popular vote.  Thus, as we see by the subtractions one state – with Hillary Clinton, California – can override the voters in 49 states. If we add New York City, the two can take control of the nation.

It's a neat end-run around the intent behind the Electoral College which would grant absolute power to California and New York. If you live in a small population State like Wyoming, your vote would cease to count, because the New York City borough of Brooklyn has more people and more votes than the whole state of Wyoming.

It's a great gerrymandering technique; one that can easily be augmented by an open border policy that allows illegal migrants into historically Hispanic states where they are counted but have no legislative voice. Naturally, the gerrymandering reality must be hidden, so the census cannot ask about citizenship – because to do so would also reveal the actual voters associated with the Electoral College and Congressional allotment.

NPVIC is a very nice means of circumventing the need for a Constitutional Amendment to end the Electoral College, removing the power of small states to have a voice in who becomes President. Once established, the next logical step would be to eliminate the Senate – which is the Legislative Branch equivalent of the Electoral College.

# CHAPTER SIX - THE Elephant

**"As a young member of a Foreign Relations Committee, I wrote and I said and I believed then what I believe now: That a rising China is a positive, positive development, not only for China but for America and the world writ large." ~ Joe Biden, May 2011**

One might expect the Biden quote to have said *'at large,'* not *'writ large,'* but, a 'Wiktionary' definition reveals the idiom to be *"From writ ("written")+large; a reference to Plato's Republic, wherein he describes the state (like the city-state) as being like the individual, but larger and easier to examine."*

His use of the term infers that benefits derived from the rise of China are something that would be obvious to the world.

If that were true, the reality of the effect of Climate Change is certainly *'writ large'*, and avoided while the media encouragers a narrow-minded debate over the causality. If major economies shift to solar and wind for their electric, and all other economies continue on the path to electric vehicles, within the three decades, when the Baby-boom generation has passed into history, the problem will be solved.

Granted, the planet will be hotter for many centuries. That only reflects that the climate needs to stabilize before it can reset – unless humanity chooses the nuclear option. In that case, there will be a sharper than anticipated decline human life, instead of a quarter to a third, half to two thirds will die. This is accompanied by a *Nuclear Winter* which would supposedly result from massive firestorms ignited by nuclear explosions.

Of course, it assumes the smoke clouds caused by the fires would cool the earth. But, as we are seeing from numerous fires generated because of current climate change conditions, the gases and such generated by wildfires have only served to add warmth to the planet and expedite glacial melting.

When it is *'writ large,'* reality takes on a meaning so fearful to the average person that they focus on irrelevant trivia. But the reality Climate Change is the *'elephant in the room'* of the 2020 campaign season.

On 16 August, California residents in San Jose, Santa Cruz,

and Marin County, experience power outages across as a result of warm weather and equipment issues.  In part, this is because air conditioning is a major part of American life – other nations, just suffer the heat.

As the planet warms, and because America's power grids are centralized, power outages will become more common.  The same centralized power network also serves to make the United States vulnerable to enemy attack – the same position Nazi Germany was in when America attacked its hydroelectric facilities as 'Operation Chastise', which became a post-war movie, *"Dam Busters"* {1955}.

We have a room full of elephants.

When communities turn to solar and wind for their energy, they reverse the purpose of the Grid and the direction the energy flows, which enhances American energy security.  We might say, the Grid becomes socialist – sharing wealth created by individual communities, rather than have that wealth *"trickle-down"* from a central source.

If an enemy targets the Grid, the best they can hope to achieve is cutting the line that shares surplus energy generation – they cannot eliminate that energy with one of two attacks.  They create an intentional repeat of the 9 November 1965 blackout which covered 80,000 miles and affected more than 30 million people from Canada down through the Northeaster States.

Because it occurred at 5:27 p.m pm a workday, it trapped 800,000 New York City subway passengers; it also knocked out air traffic controls and prevented plains from landing.

It was later determined that the cause was a faulty relay at on the Ontario, Canada side of Niagara Falls.  One relay was all it took.  Power outages can be caused by power outage is caused by inclement weather, grid failure, or terrorist attack.

Fortunately, to date, terrorists have proved stupid and have attacked structures and people, rather than infrastructure.  In 1965, the computing power of a modern tablet required roughly ten thousand square feet of air-conditioned office space.  In 2020, a terrorist could cripple the nation with a coordinated attack on multiple relay points – they need not commit suicide.  But, we are lucky that they are inherently suicidal and confine their attacks to events like the 17 August suicide bombing of a wedding in Kabul, Afghanistan – killing 63 innocent people and wounding 182.

It had no military purpose, no rational justification, it was no different from the attacks of people heading to their Mosque for prayer or shopping in local in market places.  It is every bit as irrational as the dual shooting in Texas and Ohio on 4 August.  It is, however, characteristic of an age in which people love to kill and really don't care if they also die.  In October 2019, terrorist leader Abu Omar al-Baghdadi killed himself and his two children, rather than be placed on trial for his part in terrorist mass murders.

If we think of the World Trade Center and events of 9/11, we forget that the architect to that destruction is on video saying it surprised him.  He thought he was sending people to their death to destroy a floor in a building while killing whoever was on the plane.  Bin Laden didn't expect that level of death and destruction.

The day will come the words of General George S. Patton are known to terrorists and they realize that only idiots die: *"No bastard ever won a war by dying for his country.  He won it by making some other poor dumb bastard die for his country."*

Cut the power to hospitals, airports, subways, and anything else when the target is also experiencing a heatwave, and you can have a lack of power do your killing for you; at the same time you knock-out the internet and every computer in the affected area.

It's the *'elephant in the room'* that nobody mentions.  It is the reason you need renewable energy that is not derived from a centralized grid.  But to acknowledge this elephant would mean candidates would need to address National Defense – not as a budget item whose cost exceeds the combined military budgets of the next ten highest budgeted nations, but as a defense cost with real civilian benefits.

As we know, but treat like an *'elephant in the room'*, we can support defense in a way that provides immediate civilian benefit – Border Security, crowd control for the Climate Migrants now referred to as asylum seekers, would allow them to be brought in in an orderly fashion which does not destroy the economy.  But we prefer to destroy the economy – commit economic suicide.

Forget about Climate Change.  The United States cannot do more than another nation is willing to do and certainly cannot undo the damage they are doing.  Candidates can address the issue on an America First basis – China did so when it decided it would mandate all new vehicles sold after 2025 would be electric.  Were the United

States to do likewise, it could cut the dependence on oil and repatriate the manufacture of vehicles now being produced in China by American companies.

That would eliminate a need for 'fracking', which provides half of the crude oil produced in the US, and accounts for roughly 80% of the global oil production growth.  The process is associated with earth tremors and minor earthquakes, but more importantly, it releases climate change-related gases like methane.

Typically, images of oil fields show the pumps or gas being burnt.  That natural gas is mostly methane, which is worse for the climate than carbon dioxide.  Shale oil and associated shale gas are now recognized as a source of greenhouse gases responsible for a sharp increase since 2008.

A peer-reviewed article by Robert W. Howarth, published 14 August 2019 in *Biogeosciences – "Ideas and perspectives: is shale gas a major driver of the recent increase in global atmospheric methane?"* – concluded *"increased methane emissions from fossil fuels likely exceed those from biogenic sources over the past decade (since 2007). The increase in emissions from shale gas (perhaps in combination with those from shale oil) makes up more than half of the total increased fossil-fuel emissions.  That is, the commercialization of shale gas and oil in the 21st century has dramatically increased global methane emissions."*

Just a day before publication, the news reported President Trump visited a Pennsylvania petrochemical plant where he was rather proud of US energy dominance and was in Pennsylvania to welcome the completion of a facility constructed to produce plastic made from byproducts of fracking for natural gas, and employ 600 permanent workers.

Naturally, the plastics produced are expected to increase the plastic waste in the environment, while fracking adds greenhouse gases to the environment thus accelerate global warming.  Over twenty years, methane is 86 times worse than the CO2 emissions the media generally focuses on.

Early 2018, as part of his international trade war policies, Trump imposed a tariff on solar panels, which the Solar Energy Industries Association estimated would result in the loss of some 20,000 solar industry jobs. The previous April, Trump went so far as to make the claim: "*If you have a windmill anywhere near your house, congratulations, your house just went down 75% in value."*

It is a claim that can be proved true in upscale rural areas where people are buying a view but is bogus where the windmill provides free energy for the homeowner.

Trump then went on to assert he was repeating something he was told – thus effectively disavowing the accuracy – *"And they say the noise causes cancer. You told me that one, OK."* He then went on to add, *"... and of course it's like a graveyard for birds. If you love birds, you'd never want to walk under a windmill because it's a very sad, sad sight. ... You know in California if you shoot a bald eagle they put you in jail for five years. And yet the windmills they wipe them all out. It's true. They wipe them out. It's terrible."*

Of course, this is the typical Trump rhetorical technique we touched on in other volumes in this series. He attributes stupidity to unidentified or unspecified third parties. But as stupid as it might be, there is truth in the fact that windmills, like skyscrapers, have resulted in the death of birds. As with those who walked into turning propeller blades at airports, birds often cannot detect the blade turning at higher speeds – since they fly in flocks, you often find multiple casualties.

Trump also pointed out a manufacturing flaw in any self-sufficient economic structure, when he said: *"No, wind's not so good and you have no idea how expensive it is to make those things. They're all made in China and Germany, by the way, just in case you, we don't make them here, essentially."*

China and Germany are easily out producing America – a fact demonstrated by the balance of trade numbers. Part of that reality is derived from the fact that they are building for the 21st- century, while America is still living in the early 20th-century.

It is a curious reality that, while immigrants or their first-generation children have moved American technology well into the future, its older generations tend to keep it in the past. It is only when America goes to war that the older allow the newer to lead the way.

But, once again, Trump's need to speak to his base and their backward simplicity has him speaking out of step with reality. While still a small part of the economy, as of 2017, the fastest-growing occupation was wind turbine technician. Looking at developments in the technology, the tall towers with their rotating or omnidirectional blades are yielding to deigns once seen on the roofs of rural barns as ventilation – small peak mounted omnidirectional turbines that can be used in conjunction with roof-mounted solar to provide all-weather year-round energy.

If Trump was a better salesman, he would promote national security, energy independent, job-creating, wonders of renewable energy.  The same renewable that is on the roof of a building he should be familiar with – the White House.

Trump has also made a foolish claim that windmills cause cancer.  However, we do need to acknowledge – close proximity to wind farms has been directly connected to *"decreased quality of life, annoyance, stress, sleep disturbance, headache, anxiety, depression, and cognitive dysfunction. Some have also felt anger, grief, or a sense of injustice. Suggested causes of symptoms include a combination of wind turbine noise, infra-sound, dirty electricity, ground current, and shadow flicker."* {Bulletin of Science Technology & Society, 2011 31: 296}

Trump is in a curious position.  His legacy is proving to be one of economic growth and environmental destruction.  Worse for him, the forces that are destroying the environment will also undermine the growth – and will be seen in his second term, or be a defining element of the first and only term of whoever replaces him.

As the forces driving Climate Change grows so do the forces that are causing the border crisis.  Climate refugees will define the mid-21st-century; they will be the source of economic collapse and prosperity; they will also be the driving force for what could result in the much-awaited Third World War.

Will curbing fracking save the planet or avert population shifts that will, as they have done throughout history, contribute to the changes?

Not at all.

As this is being written, Siberian permafrost is melting and releasing far more methane than the fracking – and the oil from that fracking is contributing to the economy. But, it remains '*an elephant in the room*', because it is depleting domestic oil reserves and, should there be another World War, it is placing America in the same position Nazis Germany was in when its access to Middle Eastern oil was severed.

Scientists had expected the Arctic permafrost to gradually melt. As soils soften they slump and collapse, releasing millennia-old carbon-based remains of ancient eras. Trapped greenhouse gases enter the atmosphere as methane or carbon dioxide destined to accelerate climate change. It is beyond human intervention; a matter of nature; it's the planet's reaction to the excessive size of the human population.

It is now believed that, as the planet warms, the carbon will escape faster – global warming will accelerate with every degree Celsius rise in the average global temperature, with permafrost releasing the equivalent of four to six years' worth of coal, oil, and natural gas emissions.

By 2040, permafrost will account for as much greenhouse gas as China – the major source of such emissions in 2018/19. The effect can be mitigated by the simple act of curbing fossil fuel use through the increased use of solar and wind-based electrical power. As the U.S. military has already determined, their conversion to renewables is critical for national security – both domestically and in future combat situations.

The 2020 campaign should get interesting. Trump has the Wall as an issue; Kamala Harris is on record, in August 2010, as telling the Silicon Valley Leadership Group her position on illegal immigrants was that they should *"stand in line"*. At the time, she agreed with President Obama: "*As the president has said and I agree, not letting them jump to the front of the line but stand in line like everybody else. So that's where I am on the issue. We need to have meaningful laws around this issue instead of approaching it like ostriches because it's not going away.*"

As a Senator and presidential hopeful, Harris has adopted the position: "*There has to be leadership around recognizing that we have to do what is necessary to enforce the borders, but we also have to do something with the 12 million undocumented immigrants that are in this country, recognizing that it is just not feasible or viable to believe that they're going to quote-in-quote go back. So let's figure out a way to integrate them in a legal way.*"

In 2012, Senator Elizabeth Warren expressed a similar opinion in saying, "*It's partly about making sure that people obey the law. It's about saying the people who are here need to be caught up on taxes. They need to go to the back of the line. There should be a path to citizenship for undocumented immigrants, but one that would require them to pay taxes and go to the back of the line."*

In 2019, the prevailing view seemed to become that the illegals should be jumped to the head of the line – all they need to do was assert the word "Asylum." This is a reality that Joe Biden made clear when, on the campaign trail in Detroit, he said, *"When people cross the border illegally, it is illegal to do it unless they're seeking asylum. People should have to get in line. That's the problem. And the only reason this particular part of the law is being abused is because of Donald Trump. We should defeat Donald Trump and end this practice."*

Of course, Trump is not the problem.  He simply continued the Obama-Biden policies based on a *"Secure Fence"* – one secure enough to be termed a *"Wall"*.  But with Congress opposing what had been Obama-Biden policies, Biden has been seen to quickly changed course and effectively renounced those policies.  With the numbers at the border hoovering around 1.2 million, Biden went so far as to proclaim he'd accept 2 million.

If we look to the platform of Bernie Sanders, we find he is in agreement with the Trump call for immigration reform: *"America's immigration system is 'profoundly broken' and must be fixed."*

Those undocumented immigrants who are already residing in the US should have the opportunity to acquire documentation and possibly have a road to citizenship – Dreamers need a place on that road.

Sanders believes we need visa reforms both to stop the use of cheap labor and then to *"increase opportunities for qualified individuals to take steps towards permanent residency."*

Sanders also lives in a fantasy world where border security can be increased without the use of a fence – something consistent with his Vietnam Era status as a Conscientious Objector, and what serves as a good reason why he should not be Commander in Chief of the nation's military.  He is a man who would hesitate when the use of force is advised; Trump dropped a MOAB on Taliban forces and killed them without harming civilians – in August 2019, the Taliban saw the wisdom of talking peace with someone who believes in knockout punches rather than Obama-era sparing.

Sanders' platform also reveals the delusional belief, *"We can have a fair economy that accommodates undocumented immigrants and American workers without discrimination and manipulation of wages."*

But, by definition, undocumented workers lack documents related to paying taxes. As Warren stated, the path is *"one that would require them to pay taxes and go to the back of the line."*

Economically, Sanders' "Feelthebern" website platform does make a point in saying that the wages of immigrants after they are naturalized increase – *"In the first two years ... increase 5.6 to 7.2 percent, ... after 12 years ... up to 10.1 to 13.5 percent."* And, without expressly mentioning the economic multiply, the page states that *"the increase in wages can also assist in growing the overall economy."*

The economic multiplier is the description of the circulation of a dollar – in a healthy economy, seven to ten dollars of income is generated across the economy or GDP by each new dollar earned. In terms of employment, as more people work, more money is spent and that generates the basis to create more jobs to fill the demand for goods and services.

Welfare is a curious economic necessity.

Because it doesn't fall into the classification of disposable income, welfare does not create jobs – instead, it maintains them. Those on welfare buy necessities and create a baseline of sales for grocery stores and utility companies that prevents cutbacks by those service suppliers. The economic multiplier applies to firings as well as hiring. Without welfare, in a recession or depression, every individual fired or laid-off would result in the laying-off of multiple others as the decline in disposable income filters through the economy.

However, to artificially cause the welfare rolls to grow is a formula for increasing taxes without any increase in GDP. Biden's call to accept 2 million migrants – mostly children – increases all costs rather than sustain established economic structures in the way that they are when we enter a temporary recession.

It's *'the elephant in the room'*.

The Republican calls for cuts to welfare or Social Security are calls to undermine the economy. They are calling to destroy the national economy by removing the economic base that we call "life's necessities" – food, clothing, shelter, and medical care – we all need before we can move forward to make surplus money that is the basis of disposable income.

The problem is complicated by the Reagan-Democrats who are also working to undermine the economy and social structure. But, they only reflect the same movement for change and rebellion that is consuming cultures around the globe.

On 18 August 2019, the world witnessed an estimated 1.7 million Hong Kong residents ignore torrential rain as they staged a peaceful Human Rights rally during which they shouted *"Stand with Hong Kong! Fight for freedom!"* The freedom in question appeared to be pro-democracy in opposition to the authoritarian approach taken by the government in Beijing.

Eleven weeks into the protests, Trump decided it was time for his Chinese counterpart Xi Jinping to sit down with protesters and resolve matters before any further consideration of Trade War issues.

While there are contradictory assertions as to the realities related to the Trade War or effectiveness of tariffs, there seemed to be an effect on the Chinese economy which revealed what might prove to be a shift in alliances destined to shape events after 2030. Exactly how the Hong Kong protests will play into this is unclear, but the city does appear to be China's critical link to the global economy that is critical to its New Silk Road initiative.

What was witnessed in Hong Kong was, in many ways, just a Chinese version of BREXIT and counter government protests seen to some extent in all the leading nations. Thee protests are what Trump tapped into with his campaign call to "Lock her up", and what is now the call to invent a reason to impeach him.

On several levels, these are global protests without a clear and positive political vision. There is no sense or indication that the protests can address the "what comes next" issue.

There are calls for a 'return to civility' as represented by some vision of days-gone-by when things were supposedly better and more civil. As can be seen, Biden is old-school to the point of being Roaring Twenties touchy-feely, with a pathological need to openly express himself through physical contact. That type of action is now seen as invasive and rude.

Biden has also shown inconsistency in his policy positions and that he would lack any policy direction which evidences an awareness of the long-term ramifications and outcomes related to his short-term positions.  We looked at one such gaffe in Chapter 5 – that he would welcome 2 million migrants, of which, probably 1.2 million would be children in need of basic education, and did not grasp the reality that he was imposing that burden on local communities.

In 2012, it was estimated that *"On average, it costs $10,615 to send a kid to public school for a year.  (That's federal, state and local government spending combined.)"* This means Biden has advocated increasing expenditures by about $12.738 Billion each and every year until such time as planetary warming and the promise of a better life has ceased to drive equatorial populations north.

In 2014, the average coat was *"$16,268 a year to educate a pupil from primary through tertiary education, according to the OECD annual report of education indicators."*  So, about 60% higher; teachers still earn about 68% of what a comparable college education. The most recent data is the 20017 U.S. Census data.  In that we find a cost per New York public school pupil of $23,091 – obviously, it is higher in 2019.  Thus, exclusive of any welfare cost, Biden advocated imposing a $27.6 Billion debt on communities.

Since the key costs are carried by local property taxes, Biden's 'open border' assertion is covertly an increased property tax in communities where those migrants settle.

The global electorate is screaming for change. In the States it's Trump, in Britain BREXIT -- even the Islamic State Terrorists can be seen as seeking mindless change through the same suicidal death and destruction characteristic of American mass shootings.

As with all mindless protestations, the new generation reflects the parasitic Hippy behavior of the Vietnam era and depends on the continued existence of the focus of its protest.  We saw this when Nixon gave way to Carter then collapsed into Reagan Conservative; it was repeated with the Right-wing Tea Party movement and other attacks on Obama masking racism with Birtherism.

Denied Obama or another Clinton, when Trump's election spawned a mindless protest attacking the Fence or Wall that was Obama's signature symbol of national security and labeled Trump a racist for continuing Obama policies.  Trump has provided those in Republican base with those things they seemed to want. Those in the Swamp immediately decided Trump needed to be stopped, and that they would be better off with a Mike Pence or Joe Biden.

On 7 August Trump Tweeted: *"The Dems new weapon is actually their old weapon, one which they never cease to use when they are down, or run out of facts, RACISM! They are truly disgusting! They even used it on Nancy Pelosi. I will be putting out a list of all people who have been so (ridiculously) accused!"*

He was repeating things mentioned in this book series and related online posts. Invoking racism is a standard *"dog-whistle"* dating back well past the American Revolution and the writing of the Constitution. Many of the founding fathers were Scotts-Irish, but, with the 1840s influx of immigrants caused by the potato famine, America saw "No Irish Need Apply". That represented the traditional schism between Ireland Irish, the British and Northern Scotts-Irish which is being revealed again in the 'hard border' separation caused by BREXIT.

As expressed in the Bible – *"the sins of the fathers unto the third and fourth generation."* Otherwise known as 'tradition', or, in genealogical terms, the way different species have evolved from a common root.

The author Douglas Adams expressed a concept which has been applied to society in terms of age and our approach to ideas:

*"1. Anything that is in the world when you're born is normal and ordinary and is just a natural part of the way the world works.*

*"2. Anything that's invented between when you're 15 and 35 is new and exciting and revolutionary.*

*"3. Anything invented after you're 35 is against the natural order of things."*

When our politicians reach thirty-five they are eligible to be president and they bring with them a resistance to change that produces social stability. When they are over seventy, they are, if they conform to the pattern, two generations behind reality.

Prior to the Industrial Revolution – the period in which the United States came into existence – change was sufficiently slow, and the average life expectancy sufficiently low, as to allow change to go unnoticed. But now, that first fifteen years is accompanied by the dramatic change; the second fifteen is as dramatic as the first; *"the natural order of things"* reflects whatever existed after 1985, and, in reality for that generation, whatever existed in 1991 – when they entered the first grade.

For members of the Baby-Boomer generation, the Reagan Era defined *"the natural order of things"* which imbedded the cognitive dissonance between Hippy and Conservative in which *"a red scare"* childhood gave way to individuals who preached *"peace and love."* We see the conflict echoed in the attacks on Trump as a "Draft Dodger" – a pro-Vietnam War mentality approach that was once the anthesis of "Liberal" thinking and the definition of "Conservative."

Why is it being raised by 'Liberal' or 'Progressive' minions? And why haven't they asserting it against those who, in the 1960s, were seen as actual Draft Dodgers – Joe Biden, who invoked an alleged childhood bout of Asthma when he couldn't hide behind a student deferment, or Bernie Sanders, who, consistent with his life and philosophy, claimed Conscientious Objector status?

For Baby-Boomers, and those who fall into the generation of the Biden and Sanders that preceded them, the mid-1960s can be seen as a real period of *"new and exciting and revolutionary"* change. It was the Vietnam era, an era of *"make love not war"* when cannabis and LSD replaced alcohol and tobacco and, in the process, differentiated the Hippy from the Conservative youth – which also meant it separated college student or the creative from a blue-collar worker and the lower classes who were generally also members of other or minority races.

It was the era of integration and the TV series 'Star Trek' where the nation saw Nichelle Nichols, as communications officer Lieutenant/Commander) Nyota Uhura, break the cultural mold to become the first black actor portrayed in a non-menial role on an American television series. The series also had a subplot where the racially superior, more intellectually advanced, Vulcan {named for an ancient Greek Deity – the God of Fire}.

Thus, subliminally, the 1960s became an era in which what supremacy was subjugated, but still, a force for exploration and a level of interracial equality represented by the half-human Spoke.

In 1966, when *Star Trek* was first televised, *"the natural order of things"* was the mentality of the Great Depression and the Second World War. For grandparents of the Hippy Generation, *"the natural order of things"* was the *"normal and ordinary,"* and for their parents, it was a vicarious return to the *"new and exciting and revolutionary"* which had defined the Roaring Twenties and

Prohibition Era.

In the post-war era, when the Korean War forced the young to revisit or experience the loss of family, 1950's America entered a unique period of confused thinking. It shared McCarthyism with an economic boom where the dreams denied in the Depression – a car, home, lawn, the ability to 'spoil' your children – could be fulfilled.

The era in which the majority of Baby-Boomers were born was one in which society was butting heads with itself. It was seen as a period of segregation, and an end of segregation; a time in which anti-Semitism made you a Nazi and a representative of the very things loved ones had died fighting; it also was a period when the Asian racism that had been expressed before and during the war was giving way to *"Made in Japan"* and Japan as Allie against Chinese or North Korean Communists.

The idea of racism became confused with political ideology.

In the Era of Trump, it has been reduced to a *'dog-whistle'* to be blown whenever someone wants to use their own race as a weapon to accuse others of being bigots – while the real goal is to elevate use your own race (or gender) for personal advantage.

A sociological research paper with a rather long title, *"Who Is Called by the Dog Whistle? Experimental Evidence That Racial Resentment and Political Ideology Condition Responses to Racially Encoded Messages"*, appears to affirm *"that implicit racial appeals can harness racial resentment to influence policy views, though* **specifically among racially resentful white liberals**. *That dog-whistle effects would be concentrated among liberals was not predicted in advance, but this finding appears across two experiments testing effects of racial appeals in policy domains—welfare and gun control—that differ in the extent and ways they have been previously racialized."*

Based on the study, and one of its assertions, The Squad is helping Trump through its persistent invocation of race, gender, and religion when seeking to oppose what are, in fact, rational policies addressing terrorism or Climate Change problems. This is shown by an assertion of *"representative survey data showing that racially resentful, white liberals were particularly likely to switch from voting for Barack Obama in 2012 to Donald Trump in 2016."*

Assuming there is validity to the observation, we see that it gives Trump cause to stir the pot in a way that forced members of

The Squad to double down on their accusations. The Squad is curious, its members fall into category 2, but that act like they are trying to redefine category 3 before they are forced to be part of it. But their redefinition is simply a retasking of all that is deemed *"the natural order of things."*

It's rather weird and extremely counterproductive.

Looking at the leading Democratic candidates – Sanders, Warren, Biden – we see individuals who are 70 or more, and they are at the end of their natural cycle, they no longer thinking of the future, because they know they will not be living there.

Sanders, because he has held the same core political policy objectives for the past 35-years, is the exception. But, so is Donald Trump. The difference is, Trump has an eye on the History Books and what they will say when he has expired; he is also concerned with the world as it will be for his children and ten grandchildren.

It's another *'elephant in the room'* – the personal posterity element motivating the actions of the political leads reveals their real agenda. Trump has a posterity that is front-and-center in the administration. And he's attacked for it.

When the attacks became closed-door hearings over a phone call to Ukraine. People yelled about "due process." As a result, the House voted on formal investigation rules and became the formal impeachment process which, in the impeachments of Nixon and Clinton, resulted in the Stock Market (DJIA) losing 48% or 22% of its value.

This time, *"the elephant in the room"* was the emerging reality of Joe Biden's history. So it was that, concurrent with the House vote on the rules there were revelations about Biden's *quid pro quo* when, apparently with Obama's blessing, he allowed only six-house for the termination of a Ukraine prosecutor – the type of deals Biden conducted were in an early summary by The Federalist: "*When Joe was running our Ukraine policy, Hunter landed at Burisma. When Joe was the linchpin of our China policy, Hunter was busy shoring up investors in Beijing.*"

While in 2018 Biden implicated Obama in a *quid pro quo* situation, The Federalist documented Biden's behavior dating back to the Bush administration in 2007.

With the House vote on impeachment rules, Joseph Biden was

elevated into the role of *"The Elephant in the Room."*

Another elephant is wealth and where it is located. Is there a correlation between those who voted as a majority for Hillary Clinton in the 2016 election?

Is there also a correlation to those who are attacking Trump in a way tailored to help him in 2020?

And YES! We must consider that Pelosi, Schiff, Nadler, and the California or New York City Swamp Denizen elements attacking Trump are botching things intentionally. We must consider that they have built a case on obvious lies and hearsay for the express purpose of ensuring an across the board Republican victory.

Consider the Machiavellian perspective on politics where the Swamp Denizens display their characteristic unscrupulous cunning and scheming in a way that appears to be an attack, but seems to be so obviously incompetently done as to result in the opposite of what they say they are intending. Consider the Biblical admonition – *You will know them by their deeds and not their words.*

In the Impeachment Hearings – which resulted in no charges based on the testimony – we suddenly see House Speaker Pelosi NOT immediately deliver the Articles of Impeachment to the Senate.

Instead she talks of holding them until she is assured of *"a fair trial"* – but what does that mean? Does it mean a Kangaroo Court to rubberstamp vague and undefined Articles?

# CHAPTER SEVEN – Crisis Time

**"Today I'd like to speak to you about a gathering crisis in our society: It's a family crisis. To some, it's hidden, concealed behind tenement walls or lost in the forgotten streets of our inner cities."**

**~ Ronald Reagan, 1986**


*"You lied to me, by telling me the truth."* It is a great movie line and expresses how people are convinced to do things that go contrary to their basic instincts. Phrased properly, the truth can hide the truth, or hide the true agenda of the speaker.

Reagan was referencing reality and presenting the idea he was going to act appropriately to address it. But his true intent was to launch a race-based attack on an economic segment or niche of society which required strengthening.

Thirty-three years later, The Squad inferred race whenever a descriptor could apply to a group which is a minority within the United States – even though the actual topic is a nationality whose social practices are disruptive and generally associated with some radical minority within that nation. The dual effect is to approve of the practices of that minority and then shield them from media attention.

The reason they can get away with their tactic is embodied in the premise of "The Emperor's New Clothes" as it is married to the attack on elites and therefore in the growing attitude toward higher education. The latter being revealed in a PEW report dated 19 August 2019: "The Growing Partisan Divide in Views of Higher Education".

While Americans acknowledge the value of having a higher education, and there is a clear understanding or acknowledgment of the economic advantages college graduates have over those who lack a degree, *"there is an undercurrent of dissatisfaction – even suspicion – among the public about the role colleges play in society, the way admissions decisions are made and the extent to which free speech is constrained on college campuses."*

About 38-percent of Americans believe colleges are having a negative impact and reflects an increase among Republicans or those who lean toward Republican policies. This is interesting in the context of persistent Democratic attacks on "political elites" and a so-called "1-percent" controlling 32-percent of the national wealth. Bernie Sanders routinely targets them and also makes a pitch for free college education and what is called "The Green New Deal." By definition, Sanders is saying college is for the elite, it's for those who can afford it without going into debt.

The most prestigious colleges are those located in Liberal states; the Republican base isn't generally associated with a college education, even though their leadership tends toward Ivy League educations – both the Bush Presidents attend Yale University, and Senator Ted Cruz graduated Harvard Law. The base can relate to Trump because his education and intellect are routinely attacked.

Rep. Sean Duffy {R-Wis} attacked the Green New Deal as a Liberal elite issue, asserting: *If you're a rich liberal from maybe New York or California, it sounds great because you can afford to retrofit your home or build a new home that has zero emissions, that's energy-efficient.*

The intellectual and psychological dynamic is complex, it's a selective association. Hitler used it to attack the Jews – not as the workers, but as the college-educated elite sitting safely at their desks while the average German was facing death in the trenches.

When Shakespeare's *"Merchant of Venice"*, is presented in schools, the students are taught to ignore the nobleman and the self-destructive economics he lived by. Instead, the focus is on the moneylender who, having been repeatedly cheated, asks for terms one would assume would ensure payment. Instead of focusing on the cheat, the focus is on the extreme penalty for non-payment, a pound of flesh.

Schools don't even bother to teach that the law against a Jew drawing Christian blood – the law used to void the agreement and punish the Jew – existed to deny Jewish medical knowledge and treatment to Christians. But, history and truth have no place in teaching traditional interpretations.

Shakespeare's narrative was a basic variation on the 'Blood libel' leveled against Jews in the Medieval era. The subliminal is that, for money, a Jew would cut the heart from a Christian. The original 'Blood libel' effectively accused Jews of celebrating their holidays by violating scriptural prohibitions against both contact with or consumption of blood. Subliminally it is accepted because the

Christian community indulges in symbolic sacramental blood consumed in the Eucharist or Lord's Supper.

If Christians consume the Blood of Jesus, why wouldn't the Jews consume the blood of Christians? People quickly accept any allegation which had the effect of raising them to the level of Jesus and, symbolically, made them 'divine' while allowing them to deny that divinity to the Jews (forgetting that Jesus was of the Kohanim Rabbinical line that was authorized to enter the inner sanctum of the Temple, '*The Holy of Holies*' and that he chose an Orthodox Jew to be the foundation of his 'Church').

For the Lutherans, the symbolic body and blood of Jesus are literally present within the bread and wine of the Eucharist. Thus, they are, within their belief system, literally being cannibals and displaying a cognitive dissonance Hitler built upon – Lutherans were 60-percent of the German populous and were the easiest to gathering to the Nazi banner. This cognitive dissonance is one that defines Christian Anti-Semites: Jesus, will resurgent, as a Jew worshiping his Jewish Deity father, so it is important to kill all Jews before the resurrection – in effect, killing Jesus before he can return or reveal himself.

Blood Libel was connected to the *Miftah*, the organization that was to sponsor the Israel visit of Congresswomen Omar and Tlaib.

Apparently, on 27 March 2013 *Miftah* published an article by Nawaf al-Zaru in which he said, "*Does Obama, in fact, know the relationship, for example, between 'Passover' and 'Christian blood'..?! Or 'Passover' and 'Jewish blood rituals?!'*" read the post. "*Much of the chatter and gossip about historical Jewish blood rituals in Europe are real and not fake as they claim; the Jews used the blood of Christians in the Jewish Passover.*"

Because it published the article, *Miftah* was branded anti-Semitic. In response to the immediate backlash, five days later, on 1 April they posted: "*The Palestinian Initiative for the Promotion of Global Dialogue and Democracy, MIFTAH would like to apologize for the recent and brief publication on our website of an article penned by Nawaf Al Zaru that discusses Jewish blood libel during Passover.*"

The supposed apology went on to deflect blame by saying, "*the article was accidentally and incorrectly published by a junior staff member.*" But, isn't it always the "*junior staff member*" who gets responsibility and blame?

An anti-Semitic and irrational medieval lie is cited as fact. But, as Jonathan Swift wrote on 9 November 1710: *"Falsehood flies and the truth comes limping after it."*

Falsehood traverses time and culture. The initial lies tend to reveal various truths about the liar.

A common tactic among the dishonest is accusing others of the improprieties they engage in. Of course, they seldom provide any specifics or supporting evidence – we consistently see this in the social media assertions of criminal conduct by Trump. Were their assertions true, the members of Congress who fail to support an indictment (Impeachment) must be co-conspirators and must be replaced with honest Representatives – meaning, in 2020, all the sitting Democrats must be replaced with honest Democrats; we can assume the Republicans will refrain from attacking Trump.

As previously touched upon in this series, part of Trump's technique is to toss out assertions that are easily attacked. He has a habit of playing with cognitive dissonance. His approach reflects the establishment of the Willy Wonka character: *"From the start, no one can know if he's lying or telling the truth, because he gives them an obvious lie in the opening segment."*

As a result, the media has no problem saying he's a liar – it is far easier than actually doing their job and examining the facts.

In *The New Republic*, Matt Ford wrote of *"Trump's Tax on the National Psyche"* {21 August 2019} in terms of Trump's habit of forcing things into the courts, rather than playing the politician and attempting to get Congress to act.

Historically, Congress lacks the ability to be focused and act in a deliberate manner – Trump's sister (a retired Federal Judge) would have taught him that simple legislation is often weighed down with unrelated amendments and wrapped in vague language that hampers proper management or executive action. Of course, if one has a qualified accounting staff, the rare specificity that can be found is generally confined to the tax code or laws designed to serve and reward a narrow special interest group. This makes things easy when seeking to minimize taxes or take some action that will disrupt the environment – however, when their goal is to deny citizens the benefit of the government, the language becomes painfully specific.

Because Trump understands this reality, he routinely turns to the courts – which means, in business, he engaged in a lot of litigation.  Now, as President, he encourages lawsuits.  Raised in a powerful Manhattan Law Office, I learned that the system could be leveraged from inside and that there was little need to litigate – but, when you did, you always made sure you won, even if that meant you had to structure things to ensure you lost.  And YES, as Trump knows, it is often possible to win more by losing.

In describing this technique, Matt Ford asserted, *"Trump's haphazard style of governance, forces journalists, lawyers, and government officials to expend innumerable hours on doomed initiatives and errant tweets.  His corrosive effect on American politics forces Americans to devote far more hours of their life to thinking about him than they should.  All of this amounts to a tax of sorts on the national psyche—one that can never be repaid."*

But isn't that the objective?  You want to distract spectators – distract your audience in the way PT Barnum perfected to make his sideshows and circus *"the Greatest Show on Earth."*  Trump used Barnum style showmanship to make a success of the reality TV show, *The Apprentice* – and the catchphrase *"You're Fired."*

As President, creating a catchphrase is a bit more difficult.  Though Trump has grabbed media attention through his pattern of having staff leave – it doesn't matter if they were terminated, or quit, or, moved on to more lucrative positions from which they could still represent his goals.

In 1933, Franklin Delano Roosevelt {FDR} introduced the *"Fireside Chat"* to the Radio – by the following year 60-percent of homes had one and were tuned in.  Later, FDR became the first president to use the newly invented Television, but they were too expensive for them to achieve serious audience levels.

In January 1947 – 2-years after FDR's death – his former VP, Harry S. Truman, became the first POTUS to use the medium to give a speech to the nation.  Of course, we have the first actual televised Presidential Debate in September 1960, and that taught VP Richard Nixon that image was now important and that sweating on-camera turned off voters.

When we get to Trump, the medium became Twitter and its limited characters – communication by *"Elevator Pitch"*. Quick and short, get an image across that both defines and sells a script or concept.  The classic example is one which describes the movie "*Twins*" – 4'10" Danny DeVito and 6'2" Arnold Schwarzenegger as fraternal twins separated at birth.  The "*Elevator Pitch*" is a one-liner: "*Danny DeVito and Arnold Schwarzenegger as twins*"

When Trump delivers his "*Elevator Pitch*", no matter how inane the tweet, no matter what the seemingly half-baked policy, somebody will react and it might go viral.  If it does, the next news cycle is owned and controlled by Trump.

Trump continually replays our first view of Willy Wonka.

The Tweet has no reason to be truthful, it need only be a lie that tells the truth.  Media Pundits decide if words shall be treated literally or figuratively – they are free to ignore the formulation or context. They dismiss the words as lies, meaningless or gibberish – maybe some combination of the three.

Trump's words can easily invoke a level of anxiety, concern, and stress.  They can also instill calm to the segments of society they are targeting.  But the stress element is greater in areas that voted for Hillary – not because of Trump, but because of the technology they live with and are attached to.  That stress involves silly things like robocalls.

Americans are barraged by a daily routine of robocalls that clog phone lines and disrupt daily activities – this includes the estimated 4.7 billion illegal spam calls which disguise themselves as local numbers on Caller Ids – that disruption introduces stress which is then released through either heightened rude behavior or attacks on political leaders.  Because they are lies, spam calls are psychologically grouped with behaviors.

Trump "*lies to you, by telling you the truth.  And, as events unfold, you don't know if he's lying or telling the truth.*"  Only the outcome reveals reality.  But, his evangelical base understands that – if only subliminally – because they once read, or were told, they would know them by their deeds and not their words.  This is presented in Matthew 7:16: "*Ye shall know them by their fruits.  Do men gather grapes of thorns or figs of thistles?*"

The idea is to not listen to the words but look at the actions or achievements.  The false prophet has a silver tongue, but all his actions bring harm.

In the modern world, the ability to harm resets with those who control mass media and wield the power to manipulate public opinion in America, and around the globe.  Mass media can now mold and shape the thinking of every citizen, without regard for their age, socioeconomic class, or intellectual level.  News Media is biased – we accept that we have been taught to accept Fake News as defining reality.  But that allows us to be lied to by being told the truth.  When it comes to being indoctrinated, that job has been relegated to commercials and theatrical presentations which define normal through the presentation of contextual normality.

If the central figures are gay or interracial couples, that is the premise for normality.  The media presents us with a changing range of racial and religious stereotyping combined with symbolic clues to the person's character.

The symbolic has always been an integral part of human culture – something which explored in my 2012 book *"Genesis of Genesis."*  In their childhood, Baby-Boomers came to understand that, in Westerns, the good-guy wore the white hat, and villains the black. But then, came "Have Gun - Will Travel" – Richard Boone as *"Paladin"*, a gunfighter whose custom gun fit inside a custom holster emblazoned with a chess piece, a knight.  He was the knight renowned for heroism and chivalry, the gunfighter for hire dressed in black.

In the modern computer age, the symbolism evolved into references to the *"white hat hacker"* whose skills are dedicated to being a computer security specialist hacking systems and exposing their flaws.  Those same computers allow us to stream programs where other classic symbols of old have changed. Where once movies depicted sophistication in the handling of a cigarette or the smoking of a cigar, today, when a character smokes they are seen as flawed or lower class and likely a drug addict.

Sophisticated psychological techniques are often employed to guide our thinking and opinions.  We are allowed to learn of the secret behind the "Emperor's New Clothes", so that we know we are to see them and, in seeing them be in tune with the "in" crowd of astute observers who cannot be fooled.  We, therefore, know that Trump became the criminal upon announcement of his election victory; we knew he had to be impeached.

Does it matter that, on 4 November 2016, the DJIA was at 17,888 and that by 26 January 2018 it had climbed to 26,617?  Or that on 1 November 2019 it had topped reached 27,347?

Clearly, Trump was doing a horrible job with the economy – and all his actions were bringing about a *'Great Recession.'*

The New York Times routinely portrayed Trump as an Anti-Semite, while simultaneously defending  Ilhan Omar (D-MN) and Rashida Tlaib (D-MI),  and it had no problem with its Senior Staff Editor Tom Wright-Piersanti having tweeted: "*I was going to say 'Crappy Jew Year,' but one of my resolutions is to be less anti-Semitic.  So... HAPPY Jew Year.  You Jews.*"

Gee, in his 2010 Tweet, he admits to being an Anti-Semite, so it follows that Wright-Piersanti would support those who also are, and, in keeping with tradition, that he would accuse Trump of the same improprieties he seems so proud of.

Supporting Anti-Semitism is a New York Times tradition we know dates back to 21 November 1922, when the wrote, "*Hitler's anti-Semitism was not so violent or genuine as it sounded.*"  And revealed some admiration in the fact, "*He exerts an uncanny control over audiences, possessing the remarkable ability to not only rouse his hearers to a fighting pitch of fury, but at will turn right around and reduce the same audience to docile coolness.*"

In this series on Trump's technique, we utilize the example of how a lead stallion will turn a stampeding herd.  In 1922, the Times observed of Hitler, "*It would be politically all wrong to tell them the truth about where you really are leading them.*"

That violence appears to accompany change is something which did not seem to occur to those excusing Hitler's reliance on millennia-old Anti-Semitic indoctrination as the path to power, nor does is it apparent to any viewing the current global environment.

Was it Hitler's intent for things to go as far as they did?  Or was he trapped by his own rhetoric?  Remember, the Times article was in 1922 and Hitler's biographical bestseller wasn't published until 18 July 1925.  Traditionally we have the Shylock connection between Judaism and economics – which ties to the Biblical tribe of merchants – which means there was a 'next step' connection to the events that followed the 29 October 1929 Stock Market crash.

In earlier volumes in this series and related works, you are given the Right-wing objective as *"The Most Harm to the Most People."* You see it when they attack Healthcare or refuse to raise the

Minimum Wage to above poverty – they keep working people on welfare so that they have vast numbers to attack as "welfare kings and queens."

Their Right-wing counterparts, the other half of the Swamp Denizens lurking in the shadows, are no better.  They must back the Liberal or Progressive Programs which will help people, but they will do so by crashing those programs.  We all saw it during the First Debate, asked if they would support free Healthcare for illegal immigrants, all raised their hands to signify yes.

Sounds good, if they are also giving free healthcare to legal migrants and citizens.  But they also, as Joe Biden showed, what to flood the nation with migrants ill-prepared to contribute to the American economy.  They want to gerrymander electoral districts by replacing trees with bodies that cannot vote and aren't even in the country legally – nor can they be deemed legal until after their asylum claims have be adjudicated, so the point is made to avoid funding additional judges.  This ensures that various individuals are a drain on society for at least two years.

Is that a form of racism?  To create a class of individuals as people without status or proper legal standing.  Biden assured the Iowa voters that *"Poor kids are just as bright and just as talented as white kids."*

Immediately, we see racism – white kids aren't really poor but are *'bright'* and *'talented'*.

But what if those poor aren't permitted to participate in the mainstream society because they and their families lack the status necessary to differentiate them from trees and acres?  And, while they must be educated at enormous expense to local taxpayers in the communities where they are housed, there is no pathway for them or their parents to be integrated into the culture.  That does seem to be what the racists are presenting – while they call Trump a racist for opposing them.

Biden has stated America can accept 2-million non-citizens into the census count every year.  Where will they live?  And why doesn't he or 'The Squad' seek to provide that housing to citizens ion poor communities?  Trump pointed to a rat-infested Baltimore. If America can afford to house 2-million migrants a year until such time as those escaping the sauna temperatures developing in the equatorial latitudes are in the USA, certainly, it could easily reverse housing problems in Baltimore and other areas of the nation.

Trump was called a racist by Bernie Sanders, who claimed, *"What a president is supposed to do is bring us together, and we have a president intentionally, purposefully trying to divide us up by the color of our skin."* {21 January 2019, Martin Luther King Jr. Day speech} Sanders went on to say, *"We now have a President of the United States who is a racist."*

But where is the evidence of racism?

Is it in the desire to avoid having people from nations that advocate or support terrorism enter the United States and repeat a variation on 9/11?

Could it be in wanting to protect local communities from an economic disaster of a type that would follow increasing property taxes associated with the $27.6 Billion cost of properly educating the migrant children which Biden asserted the nation could afford – while failing to explain how small communities could afford it?

There is the avoided reality of the migrant issue. If a migrant had skills the nation needed, they would have no problem entering the country legally. It's estimated the United States has a half-million jobs that currently lack qualified applicants, and as a result, requires immigrants to fill those positions.

If the migrants are unqualified for available work, they will become a public charge – at about $100 per month each for SNAP, which means $200 Million a month or $2.4 Billion a year just to feed them, with the cost being carried into the subsequent years and increased by another $2.4 Billion until such time as the adults can find work which pays 150% of poverty.

In an economy where unemployment is pushing what is – in a very real sense – full employment, and where all the known available positions are those requiring higher education and some levels of specialty training, where will migrants be employed?

That' a real question that must be addressed. The nation is not taking people in temporarily – as would happen if a natural disaster displaced them and they needed time to rebuild before returning to their homes.

People like to point to America as "the land of immigrants" and a place where people can build a new life. But that was in the last century – and all the centuries before it. America was a land of open space and "lawless territories" to which the newly arrived immigrants could venture, settle, and bring "law and order."

To facilitate this and ensure there was room for expansion, in 1803 President Thomas Jefferson dispatched James Monroe and Robert R. Livingston to secure *The Louisiana Purchase* from France. This added roughly 828,000 square miles of land which would eventually become 15 additional states which now define fully half of the agricultural Midwest – America's Breadbasket – and, extending southward, the central core of the nation providing home and sustenance to a fifth of the United States population.

Fifty-four years later, in 1867, we saw an acquisition known *"Seward's Folly"*, the purchase of Alaska from Russia negotiated by Secretary of State William Henry Seward on behalf of President Andrew Johnson. Consistent with the denunciation of actions or ideas associated with President Trump, *"Seward's Folly"* was seen as something worthy of media and public attack.

It was a waste of $7.2 Million – in 2019 dollars, about $125 million. The amount is legal because the post Civil War era had a negative inflation rate, and, in America, real inflation only began with the birth of the Baby-Boom generation and the inflation rate of 14.36% which defined 1947 – as determined by comparing the Consumer Price Index for the years under examination.

While France and Russia were unloading their territories, the Danish government appears to have offered to sell Sec. Seward the Virgin Islands. During World War I, it seemed like a good deal for America when President Woodrow Wilson determined it had a strategic military value that should be in German hands. These became the United States Virgin Islands on 31 March 1917.

After the Second World War, and recognizing the strategic importance of the region in what was becoming The Cold War, in 1946, President Harry S Truman offered Denmark $100 million in gold for the frozen island known as Greenland. At the current $1,525 market value of gold (vs $35 in 1946), that would be about $4.35 billion.

Just before the August 2019 G7 meeting in France, Social media laughed at President Trump for repeating that offer to buy. But Representative Mike Gallagher (R-Wisconsin) Tweeted: *"This idea isn't as crazy as the headline makes it seem. This a smart geopolitical move. The United States has a compelling strategic interest in Greenland, and this should absolutely be on the table."*

Of course, as with most other looming crisis situations, the common thread is Climate Change. As previously mentioned, the Greenland glacier is melting; the process that will raise sea levels is also exposing extensive mineral and rare earth deposits which an industrial nation like the United States could make excellent use of.

With the melting of the Arctic glaciers and icebergs, which is now creating the historically sought after shipping route known as "The Northwest Passage." As Climate Change progresses, the Arctic shipping route will take on major significance.

But before that, since 1941, there has been a United States military base in Greenland – The Thule Air Base, home to the 21st Space Wing's sensors network which provides early missile warning, space surveillance and control via its 240-degree horizon scanning ability.

Trump was laughed at for being rational and working in the long-term interest of the United States. And when he was rebuked by the Danish Prime Minister, who also understand the long-term value of that real estate. Naturally, those opposed to American economic and strategic interests were mocked by a mime Trump posted of a 50-story "Trump Tower" set among Greenland houses.

But there was an interesting aspect to Prime Minister Mette Frederiksen's response. She asserted, *"Greenland is not for sale. Greenland is not Danish. Greenland belongs to Greenland. I strongly hope that this is not meant seriously."*

In real estate parlance, she was asserting Denmark does not hold title to the territory, Trump would need to discuss the matter with the Greenland Prime Minister and Parliament. Naturally, Trump's response was to cancel his trip to Denmark. If Denmark lacked the necessary legal authority to negotiate a sale, there's no real reason to meet with its Prime Minister, when there were G7 matters to consider.

Bringing Greenland into the American economic sphere of direct influence would benefit its roughly 57,000 inhabitants who are subsidized by the Danish government. The matter is internal Greenland politics.

Projecting political events and elections is a guessing game. A decade ago, how many would have guessed Britain would decide to commit what, by the time of the 2019 G7 meeting, had taken on the appearance of economic suicide resulting from the June 2016 vote to exit the European Union?

Polls are nice, but people will answer or respond differently when the results don't count.  But, when it comes down to actual elections, and the influence of easily manipulated "Groupthink," we see why we have a Representative Government, and the reason America's Founding Fathers balanced population representation – The House of Representatives – with territorial representation in the form of The Senate; and why, because of the unique role of the President, they created the Electoral College to promote the joint interest of both and the nation as a whole.

Variables like the Electoral College are impossible to gage.  In 1876, the election of Rutherford Birchard Hayes as the nation's 19th President in one of the most contentious elections in national history.  His opponent was Samuel Jones Tilden – it's interesting because there is no record of Tilden ever being married, which we can say infers he was the Mayor Pete that era.  It's also interesting that the family business was based on *"Tilden's Extract"* a patent medicine derived from cannabis.

Had it not been for the Electoral College, the United States might have had a Gay Marijuana Dealer POTUS – how would that have affected subsequent history? Especially in the context of Tilden later becoming the focus of an investigation into corruption and fraud.  The Potter Committee as the Mueller Report of the era and the result was the same Tilden himself was not implicated of any wrongdoing.

As we know, Clinton lost the Electoral College against the background of "Lock Her Up" and missing emails.  With Tilden, it was Western Union telegrams which had been sent during the campaign –  29,275 were sent, all but 641 destroyed; it is said that 31,000 emails were deleted by Hillary Clinton.

In his first run for the presidency, Andrew Jackson won the popular vote, the Electoral College was indecisive, and Congress made John Quincy Adams the 6th president; 4-years later Jackson won, to become the 7th president.  While in office, Jackson set the tone now adopted by many far Left-wing types – routinely calling for a Constitutional Amendment to abolish the Electoral College.

President Grover *"Ma, Ma, where's my Pa?"* Cleveland had

been attacked for fathering a child out of wedlock – one which he acknowledged and supported.  Cleveland was elected by a small popular vote victory and the Electoral College, but even though he carried the popular vote by a significant margin, his reelection was lost when the Electoral College vote went to Benjamin Harrison.

However, four years later, Cleveland made history by again being elected – thus being both the 22nd and 24th POTUS.

In each of the Presidential elections, the Electoral College has done what it was designed to do – which is exactly what the House and Senate were designed to do.  The popular vote reflects reprehension in the House of Representatives, while the Senate has the function of representing the individual States in accordance with the will of their residents.  The Electoral College represents the combined will of House and Senate, based upon the popular vote within each state – thus, the popular vote reflects the will of the nation as asserted by all the states, and not just one or two.

Seventeen months before the 2020 election, polls asserted Biden, Warren, or Sanders could defeat Trump.  Interestingly, this infers a two-time loser, a woman, or Jewish Socialist, could win against a New York Billionaire businessman who kept the national economy moving into record territory.  It infers America changed significantly since the days when it was said, *"It's the economy, stupid."* As a Jew, I like the idea of a Jewish POTUS, but I doubt the nation could accept an 80-year-old Jewish Grandfather.

On 19 August {11:26 AM},  Trump tweeted, *"Our Economy is very strong, despite the horrendous lack of vision by Jay Powell and the Fed, but the Democrats are trying to 'will' the Economy to be bad for purposes of the 2020 Election. Very Selfish! Our dollar is so strong that it is sadly hurting other parts of the world. ...The Fed Rate, over a fairly short period of time, should be reduced by at least 100 basis points, with perhaps some quantitative easing as well. If that happened, our Economy would be even better, and the World Economy would be greatly and quickly enhanced-good for everyone! "*

At the time, economists were pointing to an inverted yield curve – meaning the long-term interest rates were lower than the short-term ones.  This denotes a belief among investors that the short-term economic risks were greater than the long-term ones.

An inverted yield curve is a harbinger of a recession, and it warns of a crisis.  But what is the cause of that warning?

A month earlier, The New York Times reported that the Trump Tax Cuts were working and the nation's largest banks were earning billions.  At the same time, there was a general decline in Wall Street trading and, as mentioned, long-term interest rates were falling – meaning mortgages were getting cheaper.  This had the effect of decreasing loan revenues, which freed income for use in consumer spending – resulting in increased revenues caused by a boom in the bank credit card business.

We need to note, even when the consumer avoids credit card interest by paying their balance before it is due, the issuer receives a fee from the retailer.  A "cashless" society, increased consumption results in increased credit card company revenue.  This produces more capital for banks to lend for long-term investments, like new cars or homes.

Could it be the probability of the next POTUS having no economic common sense and offering up programs that have not been thought through and, without difficulty, would bankrupt the nation?  Or, is it they have no international negotiating experience and are likely to get us into war – because their constituencies believe in antagonizing and insulting the leaders of nations who could become a threat to peace?

We know they yell, whenever Trump praises a dictator or fascist who controls nuclear weapons, or has the power to disrupt critical regions of the global economy. They oppose Trump and Putin talking.  It appears they never heard the adage *"Keep your friends close and your enemies closer."*  Or maybe they lack the comprehension necessary to grasp its practical application.

Either way, they do not grasp the idea that it is unwise to anger a beast that is an imminent threat to your survival.  This is especially true when you are both locked inside the same cage.

As will be explored in Chapter 9, historically, every POTUS has been a POTUS Cousin – an individual who, since 1575 and the founding of the original colonies, has shared a grandparent with an otherwise unrelated President.  In Chapter 9, we begin looking at, and eliminating, candidates based on another strange common quality of their ancestry – every president, and many of the First Ladies, SCOTUS justices, and House or Senate leaders, are all descended from one person – Charlemagne The Great.

As we know, at one time his family ruled Europe.  What is not generally recognized is the correlation between their being removed from power and the fall of the respective nations.  In the modern era, the most consistently dominant nations are Britain and the United States – whose leadership are descendants via William the Conqueror via the daughters of Hugh of Cyfeiliog, 5th Earl of Chester {1147-1181}.

Given the mathematical probabilities and the fact that each person is also the product of genealogies which echo the tribal class "marry-back" pattern genetic trait element akin to that seen in the Biblical marriage laws, it becomes clear that there is an instinctive tribal class structure.  We might refer to it as "Marrying Up", or "marrying above your Station", if we are speaking of those who do not share the common genealogy.

"Commoner" Meghan Markle marries Prince Harry and we think Black-Jewish commoner married above her station.  But the fact is that she and Harry have several common ancestors, such as Sir Edmund Sutton and Lady Matilda CLIFFORD {circa 1460}.  In context, the relationship is as close as the of Harry's siblings and their respective spouses.

Based on history, the genealogy infers that, should a non-POTUS Cousin be elected, America will lose its preeminent place in history.  In terms of a crisis, that could be the most significant  one facing the nation in 2020.

# CHAPTER EIGHT – Reality

*"Sarge, I'm only eighteen, I got a ruptured spleen...,*
*and my asthma's getting worse. ...*
*Besides, I ain't no fool, I'm a-goin' to school, ...*
*Sarge, give 'em Hell!  Kill me a thousand or so."*
**~ Phil Ochs, *The Draft Dodger Rag*,1965**

Phil Ochs was singing about the Vietnam Era reality.

*The Draft Dodger Rag* could be an ode to Joe Biden – who both went to school for the deferment and claimed to have asthma, yielding a back-up medical deferment excuse.

The Vietnam War began on 1 November 1955, in 1972, the United States and other foreign nations had begun to withdraw their troops, the draft was winding down, and by March 1973 all the foreign troops had been withdrawn.

Every now and again someone will point to Trump and yell "Draft Dodger."  It's even been asserted by 37-year old Mayor Pete Buttigieg that Trump bribed his doctor to falsify a medical exam.

It's a counterproductive polemic – attacking Trump based on the idea he bribed a doctor to falsify medical records – or, as Pete was quoted in a 26 May article in *Slate: "There is no question, I think, to any reasonable observer that the president found a way to falsify a disabled status, taking advantage of his privileged status in order to avoid serving. ... You have somebody who thinks it's all right to let somebody go in his place into a deadly war and is willing to pretend to be disabled in order to do it.  That is an assault on the honor of this country."*

In theory, a medical report detailing a bone problem would, if the problem existed, be supported by x-rays showing the affected area; a Draft Board would require such documentation.  Obviously, any false medical report would place the doctor's medical license at risk.

More important, after years of having a 1A classification with a high draft number which made it unlikely he'd be called, the medical finding was concurrent with the troop withdrawal that was accompanied by an end to the draft and Trump attaining the age of exemption from the "peacetime" Vietnam related draft.

As the record shows, the decision to give Trump a medical-based 4-F classification was an administrative action with no real Selective Service related meaning.  Those who had deferments for temporary medical issues were granted permanent status based on an administrative decision – if it was unlikely the problem would be resolved before the individual attained the age where it would require a *Congressional Declaration of War* for them to serve.

Looking closer at the Selective Service timeline, we see that the draft law governing Joe Biden and Bernie Sanders expired in June 1971, but the Nixon administration Department of Defense determined they needed a two-year extension, to June 1973.

Trump maintained a *'ready to serve'* 1A status classification throughout a period defined in Selective Service Law and received reclassification halfway through the temporary extension period – when he was already too old for basic training unless there was a formal declaration of war.  There is no rational basis to assert he evaded the Draft – the applicable law expired a year earlier and he was within months of age exemption.

The Vietnam conflict period began at the end of the Second World War, and its end triggered the Vietnamese resumption of the pre-war expulsion of colonial powers.

Mayor Pete was using Trump as cover for attacking anyone and everyone who opposed the Vietnam War that ended a decade before he was born.  Mayor Pete was creating a foundation upon which to frame attacks on those who oppose the longer imperialist "War of Terror" both Bush Presidents initiated at the behest of the Saudis.

Those who opposed America violating its WW2 promise to Vietnam – a promise that, if they helped in the war against Japan, it would be free of "Colonialist" influence, with an absolute right to self-determination in its governmental system or structure.

After the war, western powers repudiated the agreement and France was again granted its colonial power and authority, which reignited an anti-Colonialist War lasting from 19 December 1946 to 20 July 1954.

In 1954, Eisenhower decided to support the former French puppet government, introduced "advisors" who transformed it into an American puppet government combating a "red menace."  This then escalated into the Vietnam War.

As President, the best General Eisenhower could do against North Korea was restore the pre-war borders and sign an armistice that technically kept the "War" going until Trump became the first POTUS to enter the North Korean territory.

As history shows, American Superpower Military force could not even defeat the small nation of Vietnam, and the conflict lasted from 1 November 1955 to 30 April 1975 – a duration which will soon be matched by Bush's "War on Terror" which began with the 11 September 2001 destruction of New York's World Trade Center.

Of course this served as an excuse to continue the Wartime Selective Service Draft – which sent young American males, who could not legally vote for the Commander in Chief, off to foreign lands where they would use napalm and Agent Orange to kill Asian children (just as Nazis killed Jewish children) and inflict survivors with effects of chemical exposure such as non-Hodgkin lymphoma, prostate cancer, and multiple myeloma or Parkinson's disease and ischemic heart disease.

Opposing this criminal imperialist, possibly Fascist form of behavior was, in Right-Wing parlance, clear evidence symbolic of "anti-American" attitudes. Mayor Pete appears to hold that same position. For him, opposition any right of people to decide upon the government of their choice, and to do so by killing innocent people and burning children with napalm, *"at is an assault on the honor of this country."*

Of course, Mayor Pete does not fit the POTUS profile, he is NOT a JPC. Readers of Jonathon's POTUS Cousins are aware the cut-off year used was 1575, and that Trump was not a JPC – though he had been married to one. Tracing back before 1575 revealed that every POTUS, all the founding fathers, and renown people are in one common family line that traces directly to Charlemagne.

If the issue of Draft Dodging is to be meaningful, it is not one that should be raised by a person whose sexual orientation had rendered them ineligible for service. Nor should it be directed at someone who went to Military School and maintained a 1-A status throughout his period of age eligibility. Having gone to military school – Trump knew what to expect of military service and had experienced the disciplined structure of the service – with that background, he had done nothing to avoid the Draft. But, that can not be said for two of the potential Democratic nominees.

Bernie Sanders, who was born in 1941, avoided the draft by registering as a Conscientious Objector on 18 September 1959, and so had a 1-O classification in the period between the Korean and Vietnam wars. By August 1964, the United States began bombing Vietnam, Sanders had not been drafted and, by the 1968 Vietnam War Protest Era, when he relocated from New York to Vermont, he was two years past the Draft exemption age – while consistent with those of a draft evader, demonstrated his life-long aversion to the killing of his fellow humans. Can a POTUS be averse to killing?

As with Mayor Pete, Bernie has no JPC links. The mindset of a Conscientious Objector renders him unfit to be a Commander in Chief – a role requiring life-and-death decisions such as ordering another Hiroshima or Nagasaki. Could order, as Trump did, the use of a non-nuclear MOAB against Afghanistani terrorist forces?

Joe Biden, who was born in 1942, 14-months after Sanders, would have registered with Selective Service in late November or December 1960. In accordance with the song, Biden had received an educational deferment; when it was due to expire, on 5 April 1968, he was given a pre-induction medical exam and suddenly, consistent with the Phil Ochs medley, we see the football playing athlete claim *asthma* and receive a 1-Y classification.

When the Selective Service ended the 1-Y classification, our "Draft Dodger Blues", former Vice President was thirty and beyond draft age – having conformed perfectly to song's stereotype. Papa Joe is a JPC; had events warranted it, he would not have changed tradition by fulfilling his Constitutional role and succeeded Obama without disrupting the historical system.

In Iowa, Biden declared: *"We choose unity over division. We choose science over fiction. We choose truth over facts."*

His declaration presents us with a problem. He has invoked a Russian psychological propaganda technique known as *reflexive control* – in this case, stating a series of two acceptable ideas before asserting an irrational one. In sales, you should begin by invoking affirmative responses before the sales pitch, because, once they are nodding acceptance they will instinctively respond by accepting.

Can something be truthful without being factual? If you are a lawyer you tell a *Lawyer's Lie*, the Johnny Depp as Jack Sparrow line, *"You lied to me, by telling me the truth."* People will hold a thing to be true, even when it is not supported by fact – they will see the Emperor's New Clothes, even though the Emperor is naked.

Biden is saying those who comprise his base demographics will see in Trump what they have been told they should see and not what is real or factual. By the same token, they will ignore the facts about him and support the "truth" they are told they should accept.

Maybe he's just senile. We know he advocated opening the borders to two million migrants a year -- 60% of whom would be children in need of training in the English language, before they can be educated in conventional schools. Maybe Uncle Joe plans to create school systems that are Spanish language-based. Of course, these could not be conventional locally funded schools – schools funded by local property taxes paid by citizens who speak English. He might be considering creating a Spanish speaking State equivalent to the territory of Puerto Rico.

Or it might be his goal to let local communities worry about the cost – after all, it's only 2-million people in the first year and then another 2-million every year until the sauna temperatures in Central America have driven the whole of their populations into Mexico and then into the States and local communities that will be footing the cost.

After all, under Biden's grandiose assertion of America's ability to absorb Climate Refugees, by 2031, local property taxes would have increased by at least $270 Billion – just to cover the educational costs. There are no credible means of calculating the additional cost of public services which would further add to the tax burden and drive average citizens to relocate to communities with lower tax burdens.

There is also the problem of medical care.

During a 27 June 2019 Democratic primary debate, one of the moderators first asked, *"Who here would abolish their private health insurance in favor of a government-run plan?"* And they all did. With that commitment, the next request was *"Raise your hand if your government plan would provide coverage for undocumented immigrants."* And again, all raised their hands.

Universal healthcare, based on the same Medicare coverage now available to those on Social Security, or what is effectively its equivalent available to military servicemen through the Veterans Administration, makes sense and need not affect private policies

Under Social Security, retirement benefits are earned after ten years of contributions. Medicare could be made available as soon as that ten-year mark has been reached – the income benefit would still require attaining the retirement age. Employer and private medical plans would still be available as primary coverage and later, when Medicare kicks-in, as supplemental coverage.

Thus, the first show of hands can be seen as reasonable and economically sound. However, that second show of hands means an irrational government expense made more so when placed in the context of Biden adding 2-million a year to the rolls.

Comically, two months later, while campaigning in New Hampshire, Joe Biden was asked about his healthcare plan. He replied: "*We'll make sure it's **not quality**, we'll make sure it's only affordable.*"

This seems to mean his idea is to provide crap medical care – the type of care Obamacare has been accused of being. Or, that response can be added to the extensive list of misstatements and gaffes which infer Biden is in the advanced stages of dementia or senility which would result in a President Biden being the first to be the subject of Constitutional *"Amendment 25:4 - Presidential Disability and Succession"* due to his being *"unable to discharge the powers and duties of his office,"* based on a mental disability.

Almost immediately after the raise of hands declaration, Trump tweeted: *"All Democrats just raised their hands for giving millions of illegal aliens unlimited healthcare. How about taking care of American Citizens first!? That's the end of that race!"* {27 June 2019, 9:37 PM}

If we look at a disease like mumps, healthcare take on real significance. Why focus on mumps?

It is NOT a scare tactic, rather it is documented evidence of why Obama and Trump are correct in supporting and advocating for a Fence or "Wall" to control entry into the county. It reveals that the Reagan-Democrats and The Squad are now advocating a Right-wing "Most Harm to the Most People" agenda. It also infers that Joe Biden is one of them

In the Vietnam Era of 1967 there were about 186,000 cases were reported each year – and evidence of many unreported cases. In that year, U.S. implemented a vaccination program significantly reduced infections.

Before 26 April 2019, there were 736 confirmed cases, by 19 July that number had reached 1799.  In 1989,  the two-MMR dose vaccination program was introduced, and cases of mumps had decreased by more than 99%, with only a few hundred cases reported most years.  So, the first 7-months of 2019 have already shattered the average annual thirty-year rate – as reported by the U.S. Centers for Disease Control and Prevention.

In the United States, the disease increase can be blamed on the migrants; in Britain, a similar increase in both measles and mumps infections has been linked to anti-vaxxers.

Up until 2019, the World Health Organization {WHO} had granted Britain a "measles-free" status.  With the sharp increase in cases – even though there are 301 – the "measles-free" status has been removed.  Apparently, the increase in mumps is connected to outbreaks among university students, and produced the highest quarterly figure since 2009.

In Britain, the outbreaks confirm that something is going wrong in the preventative treatment against diseases once thought to be safely eradicated.  In the States, the attacks of the healthcare area precursor to the rise of similar problems.  Proper use of MMR (measles, mumps, rubella) vaccine helps mitigate the problems – anti-vaxxers and unvaccinated or infected migrants complicates matters.

The  Morbidity and Mortality Weekly Report issued by the Department of Health and Human Services Centers for Disease Control and Prevention {MMWR/30 August 2019/Vol. 68 /No. 34} stated: *"During September 1, 2018–August 22, 2019, a total of 898 confirmed and probable mumps cases in adult migrants detained in 57 facilities (18% of 315 U.S. facilities that house ICE detainees) were reported in 19 states; an additional 33 cases occurred among staff members."*

The report also states: *"Based on detainee custody status during their incubation period (12–25 days before symptom onset), most (758, 84%) patients were exposed while in custody of ICE or another U.S. agency; 43 (5%) were exposed before apprehension; and the custody status at the time of exposure of 97 (11%) was unknown."*

Ignoring those of unknown status, it would appear that 43 individuals inflected 758.  We can assume these cases are separate from the 1799, because *"Forty-four percent (394) of cases were reported from facilities that house ICE detainees in Texas."* Still, even if we net the ICE cases against the national ones, there are a thousand cases where only a few hundred should occur.

Based on the observed infection rate in the report, the excess domestic cases could be attributed to 45 illegal migrants. There is video documentation of more than that number evading ICE officers during one illegal border crossing. We know far more than that number were in the U.S. during the infection period.

A Nashville immigration attorney has been quoted saying: "*This has all the makings of a public health crisis. ICE has demonstrated itself incapable of ensuring the health and safety of people inside these facilities.*"

Of course, this is true. Members of Congress have so busy at photo-ops where they shed their crocodile tears over conditions at the facilities that they haven't had the time or interest to find the funds to provide the proper coverage. And the Presidential Candidates have been equally neglectful through their failure to call for such appropriations and to properly fund the "Wall" so that no infected individuals could evade medical examination.

Following Obama's lead, Trump has diligently repaired and improved the structure authorized by the 2006 Secure Fence Act; and he has done his best to extend and complete the structure we know was intended, but only partially funded, in 2006.

The influx of U.S.-Mexico border migrants resulting from the Reagan-Democrat open border rhetoric – and Biden's clear assertion he would accept 2 million a year – is taxing immigration system resources and enhancing the crisis President Trump had previously identified existed and was rebuked for.

Trump's first year in office saw the lowest number of illegal entries since 1971. But then the Reagan-Democrat initiated their open border propaganda, which was then supported by the effect of Climate Change in Equatorial regions. As a result, in 2018 the influx invasion began with the full support of the extreme Right and the Media – that intentionally avoids reporting on the various tropical disease being carried north.

Many of those infected by diseases are actually immune to them – it's similar to the disasters that befell the Mayan when the Spanish brought European diseases which ultimately decimated their population. When HIV emerged in or from Nigeria, it was later discovered that many women, prostitutes, were immune. The Climate migration will bring with it diseases that are currently unknown, but would be discovered in routine blood testing – if such testing was being done on the asylum migrants.

However, since there is a dual objective of destroying the Obama Legacy – Fence and Obamacare – while also inflicting the most possible harm on as many as possible, we can be sure the Reagan-Democrats will continue their propaganda campaign and general assault on the government.

Comically, that would explain why Joe Biden is leading the field for the 2020 Nomination. Given hid gaffes and the proven use of his office to acquire lucrative deals for family members, Biden is proving to be exactly the person the Reagan-Democrats wish Trump was. That means, if Biden is nominated, his Vice President would need to be vetted to a much higher degree than any POTUS in American history – because that VP will be elevated to the Oval at a pint where the Constitution would allow them to serve ten years.

We know Joe Biden conformed to *"the Draft Dodger Rag,"* but let's look at military service and draft-dodging again.

On 29 August, having failed to meet the criteria necessary to participate in the 3rd Democratic debate, Tulsi Gabbard simply moved on with her campaign.

Among the candidates, she was unique. A strong JPC who was also a Major who in 2004/05 served in the Iraqi combat zone and then in 2008/09 was deployed to Kuwait.

While serving her state of Hawaii as their Congresswoman, she serves the nation as an active reserve officer. Her credentials make her unique among those running for the 2020 nomination, and, assuming the self-defeating DNC handling of the nomination debate process keeps retains its desire for Septuagenarians, she will be the frontrunner in 2024, and win her second term in 2028.

In an interview following the DNC decision, Representative Gabbard stated:

*"People deserve having that transparency, …, ultimately, it's the people who will decide who our Democratic nominee will be and ultimately who our next president, commander-in-chief will be. And when you see that lack of transparency, it creates,*

*you know, a lack of faith and trust in the process.*

*"Really what they see is a small group of really powerful political elites, the establishment making decisions that serve their interests and maintaining that power while the rest of us are left outside. The American people are left behind."*

Back on the campaign trail, she reminded voters of one of her major qualifications for the Oval Office: *"Presidents of both parties have wasted trillions of tax dollars on regime change wars and new cold war. This must end. I've seen the cost of war first-hand, and as your commander in chief, I'll stand up against the warmongering foreign policy establishment clamoring for more war."*

Sadly, Tulsi is an anti-nihilist, she thinks positively, sees a purpose and direction. Her manner, her Hawaiian invocation of "Aloha" – a greeting invoking love, affection, peace, compassion, and mercy – places her at odds with a culture based on negativity, disbelief, a lack of purpose and a strong impulse to destroy which we see manifested in the mass killings in America and the suicide boomers who murder people in market places or on a religious pilgrimage to some holy place of worship.

Because they cannot believe, the nihilist rejects everything. They cannot grasp the idea behind Aloha, or the Hebrew Shalom, or even the Hindu Namaste which acknowledges there is within everyone an element of the divine.

The primary characteristic of modern nihilist thought is in the rejection of a Creator – a starting point for everything – which is different than rejecting a specific religious doctrine. They also reject the idea of timeless knowledge based on observation rather than some modern method of scientific investigation. They fail to grasp that the modern transfusion represents giving life within the Biblical admonition that blood is life. Or the idea behind blood as a biohazard, as contained in the idea that we should not consume it.

The biohazard element is in the instruction to immediately wash if you come into contact with blood – as while treating an injured person. In terms of disease transmission, there is also the idea of a menstruating woman being 'unclean' – but that was in the days before tampons or sanitary napkins, though it could also have reflected a male reaction to the serotonin level induced hormonal mood disorders.

Of course, sanitary does not mean clean and since the mid-20<sup>th</sup>-century tampons and menstrual pads have had their designs "improved" by the addition of plastics. On average, women experience menstruation for five-days a month spanning a period of about 40-years – or about 6.5 years of their life – and require between 5 and 15 thousand pads to absorb the discharged fluids.

The products are wrapped in plastic, tampons have plastic strings, plastic within the absorbent fibers, and plastic applicators; leak-proof plastic shielding covers the outer surface of pads. It is an undiscussed plastic waste that joins the bottles and wrappings that are contaminating the environment and adding another layer to the biblical "unclean."

Reality takes many forms and our reactions to it are varied, but there is an element of 'group think' – be it positive, negative, accepting, or rejecting. Humans have a need to belong, to be part of a group and to "fit in." Politicians win when they are believed to be one of the people or group that defines their base demographic.

Periodically, all nations enter into a time of change which is defined by 'need for chaos.' This is accompanied by a level of paranoia which is a combination of reality and fantasy. One basic traditionally observed reality is the targeting of the 'elite' – those we currently refer to as the one-percent. Within that tradition, the merchant class or nobility are the targets, and within those classes, the Hebrew merchants and scholars have always been the target of choice. If not the Jews, then their kindred spirits, the Chinese.

Reality is a strange thing. Trump invokes chaos, while we witness his detractors assert his strategic bankruptcies as if they were symptomatic of failure – yet he became POTUS and they are struggling to pay their mortgage, or are so poor they fail to qualify for mortgages to worry about. Trump fails in style, while others simply fail. George W. Bush was a failed President; one who got the nation into the perpetual war with no prospect of victory but continues to cost the nation trillions of dollars – even though he has been out of the Oval Office for over a decade.

There is another level of chaos, one that is associated with an idiotic focus on setting levels of greenhouse gases, rather than focusing on transitioning away from there generation – as the Chinese did when they set the 2025 goal of all new vehicles being electric. By doing so, they spawned the next-generation Ford and

General Motors as build around the concepts which created Tesla.

The idea is to decentralize through the use of electric.  If we look to California we see experiments with piezoelectric roadways, solar roads (which, based on the current technologies, appear to be structurally weak, though the basic concept might be applicable to driveways, or paved low traffic areas).

Conversations about global warming focus on icebergs and glaciers, but, to date, have minimalized the reality of heatwaves – while the nation focused on #SharpieGate (Trump's altering map of Dorian's path when it was still projected to impact Florida as it moved into the Gulf to impact Alabama) Las Vegas was declared the fastest-warming city in the United States.  That heating echoes what is happening in Australia and Central America.

In Las Vegas, temperatures of 115F (46C) are becoming the norm; homes without air conditioning are becoming death traps – the same is happening in equatorial nations like Columbia and Ecuador; countries like Guatemala and Honduras are borderline, while Nicaragua, Costa Rica, and Panama are sufficiently within the sphere of Climate Change to drive their inhabitants north.

Over the next decade, well before any proposed target date for modification of greenhouse gas emissions is reached, global warming will spawn a massive northern migration from Central America and nations on or north of the equator.  For Brazil, which extends southward, there is sufficient territory for the equatorial population to relocate within its national borders.

Because the population migration will number in the tens of millions, Mexico and the United States must make a choice – they focus on border control and the creation of rational methods by which the mass migration can be controlled, with its people integrated into the respective cultures in an ordered manner, or they can, as Biden has declared, simply open the borders and pay the price.

The Obama-Clinton bipartisan 2006 Secure Fence Act was the first step in creating an orderly integration.  Trump's Wall, or personalize designation for the Obama Fence, has rightly been declared a national security issue involving construction standards comparable to military security. Europeans are experiencing an early stage of climate migration – one driven by the economics and politics of the climate affected regions. Through NATO funding, the

Congressional appropriations will fund European Walls while opposing the Wall/Fence which is needed to safeguard America.

American media prefers reporting on the nonsense of a type labeled #SharpieGate – the President marking the extended area of Hurricane Dorian's path as reported by CNN. Then there is the hope of contributing to impeachment, rather than reporting on real dangers to the nation from climate change and future Dorian Category 5 hurricanes. Or they could focus on what was a minor story about Las Vegas and then project how soon various cities will be uninhabitable unless they are fully air-conditioned – using fossil fuels to generate the necessary electricity would then help worsen the problem by generating greenhouse gases to exacerbate the global warming problem.

Of course, Sharpiegate has become humorous. And in that vein, Ivanka Trump became the butt of jokes when she announced plans to visit Alabama and former FBI Assistant Director Frank Figliuzzi jokingly tweeted: "*Will you be surveying the hurricane damage there?*"

Actress Angela Belcamino tossed in her two cents with the tweet: "*Please do survey the hurricane destruction and don't forget the paper towels...*" which referenced Trump tossing paper towels at a 2017 news conference when he and the first lady visited Puerto Rico's Calvary Chapel disaster relief distribution center.

It's all-well-and-good to make fun of the first family and any work they do to bring equality into the workplace – the visit by Ivanka followed upon her South American mission where she was a key participant in Women's movement.

It's also neat that they ignore realities of international law, which does not recognize environmental refugee status under the Geneva Convention only acknowledges those fleeing violence and persecution – not those whose homes or even {island} nations are destroyed by the global warming, rising sea levels, or just "the weather." This lack of coverage includes earthquakes and volcanic eruptions – people are not valid refugees if they are victims of "acts of God."

Reality is nasty. Unless the people install violent dictators, they have no valid refugee status which will afford them the right to find a climate that sustains life. They must provide credible evidence that their leaders wish to personally harm them, or they have no legal right to seek asylum.  In the decade which begins in the year 2030, that will make things rather interesting for any but a "Biden-Pelosi America," where open borders and the acceptance of all will be the rule – this will make things interesting for the American economy and its survival.

In 2019, the population of Central America was about 50-million; if they headed north, the United States population would suddenly increase by around 15-percent – none of whom speak a level of functional English or have what Americans would consider a proper education.  The latter being a minor issue since half of them would likely be children who would be enrolled in American schools funded by American Real Estate or homeowners.

Because politicians elected in 2018 refuse to create border control and processing centers to handle what will become record numbers of immigrants created by global warming.  Fortunately, the United States will not face the massive population shift and related problems arising in North Africa and feeding into Europe; or in India where it will cause a "caste system" imbalance that can then disrupt Asia – with its initial impact compounding tensions that already exist with Pakistan and conflict between Hindus and Muslims.

Of course, Trump has imposed a technique similar to one that proved successful for Obama.  He "got irrationally tough" on all who entered the country illegally or through unorthodox means  – as a result, what had been a growing problem suddenly reversed itself.  In part, with Trump giving them the full credit, the fall in apprehensions resulting from a decline in crossings was brought about by the Mexican government tightening patrols along its side of the US-Mexico border, and also tighten security along Mexico's border with Guatemala – stopping the migrants before they could enter Mexico.

In effect, Trump had successfully achieved a solution to the emerging problem in Europe, where the number of migrants into Turkey and Greece was growing and had become a threat to their economic structures.  Represented by coastal migrants intercepted in August 2018 (1,311) and a year later, in August 2019 (7,834), the month-to-month patterns of increases and decreased seemed to echo the changes seen on the US-Mexico border during the same periods. That correlation infers a climate component is being masked by claims of other, more easily visualized, reasons that are consistent with the Geneva Convention on Asylum claims.

Where Trump negotiated with Mexico to increase its border security in the north and initiate security in the south – effectively shifting the cost from the ICE or Wall budget to that of Mexico – without saying "Mexico is paying," the media was reporting on the enforcement of a United Nations "Third-Country" asylum process.

Being opposed to the Administration and in favor of open borders, media reports of an ACLU challenge to the third-country transit asylum bar, issued 16 July 2019, as a domestic "human rights" issue rather than one of compliance with international law that Congress had selected to violate to encourage what was then the dominant variation on Reagan's 1980s open-border policy – which included opposition to any Fence or Wall along the border.

A September 2019 *Human Rights First* fact sheet stated that *"In the first four months of FY 2019, less than 32 percent of reasonable fear screenings resulted in positive determinations."*

So only a third of asylum claims are deemed legally valid by the courts; that means the attack on Trump's enforcement of international law is being challenged to facilitate circumvention of law by the ACLU.

Looking to Turkey, we see they were under severe economic stress and were looking to international aid, the alternative is to allow or "push" the migrants through into the European Union.

At a time when the 'open border' Reagan-Democrats were complaining about migrants dying in ICE care, it is worth noting that, 2018 had seen 174 migrants died crossing into Turkey, and 57 had died in the first eight months of 2019, while only 24 died in ICE custody. The highest recorded death rate in ICE custody was 32 – in 2004, during the Bush Administration and at the peak of illegal entrant apprehensions, and before the Secure Fence Act was signed into law.

Applying the 'Crude death rate' – which represents the total number of deaths per year per 1,000 people around the world, or 8.33/1000 – it becomes clear that 2,499-4,165 could, statistically, be expected to die during the calendar year or 10 on any given day.

Deaths in ICE custody are therefore extremely rare, and in the period ending June 2019, the agency spent over $269 million to provide *"comprehensive medical care"* for each of the 300,000 to 500,000 individuals taken into custody every year leading into the 2020 campaign season push against the fence/wall.

In addition, ICE  reviews the circumstances surrounding all deaths of those in its custody  – revealing any infectious diseases of the type associated with the previously cited MMR resurgence.  As with Ellis Island in the early 1900s, the Fence/Wall is the only means controlled entry which would allow for screening asylum seekers for infectious or deadly diseases.

Of course, while Turkey can illustrate problems American is exposed to by mass northward migrations, it also has a very real version of Trump's claim that there could be various criminals and terrorists to contend with.  Those entering Turkey are from war-torn Syria and easily include sleeper agents from various terror group members.

When we look at Trump's statements – which seem off-the-wall to many in the media – we need to remember that he seeks out and identifies patterns in known similar events.  Thus he can generalize what is evident in Greece and Turkey, or any other area of mass migration, and apply it to what will eventually emerge in the context of migrants from socially disrupted Latin American regions.  The immediate threat is economic.

Media promoting the threat of a recession began 7 January 2019 with articles like, *"How will central bankers cope when the next recession comes?"* "If you ask most central bankers around the world what their plan is for dealing with the next normal-size recession, you would be surprised how many (at least in advanced economies) say "fiscal policy". Given the high odds of a recession over the next two years – about 40% in the US, for example – monetary policymakers who think fiscal policy alone will save the day are setting themselves up for a rude awakening."

While there will be multiple minor recessions, maybe even a new Great Recession, the real problem is Climate Migration.  As this was being written, the DHS admitted the Border Wall issue was a Climate Migration issue.  The day after the admission, Prime Minister Mia Mottley of Barbados told leaders at the United Nations Climate Event Summit: *"Make no mistake, there will be mass migration by climate refugees that will destabilize the countries of the world that are not on the frontline of this climate crisis."*

She went on to explain issues related to temperature rise  and then said, *"In other words, 2 degrees needs to be taken off the table once and for all.  The real solution is for us to not keep asking people to make commitments that are small ... but the global community must accept that it is within our power to halt and reverse climate change."*

Trump avoided the Climate issue and focused on religious bigotry defining the lives of a majority of the global population.

In his own way, he was addressing a force of conflict that will define the Climate Migration and ability of people to integrate into new regions and cultures. We know that various members of Congress like to rant about Climate Change, but few do anything to address the real issue of people coming to the Southern Border while droughts are creating water scarcity, and the associated heat is making border regions of the United States uninhabitable.

The World Health Organization website warns: *"With a limited water supply in the future, there will be competition between various sectors with regards to the use of water. Water scarcity can cause a variety of health problems by reducing the amount of water available to practice basic hygiene and by increasing the risk of chemical and microbial contamination; these can lead to gastrointestinal diseases and other health risks."*

Climate Reality, the elephant in a room – one everyone is happy to discuss, but only in terms that support the delusion it is in another room and either being ignored by, or a fantasy of, other people.

In her speech, Mottley pointed to the reality of misplaced priorities with an apt analogy: *"The world finds it possible to apply resources to solving male baldness while it cannot find the resources to cure malaria."* It is applicable because, as the climate warms, mosquitoes carrying malaria will migrate north – but so will other insects carrying diseases we never heard of and have no defense against. In some cases, the infections will reach northern nations before the insects – carried by the same Climate Migrants Joe Biden and his ilk want to allow to flood into the United States without the physical exams once common to Ellis Island and other 19th and early 20th-century ports of entry.

As the summer of 2019 drew to a close, and the Democratic candidates began promoting their ideas. With 6.1 million people unemployed in the United States, Bernie Sanders was envisioning some really cool jobs. The only problem – most unemployed were hardly qualified to be janitors and were far less qualified to install solar panels or do the carpentry involved in weatherizing homes. In construction, September saw companies declare they had to turn away 43% of jobs because of a lack of people who can handle a hammer or read a blueprint.

Border asylum seekers are even less suited to file the range of green or basic occupations. Sixty-percent are children and most of the others are the women who care for them. Then too, even those with the basic skills have a language and literacy problem when working in an English speaking environment.

In many ways, the asylum seekers could be compared to the Eastern European Jews who arrived before 1900, That group were deemed to be morons and idiots – a perception affirmed by the IQ Testing of the era. But, given access to the American educational system, their children, like the children of Jewish immigrants who arrived in the 1880s, where dominating Harvard admissions did by 1915. There is no reason to believe the same will not be said of Climate Migrant children – but we will not know until 2040 or later. But, how will the economy survive until then?

Who will pay to support or educate Climate Migrants?

What is the *Green New Deal* that Democrats speak of?

# CHAPTER NINE – GRETA Thunberg

*"She seems like a very happy young girl looking forward to a bright and wonderful future.*
*So nice to see!"*

~ Donald J. Trump, 24 September 2019

*{describing Greta Thunberg}*

*"A very happy young girl looking forward*
*to a bright and wonderful future."*

~ Greta Thunberg, Twitter bio, 25 September

"I was diagnosed with Asperger's syndrome, OCD and selective mutism.  That basically means I only speak when I think it's necessary.

Now is one of those moments."

~ Greta Thunberg, November 2018

Many people have said, **"*Perception is Reality.*"**  Donald Trump Jr, in *TRIGGERED*, said: *"The narrative rules the facts."*

Reality is whatever we choose to accept and repeat.  Every Christmas we see millions of people celebrate the Roman Holiday of Saturnalia as a birthday; we start our calendar – declare as year one – a year that is seven years after the birth it marks, and four years after the death of a king who died when the birthday boy was three years old.  We like the narrative, so declare it a reality.

The original remark could be sarcasm or intended as some form of a backhanded compliment.  If you wish to see a negative, you can embrace it and have it define you.

Or, you can take it at face value and embrace it.  Forest Gump was portrayed as stupid, but said, *"Stupid is as stupid does."*  The interpretation is that a person's lack of intelligence is seen in their actions.  If we held to the biblical, we would "judge everyone according to their deeds" and accept the idea "Ye shall know them by their fruits." {Matthew 7:16}

Do not judge based on propaganda, it's actions that matter.

But, in a 21$^{st}$-century America, a scientific foundation and the basic foundation of being 'Kosher' has no place.  Ethics are the province of those who can yell the loudest or be the most destructive.

There is no rational consistency – Biden can boast of his criminal *"quid pro quo"* and be ignored; Trump adheres to his oath of office and the Congressionally approved 1998 Treaty.

President Clinton's "Letter of Submittal", dated 19 October 1999 stated, *"The scope of the Treaty includes not only criminal offenses, but also proceedings related to criminal matters, which may be civil or administrative in nature."* With the subsequent series of explanatory paragraphs means Trump's "favor" was legal.

The use of nonsense words distracts us from considering the facts or observing the actions. Take as a current example the Paris Climate Accord which says climate gases are to be reduced by 2050. But the reality is that the tipping point for Global Warming, and those effects most detrimental to life, will be reached in 2030. If science is correct than the Paris accord – assuming it goals are attained by 2050 – will accomplish a goal twenty years too late. The racer is going to cross the finish line – but only after the race is over and the spectators have gone home.

A curious reality is that the message that has been around for over a century is being brought to light through the efforts of a 16-year-old girl, who looks as if she's twelve, and speaks more knowledgeable than America's 76-year-old presidential candidate, Joe Biden. And she does so in English, despite the fact her native language is Swedish.

The message she is delivering is one that has been known and ignored for about a century. The core element that has mad human survival and progress possible – the discovery of fire – has now reached the point where it is altering the natural cycles of the climate-controlled epics which once produced the Ice Age and the warmth which brought it to an end.

As children of the global community prepared to take part in the September Climate Strike, Robert Jeffress, an Evangelical pastor who serves on President Trump's Evangelical Advisory Board and the White House Faith Initiative, termed the climate changes an "imaginary crisis." And invoked Noah's Flood, saying, *"Somebody needs to read poor Greta Genesis, Chapter 9, and tell her the next time she worries about global warming, just look at a rainbow. That's God's promise that the polar ice caps aren't going to melt and flood the world again."*

Of course, the polar ice caps lack the water volume that would be necessary to flood the world; and the Noah story was not real, rather – as is shown in the book *Genesis of Genesis* – it was a myth, taken from the *Tales of Gilgamish,* used to introduce the necessary calendar correction would maintain a chronology which would eventually become the basis for a modern calendar system  that is now common global system.

But mythical Flood proportions are not necessary. Look at the State of Florida where, since 1950, sea levels have increased by eight inches and projections in 2019 indicate it will increase by an inch every three years, with general sea levels rising an additional 15 inches by 2050.

So what?  By 2040, the Baby-Boomers will all be dead, they have no reason to be concerned about a bit of extra water along the shoreline.

But, in Florida, it's not a shoreline issue.  The state is seated on porous limestone, allowing seawater to quickly reach inland areas and raise the underground water table at a similar rate as the Atlantic Ocean, and this means Florida's low-lying geography makes the State especially vulnerable to changes in sea level.  But, again, why is that important?

Actually, it's about indoor plumbing and the septic systems, upon which about 1 in 5 American households rely.  About 15% of those septic systems are in Florida, and across the United States, as many as 60 million toilets could be rendered inoperable, as the increased groundwater makes the soil too wet to soak up the water that now moves into septic leach fields or, as they are also called drainage fields.  Those drainage fields are becoming saturated to the point where they no longer absorb septic tank liquids.

Worse, as the water table rises, decomposed human waste from the septic systems would discharge in ways that, under 2019 Environmental Protection Agency (EPA) regulations, could make things interesting.

Climate change eliminates your ability to flush the toilet or drain the bathtub.  Does anyone really care if their grandchildren or great-grandchildren can take a bath or flush a toilet?

Let's consider this in terms of an Environmental Protection Agency (EPA) violation filed against San Francisco on 2 October 2019.  The EPA violation cited San Francisco for water pollution associated with the city's homeless crisis.

The associated letter from the EPA administrator, Andrew Wheeler, stated the city's incomplete data showed *"it discharging approximately one and a half billion gallons of combined sewage annually onto beaches and other sensitive areas, including areas where recreation takes place."*

In San Francisco, the complaint was deemed a *"politically motivated ploy,"* but in the future, a rise in sea level means many coastal cities will be faced with very real pollution issues leaving two choices: abandon EPA regulations or fix the problem. One of those problems is a classic – Cholera, which is contaminated with a bacterium called Vibrio cholerae which was common before the 1900s when modern sewage systems came into existence.

Obviously, it is far more important for Congress to invent reasons to impeach Trump that it is for them to find a solution to a problem the World Health Organization says is responsible for about 145,000 deaths a year. Not many in a population of over seven billion, but in the past, cholera pandemic managed to kill about 3-percent of the population where they occurred.

Thus Florida, along with various East and West Coast regions could see similar levels of death from one water-pollution related bacteria. It's just a matter of contaminated drinking water in coastal areas.

Greta advocates, for the Federal government to address the issue now. Instead, the House of Representatives devotes time and resources to impeachment proceedings based on a "parody" by the individual who is then placed in charge of those politically motivated proceedings. Accordingly, the 116th Congress is likely to make history as the most inept and disastrous one ever elected – and that's with members like Bernie Sanders promoting a Green New Deal or other environmental fantasies dealing with periods several decades in the future.

Think about this. The universe is designed to be perfectly imperfect, a perpetual motion machine with a beginning and end that are one and inseparable – which some postulate is designed as a three dimensional Mobius Strip, which is what you get when you take a stip of paper, give it a half twist, glue the end together to form a circle, and then discover you can draw a line down the center which will join itself. That's two dimensional, in three, you can go in any direction and, while always moving forward, return to where you began.

The environment or ecosystem is a closed loop of elements joining and separating, generating heat or absorbing heat. Carbon and oxygen combine making CO2 when we breath or things burn; plants pull the elements out of the air, expel the oxygen, deposit the carbon in the soil where it provides carbon for carbon-based life. In that process, fire is a natural component; when humans evolved to create fire and utilize, they altered the system and the system adjusted. With industrialization, humans both advanced and expanded the imbalance so the atmosphere heated, melted ice, creating more water to absorb both the heat and CO2.

Human evolution is a part of climate change; evolution is defined by intelligence, and we have reached a point where that intelligence must now be used to integrate human behavior into the ecosystem. Humanity must stop demanding the environment compensate for its abuses and respecting the system's design.

Greta is telling us that here generation needs the system to be respected; the attacks on Trump which began with the election, and are therefore not related to any activities on his part, show the American disrespect for the natural order of things – not just the rejection of the Constitution, but a rejection of nature in the form of climate denial, which reflects a rejection of human evolution – what religious-types might define as the *"wisdom, knowledge and understanding"* which the Bible says is the *"spirit of God"* and, therefore, we could argue American Evangelicals and others have rejected God by disrespecting the system they claim he created.

The system is like a pinwheel that spins in the breeze. But, it's speed can be increased by the breath of a child combining with that breeze or moved simply by that child's breath. By blowing on the climate pinwheel, by burning fossil fuels when we were given wind, sun and geothermal energy to use, humans have increased climate change. Given the history of windmills and water wheels or other tools that captured energy, humanity made a conscious choice to violate nature – and nature is getting even.

Greta has stood before members of the United Nations and said, *"This is all wrong. I shouldn't be standing here. I should be back in school on the other side of the ocean. Yet you all come to me for hope? How dare you!"*

America is the Global Leader – or so it wishes to believe – it has a President noted for his ego and desire to be remembered by history, and the Congress is blowing the opportunity to really lead, the opportunity to show the world the future.

Greta told the UN members: "*You are failing us. But the young people are starting to understand your betrayal. The eyes of all future generations are upon you. And if you choose to fail us, I say we will never forgive you.*" But alleged Global Leader, America, is failing humanity, the planet, and itself – it's blowing an opportunity to be self-sufficient and economically independent. That independence would make America the leader of a "Star Trek Federation" and a world where there is no poverty. But America is rejecting it – worse, Evangelicals are rejecting it like they reject everything scriptural.

When humans industrialized they blew on the atmospheric pinwheel and the planet began to warm at a faster rate than its natural cycle. The days of fossil fuel-based industrialization are gone; we are in the era of electronic connectivity and a "Star Trek" style global community; we must cease blowing on the pinwheel. The only issue is, do we do it now, and move forward to a beautiful future, or suffer the problems that come when you fight nature?

The decision determines where in the cycle we will come to rest. For now, we have accelerated to the edge of de-glaciation. Do we cross over now or later? That is the climate change quandary.

The last time $CO_2$ concentrations were higher than current levels was over three million years ago when sea levels were 50 and 80 feet higher than they are now.

Humans will, within a decade, trigger a carbon catastrophe, we are seeing the atmosphere getting warmer, soon the oceans will become more acidic and the mass extinctions which have already begun will increase.

This is the world Greta sees and is angry about because so many supposed leaders are doing nothing, while many others are making things worse.

Of course, had Jeffress understood the reference he made, he would also know that "*you shall not eat flesh with its life, that is, its blood.*" Which is to say, any meat must be slaughtered in a kosher manner before he is permitted to consume it. He would also be opposed to any military action that is not retaliatory, for "*Whoever sheds man's blood, By man his blood shall be shed.*" It is an interesting verse that seems to mandate the death penalty for all who commit murder.

Of course, most people have no interest in the Bible, or they would be paying attention to Revelation and know it brings an end to the command: "*And as for you, be fruitful and multiply; Bring forth abundantly in the earth And multiply in it.*"

Revelation tells us that, toward the middle of the current century, a third of all life will die. If we count vanishing species and the demographics of the Baby-Boom followed by a Baby-Bust, Jeffress can take solace in that prediction appearing to be proving true. That is exactly what we are witnessing when, at the Climate Action Summit in New York, Greta declared: "*Entire ecosystems are collapsing. We are in the beginning of a mass extinction. And all you can talk about is money and fairytales of eternal economic growth. How dare you!*" {U.N. 23 September}

How dare Robert Jeffress – or his hypocritical evangelical colleagues – invoke a Bible whose verses and realities they either ignore or intentionally encourage people to violate? Is it that they are inherently evil, or do they simply lack the requisite "Wisdom, Knowledge, and Understanding" which Greta elegantly displays.

Given that Congress wants to distract from Climate Change, they fabricated a complaint against Trump to justify initialing an impeachment investigation during the week-long Climate Strike which began Friday, 20 September and ended on the 27th; they even initiated televised House impeachment hearings on the day Greta departed for a conference in Spain.

To achieve distraction, with an added benefit of furthering attempts to plunge the economy into another recession. During the Mueller investigation, Adam Schiff, in his role as the House Intelligence Committee chairman, lied about having evidence of Trump collusion with Russia; his claim was obviously false so the evidence was never produced. Had the claim been real, then Schiff could be guilty of withholding critical evidence from the Mueller investigation – which would be criminal interference with a Federal Investigation and warrant his arrest and prosecution. The lie would, had it been done under normal legal circumstances, constitute a false statement to disrupt an investigation.

With the failure of Mueller to reveal improper behavior, the phishing effort turned elsewhere, and for some reason eventually settled on the 12 August 2019 "whistleblower" letter, which had been deemed untrustworthy because it contained no first-person observations and failed to identify the third party sources alleged to be the true source of the information which, as of this writing, has proved unreliable or clearly false.

Still, with the news cycle focused on a 16-year-old, it was the perfect time to the reignite disruptive political impeachment moves had begun with the announcement of the November 2016 election results. Under normal circumstances, the media attention would have focused on the millions of demonstrators taking to the streets in countries all over the globe. Instead, that media was fed lies and distraction, which it joyfully repeated – *"if it bleeds it leads"* is the classic journalistic motto which encourages a media approach that sees or describes a glass half empty and about to spill.

On Thursday, 26 September, Schiff blatantly lied about the contents of a phone call between the presidents of American and Ukraine, and so orchestrated propaganda designed to force the start of an impeachment investigation. Schiff was called out for his false statements, and admitted the comments were invented – he labeled it a conversation "parody," even though he claimed to not have actually read the transcript of the conversation he received the day before and which served as the basis for his "parody."

In any event, Schiff successfully distracted the media from coverage of the Climate Crisis demonstrations. In the process, he also initiated events consistent with the two prior impeachments.

On 13 November Greta left for Europe, the House started its impeachment hearing game, and the DJIA closed at 27,783 with a high for the day at a record 28,806. Had the impeachment held the credibility of the Clinton model, the direction would have been down, not up. On 4 November 2016, the DJIA was 17,888 – After the low of 6,507 on 9 March 2009, Wall Street began to appreciate Obama, and then it took a liking to Trump. Under Bush, about 19-months before the 2009 low, the DJIA had peaked around 13,907.

Bush took office with the DJIA about 10–percent lower than it had been after shrugging off Clinton's Impeachment to achieve a record high by the start of the campaign season. It took six years for the DJIA to gain 40-percent, then Bush successfully cause it to crash.

Bush-43 was a swamp denizen who gifted the nation with a 19-year war and a Great Recession; now, his companion denizen, Adam

Schiff, is pushing an impeachment which would tarnish the Obama legacy, return to the recession, and ensure the re-election of Trump. Obama must be tarnished, he nearly tripled the DJIA – relative to the 2009 low.

During his two terms Clinton, like Obama, nearly tripled the DJIA. And now Trump has brought an increase in average wages accompanied by record-high minority employment, and record low unemployment for all groups. In just under three years in office, Trump added 10,000 points to the DJIA. If not for BREXIT and obstructionist Swamp Denizens he could be doing better. The Trade Wars have done no noticeable harm; even the farm problems are more related to Climate Change than Chinese tariffs.

Many bemoan the loses associated with soy, used for animal feed by the Chinese pork industry. What the media fails to connect is that, since August 2018, there has been a severe pork shortage in China, due to an outbreak of the African swine fever. As a result, the demand for feed was falling, because there were no pigs to feed. Concurrently, the Midwest agricultural regions were experiencing record heat and flood rain, which caused a delay in planting season.

Those combined forces meant the agricultural sector would suffer severe losses in 2019, and, at the end of July 2019, Trump provided a $16 billion aid package for those farmers damaged by the effects of bad weather and the US-China trade war. By the time the Impeachment hearings had been scheduled, and with no call to cite the swine fever epidemic, there would be a third set of bailout payments added to the $26 billion already expended.

The epidemic devastating the Chinese pork supply has had the interesting effect of altering the traditional Chinese diet, which is good in terms of Climate Change. Pork production is linked with Greenhouse gas emissions and by decreasing consumption of pork, which is also associated with clogged coronary arteries and heart disease, as well as decreased brain function, both climate of China and the health of its people can be improved.

While probably unintentional, Trump's trade war might well be doing more to address global warming than anything included in the Paris Climate Agreement.

On 5 June, Adam Schiff tweeted about Climate Change:

*"Scientific consensus is clear: climate change is happening. Now.*

*"The effects are cross-cutting and severe, with real impacts on our national security. Climate change causes resource scarcity, instability, and conflict."*

Schiff's statement makes it clear he understands aspects of climate issues. That understanding reveals intentional actions, as opposed to the acts of an incompetent legislator. Schiff's actions to impeach based on hearsay are tailored to ensure four additional years for the denizens to regroup and emerge from their safe haven in California and New York. It's one way that *"The Swamp Fights Back."*

Swamps give off Greenhouse gases, the political system is a neighborhood consisting of four houses built along the shores of a swamp. Those houses are Democrat, Republican, Independent, with the final house being a type of political bed & breakfast where transient groups reside.

Ignoring the negative ramifications of their actions, Swamp Denizens are emerging from the left to continue the work of their right-wing counterparts. These efforts are an attack on Obama and the economic recovery and borer security he initiated. Trump has taken those initiatives and has worked to improve upon them. It is through the use of nonsensical impeachment that the denizens are pushing real issues off the front pages and out of the purview of social media discussion.

In another time, the media might have tracked Greta as she crossed the nation triggering climate rallies that, in terms of those who turnout, exceeded the numbers appearing to support most of the Democratic Presidential candidates. Greta presents us with an almost mythological tale of a young girl who emerges as a leader in the way Joan of Arc took command in the Hundred Years' War.

Of course, Jeanne d'Arc was burned at the stake, when she was nineteen. Greta is working to see that humanity avoids some similar fate as its lands and crops suffer from global warming. Of course, since we are at a weird point in history, history has a way of being weird. So it was, as Greta sailed to Europe, an 1898 photo of three Yukon Territory children extracting water from a well was discovered in the University of Washington archives. The young girl looked exactly like Greta – and a segment of the internet went crazy over the question: *Is Greta Thunberg a time traveler?*

Before hitching a ride on the catamaran sailing to Europe,

Greta Had been touring the country and reignited the interest of 1960s activists like Jane Fonda, who, beginning 11 October, made a point of being arrested for protesting climate change on the steps of the U.S. Capitol building.

The 81-year-old activist-actress was part of the weekly "Fire Drill Friday" campaign which sought to get Global Warming loving Democrats (the California-based impeachment organizers which included Pelosi, Schumer, Schiff, and Waters) to take action on the Green New Deal initiatives. The objective is to end all new fossil fuel exploration and drilling and promote renewable clean energy which also holds the economic promise of creating a new class of employment suitable for the communications age while, at the same time, protecting communities.

Arguably, California is spearheading the Green revolution and it's in their economic interest to assure the rest of the nation falls behind. The state also produces 8.3% of the nation's oil and, if the Green Revolution were to end fossil fuel reliance before those wells are completely dry – a process which began in 2010, when hydraulic fracturing of shale oil deposits opened the way to new supplies of natural gas and increased oil production. Thus we see a strange dichotomy echoing Saudi Arabian moves toward broad usage of renewable energy – rather than draw on the abundant oil reserves.

Symbolically, fracking proclaims related oil fields are going dry and producers are scraping the bottom of the barrel.

Fracking was experimented with in Oklahoma in the 1960s and 1970s; the practice ceased when it was realized earth tremors were a side-effect hydraulic fracturing. One might suspect that it would be unwise to initiate earth tremors in a state defined by a major earthquake fault line.

However, this is a state that still supports Ronald Reagan's open border policies, strives to increase undocumented aliens, but has elected members of Congress who consistently fail to make the effort to address the DACA issue, and whose state representatives can boast of having more than 20% of America's homeless people. One is forced to wonder where the migrants will live, if California cannot house citizens, and has been regularly beset with wildfires that only add to the number of displaced persons.

Jane Fonda can demonstrate happily in Washington, but it is her home state which requires action, and will much if migrants flood in to burden an already fragile ecosystem in a state that Greta spent considerable time and energy trying to awaken to reality.

Another side-effect of fracking is the release of greenhouse gases which can easily overwhelm any positive element of the green actions symbolized by the electric vehicles used by Jane Fonda and former actor and California Governor Arnold Schwarzenegger.

In my 1978 book, *"The Prophecy Notebook,"* I mention the failed Oklahoma fracking experiments and the risks they offered if tried in California or any area where they might initiate a "butterfly effect" in which a small tremor initiates a major quake.

In 1978, my focus was on Pennsylvania and the Missouri oil fields where they use large boilers of water heated with natural gas to produce steam which is injected into the oil to thin it and help it flow. The region of New Madrid, Missouri has the Reelfoot rift that spans Arkansas, Tennessee, Missouri, and Kentucky and was the source of the horrific 1812 earthquake – said to have rung Church bells in Boston.  Of course, that meant it was widely felt across the eastern seaboard, where it awakened residents of New York City, Washington D.C., and Charleston, South Carolina.

In 1811/12, the New Madrid region was uninhabited land, but now about twenty-percent of the American population would feel its effects; meanwhile, the population San Francisco has only doubled, so less than a million people would feel a direct effect of an earthquake-recurrence rate of between 140–160 years, which places the next event in 2046 – after the death of the baby-boom population.

Many might dismiss this the way they do global warming, but with resumed fracking, Oklahoma now has more earthquakes than in California.  Fracking in California offers the real potential of triggering the San Andreas fault, which could then cause a repeat of the 1906 San Francisco earthquake, which was comparable to the Missouri quake 95-years earlier – that event was a Richter scale 7.8 to 8.8, while the San Andreas one was 7.9 to 8.3.

Because any geological disruption will release Greenhouse Gases that affect global warming, a possibility of human triggered events not only offsets and negates human efforts to curb warming, but also must take into account significant population growth in the potentially affected seismic regions. But, apparently, we wish to see the planet warmer – even at the risk of seismic results.

During the impeachment hearings, National Geographic published an article stating: *"Global governments plan to produce 120 percent more fossil fuels by 2030, drastically at odds with the 2.7 degrees Fahrenheit (1.5 degrees Celsius) warming limit they all agreed to under the 2015 Paris Climate Agreement."*

At the same time, other news spoke to medical findings that linked small particulates released by coal and oil-based fossil fuels to numerous deaths in the United States – but, after three years of attempting to invent Devine a justification, impeachment was more important than the health of voters.

As we saw, Schiff understands Climate Change, so when he and Pelosi and the rest attack Trump and the Border Wall, they are intentionally ignoring its ramifications. Some of those are reflected in the Bernie Sanders Tweet of 16 September 2019:

*"As many as 22 million people—double the populations of New York City and Chicago combined—could be displaced by global warming this year.*

*When we say that climate change is an emergency, this is what @AOC, @RepBlumenauer and I are talking about."*

None of the politicians focused is on impeaching Trump are of a mindset geared to national survival. While the 22 million are global, the American share is currently less than 2 million. Their forced migration will cause economic disruption in the nations they pass through, and enormous levels of disruption where they finally settle – unless the nation has systems in place to integrate them.

One system which Trump established is being attacked by various self-serving Resettlement Agencies.

In a lawsuit designed to attack Trump's authorization that would allow cities and communities the right of self-determination in accepting or rejecting migrant refugees – which includes all the costs related to the education of their children, along with family housing and culturalization – stated:

*"The President's order and resulting agency actions threaten to deprive thousands of refugees of their best chance to successfully build a new life and to burden thousands of US families who are waiting to reunite with their parents, children, and other relatives fleeing persecution."*

Obviously, a bogus argument. Any refugees reuniting with a

family who are already legally settled are simply joining family – this is not a real issue.  The issue is those who have no families in the United States and are seeking the *"best chance to successfully build a new life."*  For them, the ideal situation is relocation to those communities who need new residents and whose schools now require students.  As Americans move to cities, this describes a major section of rural America.

Allowing communities to decide allows for better integration into society.  Refugees should settle where they are both wanted and needed; it is only there that they can both tribute and derive the most benefit.  Since many communities have lost population and could die without migrants and their children to fill basic jobs and populate the schools, the nation benefits.  More so because those same communities generally have an abundance of vacant homes.

In terms of Climate Change and going Green, obviously, any refugees with advanced skills and educations would find work in High Tech communities.

However, the average refugee may not even fit a blue-collar image or have anywhere near that skill base.  As of November 2019, 60% of migrants are children in need of basic education.  Many of the remaining 40% might meet the emerging need for people who can be trained to install and maintain renewable energy like that associated with Solar and wind.

Many manual workers could have skills needed to upgrade vacant housing for their fellow climate refugees to occupy.  Which means they have productive work and would not be a burden of the economy.  Ans this takes us from Greta's concerns to Trump's.

# CHAPTER TEN – CLIMATE MIGRANTS

Now we have a mess you might have noticed in the previous chapter. Greta, Trump, Climate Change and any number of other matters are all locked together and feeding off each other. As they feed they also define issues that should be important in the 2020 campaign debates.

The Elephant in the room is the Climate Refugee the media treats like Jews in the hands of Nazis. They're in cages. Detention centers – are they racist concentration camps? Without them, are the migrants to live on the streets? How are they to be processed, when the American Congress would rather do tearful photo-ops and then return to an impeachment process started on 9 November 2016, which, by Thanksgiving 2019 had seen two weeks of hearings consisting of hearsay, gossip, and petty bureaucrats both second-guessing the President's policies, while asserting those very same policies were consistent with those of the Obama Administration.

Trump's resettlement order, granting communities a say in the process, was covered by the Refugee Act of 1980, which was a response to the end of the Vietnam War. At the time, Congress sought to establish a structured and rational system of immigration and resettlement based upon a clear and flexible policy.

The Act changed the definition of "refugee" to the United Nations accepted standard of a person with a "well-founded fear of persecution." As nations are beginning to recognize, that definition has no application in an era of global warming and climate-driven migration – are scorching hot days and nights or rising sea levels a form of "persecution"?

*Sec 101(b): "The objectives of this Act are to provide a permanent and systematic procedure for the admission to this country of refugees of special humanitarian concern to the United States, and to provide comprehensive and uniform provisions for the effective resettlement and absorption of those refugees who are admitted.*

Under this Act, the President has relatively broad powers in setting the numbers to be admitted. Under a different section, we find he is responsible for *"(3) A description of the proposed plans for their movement and resettlement and the estimated cost of their movement and resettlement."*   And in conjunction with other language within the Act, Trump is free to allow the communities to decide if they can handle the resettlement.

But Refugee Agencies are generally city-based and function in conjunction with the aforementioned gerrymandering operation which brings in non-voter bodies to justify federal welfare revenues which enhance voter incomes.  The last thing they want is to have a rational placement of refugees in communities not under their immediate control – places where their wallet is not filled with the support service money.

While we have members of Congress wringing their hands – they are not doing their job, and are not providing the resources need to resettle people.  Instead, the refugees must wait years to be processed when, in the days of Ellis Island, migrants and refugees were processes within hours and that included what was called *"the six-second physicals"* or basic medical classification examination.

If a migrant appeared to have a confirmed disease or was too sick or too weak to manage to work, they were not allowed to enter the US.  There was no detention, they were sent back.  Today, we can treat diseases that were once deadly.  But new ones are being driven or carried north as a result of climate change.  Congress did nothing when they should have enacted Universal Healthcare

On 4 May 2017, DJT told Australia's Prime Minister: *"You have better health care than we do."*  And, recognizing that the Australian system is Universal Health Care, Trump challenged the American Congress to create a better system.  Sen. Bernie Sanders grabbed the opportunity and is seeking the Democratic nomination for 2020 on a platform that includes *Medicare for All* – something Sen Elizabeth Warren is also advocating as part of her platform.

In May 2017 Sanders said:

*"Thank you, Mr. President. Let us move to a Medicare-for-all system that does what every other major country on earth does — guarantee healthcare to all people at a fraction of the cost per capita that we spend. Thank you, Mr. President. We'll quote you on the floor of the Senate."*

But where is the Democratic House of Representatives?  Do they even care about Americans?  Even candidates said they would provide free healthcare for the refugee-migrants.  But where is that care for voters?

With the northward migration of Climate Refugees are the wildlife and insects that carry diseases that could decimate North America's population just as diseases carried by the Spaniards in the time of Columbus did to Mayan and other native populations.

Disease ecologist Andy MacDonald at the Earth Research Institute of the University of California, Santa Barbara has said:

*"It's pretty well established that deforestation can be a strong driver of infectious disease transmission. It's a numbers game: The more we degrade and clear forest habitats, the more likely it is that we're going to find ourselves in these situations where epidemics of infectious diseases occur."*

We have Brazil intentionally burning the rainforests and the California wildfires to concern those in the American hemisphere. The problem also exists in Asia and Africa.  But it is the effect these activities have on America that concerns Trump, and which should concern California's Representatives – but they seem to be focused on politically driven impeachment and not on the nation.

The threat of disease doesn't mean America closes its border – it means it needs a border fence/wall to ensure that refugees are screened for health issues and to impede disease-carrying wildlife from entering the country.

YES!  Wildlife, the migratory animals, whose travels some groups have said would see their normal migratory or predatory patterns hampered by the Border Wall, are going to be carrying the diseases that humans have no defense against.  These hitch-hiking deadly diseases are first being discovered – in part because Brazil has decided to burn the rainforests which serve as the "lungs of the planet."

In his first three years, Trump hadn't constructed any new wall, instead, he replaced and reinforced 76 miles of existing fence and automobile barrier.  He improved upon what Obama had done, and there are those in California who hate him for that.

They also hate the fact he took Ronald Reagan's MAGA and made it his own; they hate, as mentioned above, that he advocated improving Obamacare in a way that complies with the medical care concepts advocated by Obama and Sanders – ideas that date back at least to 1880, when PT Barnum wrote and published *The Art of Money Getting: Golden Rules for Making Money,* which opens with the words:

*"In the United States, where we have more land than people, it is not at all difficult for* **persons in good health** *to make money. In this comparatively new field, there are so many avenues of success open, so many vocations which are not crowded, that any person of either sex who is willing, at least for the time being, to engage in any respectable occupation that offers, may find lucrative employment. "*

Fools dismiss the wisdom of a man who created what was, for 146 years, *"The Greatest Show on Earth."* Yet, if they read the book – which is freely available online – they would see his words apply equally well to the modern era as to the immigrant nation of 160 years ago. Without good health, achieving anything is difficult and yet we have a society that seeks to hamper itself by denying its citizens the foundational necessity to prosper. And, as we are being told by scientists studying the issue, Obama's Fence or its improved version, the Trump Wall, is an integral part of keeping the nation healthy in this era of Global Warming.

While Trump had not immediately added to Obama's Wall, he did, as Obama had introduced a series of administrative and regulatory modifications whose cumulative effect was the creation of an invisible wall.

Look at any graphical representation of illegal migration under Obama and you'll see the steady decline. That decline only ended when Trump took office and the California gerrymandering crowd started pushing for open borders. Migrants aren't people, they're bodies recognized by SCOTUS and countable in the census toward increased representation. Once the 2020 census is done and a basis for district and Congressional representation is legally established for another ten years, they can be expelled or deported.

The Trump effect was seen in 2018 when the United States population grew by 200,000 immigrants, which was 70 percent below 2017. And, as we know, Trump wanted communities, not manipulative politicians, to decide if they could handle an influx of migrants. Allowed to decide, many rural areas in the Midwest and Northeast would welcome future citizens to fill their empty houses and empty classrooms.

In New York State, a Democratic Governor was doing what he could to address Climate Change related issues, but when it came to allowing candidates to debate those issues, the Democratic National

Committee (DNC) determined it was not a relevant issue or topic; accordingly, a few of the candidates held a Town Hall on 4 September 2019, which was hosted by CNN's Chris Cuomo – the Governor's brother.

As host and moderator, Cuomo posited this hypothetical:

*"You're on the debate stage... across from the president. And he says the Green New Deal is a dream because we're 60 percent right now on fossil fuels. You're saying you want to put into research and get it done, but you don't know how right now. So you want to bet our economy on an ambition. What's the answer?"*

Warren responded it wasn't a dream, it is a nightmare, and then echoed Greta Thunberg:

*"We've got, what, 11 years, maybe, to reach a point where we've cut our emissions in half, and that's not just America. We're only 20 percent of the problem. That's a big hunk of the problem, but there's another world out there that's 80 percent of this problem. So you bet that this is a moment where we better dream big and fight hard, because that's how it is that we're going to make the changes we need to make.*

*"... Life on Earth is at risk, and if we don't make this commitment, we not only cheat our children, we cheat their future and their children's future, and that is morally wrong. We have to be all the way in."*

Cuomo knew his family was seeing that America was doing what it could. But how do you address the 80-percent, the British in Argentina, the Brazilians burning rainforests, the permafrost that is already melting and compensating for human corrective activities which have been ignored or avoided for over the century since the *Greenhouse Effect* was scientifically and mathematically established by Svante Arrhenius?

There's an interesting reality, about the 1903 Swiss Nobel Laureate Svante Arrhenius who, in 1896, associated the end of the ice age with increases in atmospheric carbon dioxide. From there, he went on to explain increases in the Earth's surface temperature through the *Greenhouse Effect* which many see as a modern term or a recent discovery.

Arrhenius postulated that CO2 emissions from the then-new

human reliance on fossil-fuels and various combustion processes would increase global temperatures. To quantify those increases in 1889 he developed his Arrhenius equation, which could explain energy activation which presents as heat.

Thus, two 57-year cycles passed from the time a Nobel prize was awarded to the scientist who postulation of an event known as Global Warming to time when his 15-year-old second cousin 4x removed would skip school to sit outside the Swedish parliament holding a sign reading, "*School strike for climate*," which, within a year, would both spawn a global movement and see her address the *2018 United Nations Climate Change Conference*. Where her cousin gave us the *Greenhouse Effect*, she has spawned the "*Greta Thunberg effect*."

Given the number of books I've written based on cycles that reflect 19, 49, or 57, it is also comical that Greta was born two 49-year cycles after her cousin received his Nobel Prize in chemistry, and would herself be suggested for a Nobel in the 19th year of the century in which she was born.

Greta's movement has brought 81-year old Actress and JPC Jane Fonda – briefly known as "Hanoi Jane" during the Vietnam War protest era – back into the protest spotlight. On her website Fonda stated:

*"I will be on the Capitol every Friday, rain or shine, inspired and emboldened by the incredible movement our youth have created. I can no longer stand by and let our elected officials ignore – and even worse – empower – the industries that are destroying our planet for profit. We can not continue to stand for this."*

Of course, with America moving in the direction of clean energy, Trump was criticized for leaving the Paris Climate Accord – but where was the criticism of Britain, which, as a signatory, had been diverting resources to non-signatory nations so that it could continue polluting while technically being in compliance with the accords?

Critics and climate organizations said that the Paris Climate Accord, which required countries to pledge Intended Nationally Determined Contributions, failed to force binding action on climate change. That being the case, it is irrational for the United States to lock itself into that system.

Trump exiting the Accord would be meaningful if his critics were able to identify any Obama Era legislation creating concrete binding actions for America, with trade penalties for signatories who failed to meet the necessary criteria.

It would also have some meaning if Trump's actions meant America failed to do its part. But, on 26 September, America was identified as a major contributor to the climate problem, with a spokesperson for the UN Environment Programme (UNEP) saying that the problem dates back to 2010, when cuts of 3.3% would have been sufficient to address the problem; now, from 2020 to 2030 nations will need to reduce emissions by 7.6% a year, to achieve the 2030 target levels. For America, that places blame squarely on the pre-Trump government which was opposing Obama and Sanders.

Trump was attacked for backing out of the Paris agreement and then praising coal minors, yet, under his administration, by shifting to gas power and renewable energy, the US has made the deepest cuts to coal power of any developed nation. By the time of the UNEP statement, coal use was reduced by almost 14% over the same annual period in 2018. This has contributed to a decline greater than the combined coal generation in Germany, Spain and the UK in 2018.

In China – the nation Trump has been attacked for initiating a trade war with, while denouncing its practices – new coal plants are being built five times faster than coal-fired power capacity is being reduced in the rest of the world. China alone is offsetting global international efforts to combat Global Warming. China is adding the equivalent of one large new coal plant every two weeks.

As a result, based on a report from Global Energy Monitor, the number of coal-fired power plants in the world is growing.

In January, as part of the 2019 Executive Budget for New York State, Governor Andrew M. Cuomo had declared the *Green New Deal*, would provide a nation-leading clean energy and jobs agenda which could place New York State on a path to economy-wide carbon neutrality and echoed words we can associate with Greta's comments the same month. But her perspective on the issue was stated in a speech given month before Cuomo's:

*"If I live to be 100, I will be alive in the year 2103. When you think about the future today, you don't think beyond the year 2050. By then, I will in the best case, not even have lived half of*

*my life.  What happens next?*

*"The year 2078 I will celebrate my 75th birthday.  If I have children or grandchildren, maybe they will spend that day with me.  Maybe they will ask me about you, the people who were around back in 2018.  Maybe they will ask why you didn't do anything while this still was time to act?*

*"What we do or don't do right now will affect my entire life and the lives of my children and grandchildren.  What we do or don't do right now, me and my generation can't undo in the future."*

Greta is looking eighty-years into the future and at all the years in-between.  American politicians have proven they have a real problem looking more than two-years ahead – this has been made clear by their focus on a Trump impeachment investigation, rather than the 12-months leading to the election to inform voters of factual reasons Trump should be defeated in 2020.

Greta addressed their behavior when she said, *"...since our leaders are behaving like children, we will have to take the responsibility they should have taken long ago."*

It seems House Democrats are behaving like children, and have been for the preceding three years.  During Obama's second term, Republican Swamp Denizens – since subdued by Trump – were the problem.

Speaking at the meeting of the *World Economic Forum* in Davos, Switzerland – at the end of January 2019 – Greta warned:

"Our house is on fire, I am here to say our house is on fire.  According to the IPCC we are less than 12 years away from not being able to undo our mistakes.

*"In that time unprecedented changes in all aspects of society needs to have taken place including a reduction of our co2 emissions by at least 50% and please note that those numbers do not include the aspect of equity which is absolutely necessary to make the Paris agreement work on a global scale.  Nor does it include tipping points or feedback loops like the extreme powerful methane gas being released from the thawing Arctic permafrost. ...*

*"The main solution, however, is so simple that even a small child can understand it.  We have to stop the emissions of*

*greenhouse gases. And either we do that or we don't. You say nothing in life is black or white but that is a lie, a very dangerous lie. Either we prevent a 1.5 degree of warming or we don't. Either we avoid setting off that irreversible chain reaction beyond the human control, or we don't. Either we choose to go on as a civilization or we don't. That is as black or white as it gets. ...*

*"Adults keep saying we owe it to the young people to give them hope. But I don't want your hope, I don't want you to be hopeful. I want you to panic, I want you to feel the fear I feel every day. And then I want you to act, I want you to act as if you would in a crisis. I want you to act as if the house was on fire, because it is."*

While leaders behave like children, they seem incapable of comprehending what a child can understand and express. Thus it was interesting to see Gov. Cuomo introduce his budget with the words:

*"Climate change is a reality, and the consequences of delay are a matter of life and death. We know what we must do. Now we have to have the vision, the courage, and the competence to get it done. While the federal government shamefully ignores the reality of climate change and fails to take meaningful action, we are launching the first-in-the-nation Green New Deal to seize the potential of the clean energy economy, set nation's most ambitious goal for carbon-free power, and ultimately eliminate our entire carbon footprint."*

Governor Cuomo's *Green New Deal* seeks to secure a clean energy future by growing the clean energy economy; this is a goal he began, on 1 January 2011, when he assumed his office as the 56th Governor of New York.

Over his first two terms, he dedicated himself and the state to protecting the environment for generations to come; doing so with the largest renewable energy procurements in U.S. history, banning fracking of natural gas, and  increasing use of solar by nearly 1,500 percent, while preparing to use offshore wind to transform the State's electricity supply to be cleaner and more sustainable.

Before the 2021 Presidential Inauguration, the state should have completely phased out coal power, with a mandated goal of 50 percent renewable power by 2030.

As a result, New York State will exceed the accomplishments of signatories to the Paris Agreement – and he moved to make this national via the establishment of the U.S. Climate Alliance.

New York resident Donald Trump knew before he withdrew from the Paris Agreement, that America was on track to exceed its goals. He also knew that, as with NATO and every other agreement entered into with Europe nations, it would be America that carried the burden and responsibility.

Only 36 Countries have made Paris Pledges that could slow Climate Change. Most have circumvented or broken those pledges, and a result presented in a study published in the PNAS journal, which asserts that as current trends in global warming continue, concentrations of greenhouse gas in lakes will, on average, increase by 1.5 to 2.7 times. This is the combined effect of the amount of dead vegetation (falling leaves, etc) in the water and the *"biological activity, namely the break down of carbon-based compounds by microbes."*

In the above context, Jens Holtvoeth, a University of Bristol expert in organic chemistry stated:

*"However, it may well be the small things that, altogether, make a big difference on a global scale. When we hear that some processes associated with climate have been found to progress faster than expected it almost certainly results from some ... minor mechanisms having been underestimated."*

When combined, small things make a big difference. Could it be that the Obama-Trump Wall along the Southern Border could be such a "small thing." Could it be an orderly and efficient means of processing climate refugees is critical to the creation of sustained resource allocation?

What is the driving force behind climate refuges, and when can we expect them?

In the United States, they have already begun to arrive, and their numbers are going to grow. We know that from the warning by the U.N. Intergovernmental Panel on Climate Change (IPCC) of 2018 – we only have until 2032 to ensure that global temperatures don't rise another 1.5 degrees Celsius above the base period mean that prevailed when the Baby-Boomers were children. (The global mean surface air temperature in that era was about 14°C/57°F.)

Most people have trouble relating to the idea that we should be concerned that the air temperature would be 15.5°C/60°F seems weird.  But that's an average from the equator to the Arctic when the Arctic is moving above permafrost levels and equatorially it will exceed 120°F – surface temperatures for objects in the sun might well exceed those of a sauna (140°F).

Form a different perspective, the typical steam bath only reaches 115°F.  As for the joke about frying an egg on the sidewalk – sidewalks can usually get up to 145*F on a good sunny day – a normal summer at th latitude equivalent of the American Country Music Capital – Nashville, Tennessee.

Once that temperature change is exceeded, droughts, floods, displacement, and conflict will ensue.  But we need not wait for the temperature rise.  In 2019, with pollution levels below those set by the U.S. Environmental Protection Agency, air pollution kills about 200,000 Americans annually.  What legislation has the House of Representatives passed that will address this problem?

We hear the uproar over less than 40,000 firearm deaths in the nation, but they ignore the five times that number from causes linked to fine particulate matter (PM2.5) exposure include type 2 diabetes, lung cancer, obstructive pulmonary, cardiovascular and cerebrovascular disease, pneumonia, and previously unrecognized common blood flow related problems -- chronic kidney disease, hypertension, and dementia.

Coal-fired facilities are a major contributor, but so are Truck and automobile exhaust fumes.  And, while some of the highest rates of air pollution deaths are in the Midwest, Appalachia, and states like Ohio, Louisiana, and Missouri, the problem is national.

As Petteri Taalas, head of the UN's World Meteorological Organization said:

> *"There is no sign of a slowdown, let alone a decline, despite all the commitments under the Paris agreement on climate change.*
>
> *"In fact, the jumps in the key gases measured in 2018 were all above the average for the last decade, showing action on the climate emergency to date is having no effect in the atmosphere.  The world's scientists calculate that emissions must fall by half by 2030 to give a good chance of limiting global heating to 1.5C, beyond which hundreds of millions of*

*people will suffer more heatwaves, droughts, floods, and poverty."*

Taalas also pointed out that:

*"It is worth recalling that the last time the Earth experienced a comparable concentration of carbon dioxide was 3-5m years ago.  Back then, the temperature was 2-3C warmer and sea level was 10-20 meters higher than now."*

Considering the current projections have the planet 2-3C (4-6F) warmer by the end of the century, if Taalas is correct about the sea levels, they'll be 33-66 feet higher and for many, it would seem as if they were experiencing the Biblical Flood.  This is, to invoke a currently popular term, this is a true existential threat displaying a nascent character that demands action.

As reported in conjunction with the CO2 levels, it appears that agricultural practices have, during the first two decades of the new century, have caused a significant increase in nitrous oxide (N2O) entering the atmosphere.

Yep, the atmosphere is flush the common gases which, taken together, increase the planetary heat levels.  If your sense of humor borders on the perverse, you see the comedy in *laughing gas* as a by-product of food production.  Or, maybe, as Trump suggested, it's all just a Chinese "Hoax" – a form of a humorous Asian deception that hides some malicious intent.

If Climate Change were real do you think Chinese would be adding coal production at a rate that ensures it worsens?

China has a sixth of the global population in an area only slightly larger than the United States; most of their population is in the southeast at the latitude of the Mexican-American border – so will be seriously impacted by any change in global temperature and weather conditions.

Aside from the major damage of their coal-fired facilities, we know China has set 2025 as when only electric vehicles can be sold; they are also the world leader in renewable energy production with twice the production capacity of second-ranked United States and about seven times that of India which is third.

Does China see Global Warming as real or a hoax?  It seems – based on renewable energy and coal usage – they don't care.

Energy policies are economically rational in a world where

energy independence will define national security.  The need to use coal or other fossil fuels is, in the short term, a necessity brought on by the conversion to electric vehicles – that electric must be supplied by traditional sources, until such time as wind, solar, and possibly hydro can meet the demand.

The second-ranked position of the United States indicates it is doing more than other nations to develop renewables – and it is doing it under Trump.  But there are so many ways to measure the issue, so many metrics that can be applied – such as per capita, which would rank India and China near the bottom.

This energy production aspect of the current changes in the environmental realities associated with this stage in evolution is emerging as a major campaign issue.  Yet, the voting population has not come to grips with the reality of climate refugee migration.  As established by a Pew Research survey published 25 November, Americans fell the federal government was *"doing too little for key aspects of the environment, from protecting water or air quality to reducing the effects of climate change."*

The Pew results infer The Green New Deal should resonate with the majority of Americans.  But a physical environment focus has the effect of ignoring the damage caused by the uncontrolled entry of tens of millions of climate migrants into fragile areas like water-poor California.  Short-term, their arrival gerrymanders the state representation in Congress.  But, over the longer period of a decade, there will be enormous damage.

Trump sought to address this potential for environmental damage by granting communities the right to reject the migrants.  Those seeking federal welfare funds challenged the order.

# CHAPTER ELEVEN – UKRAINE
**"Remember this persuasion rule:
People will put more energy into NOT LOSING
what they already have
then they will trying to get something new."**

What has happened?  Trump promised to drain the swamp and *The Swamp Fights Back.*  It turned on him the day his victory was announced and has been seeking his impeachment since then.  Are these the denizens we knew of?

Nope.  The Republican Party is Trump, it is no longer the party of the extreme Right-wing.  Even Ted Cruz bowed to Trump and has taken on the predicted, quieter, position of attacking the denizens in the Democratic camp.

Trump is *the Republican Party – the true Party of Lincoln –* and he is the Democratic Party that Ronald Reagan opposed in 1980 when he denounced the border fence.  The destruction of the World Trade Center and the huge migrant population which Regan had encouraged to storm America's southern border, all came together to create the Obama-Clinton 2006 Secure Fence Act.  At the time, nobody acknowledged this to be the first step in the war against Climate Change – a defense against uncontrolled population shifts which are the emerging Climate Migration that is undermining European Economies and will soon be felt in Asia.

As the Denizens have shown in their rants about Trump being a failed businessman because he has not hesitated to declare bankruptcy – they refuse to acknowledge that he profits from it; that bankruptcy for profit is taught, on the graduate level, at the best Business Schools in the nation.  Trump does not fear public opinion – he manipulates and uses it.  In the case of the Atlantic City casino bankruptcy, history reveals that Trump got out before the Atlantic City economy collapsed under the competition from Indian Casinos scattered across the nation.

In the decade that followed Trump bailing on Atlantic City, numerous casinos went bankrupt – with either little or no benefit to their owners.  Since then, Global Warming has affected the sea levels and tides to the point that, in June 2018 *"NOAA released a report on high-tide flooding in the United States over the course of 2017.*

*Atlantic City and Boston were tied for second place with 22 days of flooding from high tide alone."* The worst flooding was on the Gulf Coast along the Texas-Louisiana border.

Obviously, since American business is addressing it, Trump need not concern himself with Climate Change.

Trump's major holdings are in New York City, which is constructed on metamorphic rock that was once incredibly hard and hot; now it is referred to as solid bedrock. It is the stable foundation which allowed the creation of Manhattans skyscrapers and 58-story Trump Tower (664 feet high) where Trumps' 10,996 square foot, three-story Fifth Avenue penthouse is located. It is also high enough to be above the worst-case scenario for coastal flooding – but its subway system could be lost.

A quarter of a century after Trump bailed on Atlantic City, he was ensconced in the White House and Atlantic City was once again redefining itself – this time, in terms of the looming threat of hurricanes and coastal flooding. But even here, with the shuttered casinos —the city has begun to turn its vulnerability into an asset. It has begun to turn the casinos into Climate Laboratories dedicated to climate science studies; where there was a convention center, now there is a training ground for civic leaders.

The Atlantic City that began as hotels and a boardwalk in 1870, has gone through multiple incarnations – always changing with the times. Trump foresaw the end of an era which, in various forms had spanned had spanned the century-and-a-half since the city was first incorporated in 1854, and exited so he could pursue the industry he knew. Those who would like to see America fail are belittling Trump for his foresight and economic persistence.

We know a few Right-wing denizens are still hanging about, but Trump has brought most into some form of obedient order. It is now the Left-wing swamp denizens who are the threat. As the Swamp Drains, different denizens are exposed.

As we are seeing, as is being revealed, they are eating their own eggs because, if they don't, Trump will hatch them and they will call him their father.

Far Left-wingers are at death's door and seeking a savior where none is to be found – save for those of Biden's type, who are representatives of the old school opportunism and corruption. We have seen this corruption with New York Senator Chuck Schumer –

who was a diehard supporter of the Fence and Obama policies on the Southern Border immigrants, until Trump called the Fence a Wall and continued the identical policies.  Since then, Schumer revealed himself a supporter of policies that Ronald Reagan would cheer.

While the 2020 election is important, in terms of Climate Change and the survival of the Obama-Trump economic recovery, it is the 2024 election that will define America's future.

In 2024, America will decide it's true fate, but for now, as we will see, a POTUS Cousin has emerged who was in the right place at the right time.  That Cousin is Tulsi Gabbard, who will be the one to beat in 2024, unless a better candidate emerges  – one who has been in the military, knows the cost of war, knows the cost to lives and families and knows enough to want to protect America in ways that do not also harm it.  In 2020, Tulsi must go against those who have ill-conceived ideas, and, as in the case of Bernie Sanders, at least one who is not a POTUS Cousin and whose election would shatter the history of western leadership that dates back to Charlemagne, and to those who were ancestors  to the Norman-Viking line which yielded William the Conqueror and appear connected to the ancestors of Greta Thunberg.

As an aside, 2024 is also the year in which India's Prime Minister promised every home would finally have running water.  It seems strange to realize that the nation that is probably the home of the oldest civilization – that of the Indus Valley – has yet to enter the "running water" era.

For now, America is still spinning things to impeach Trump for agreeing to assist in a joint investigation of parties involved in the massive corruption which had defined Ukraine during the era concurrent with that of Bush and into the first term of Obama.

Apparently, Trump's *"High Crime and misdemeanor"* was to remind Ukrainian President Volodymyr Zelensky that, in the context of ongoing Ukranian investigations into its own  political corruption: *"There's a lot of talk about Biden's son, that Biden stopped the prosecution and a lot of people want to find out about that so whatever you can do with the Attorney General would be great. Biden went around bragging that he stopped the prosecution so if you can look into it. ... It sounds horrible to me."*

A former Vice President can boast of his blackmailing the leaders of another nation – he can force the firing of a Prosecutor

General and possibly shield his son from prosecution – and he can assert consistency with Government Policy, making those actions the responsibility of his President.  But if the current POTUS seeks to have the Attorney General provided with Ukraine-based facts surrounding the firing, that gathering of facts is *"High Crimes and misdemeanors"* warranting impeachment.

The Swamp Denizens know their system, and they believe they know the level of ignorance that defines the American Voter  – the masses in the *Emperor's New Clothes* who will see what they are told to see, for fear they might be seen to be as stupid as their foolish acts of compliance show they really are.

That means the world will enjoy the shenanigans of a world superpower turning on itself.  How can they fail to?  Democrats say Trump should be impeached for mentioning Biden, while we have a video of Joe Biden, on 23 January 2018, telling the world he told the Ukraine President that he wanted the prosecutor fired.  Biden's act of extortion reflected the behavior of a Mafia Don who protects a corrupt associate – a Ukraine corporation that gave his son Hunter a do-nothing Board of Director position that paid more in a month than the average American family earned in a year.

He bragged to the viewers, that he said: *"I'm leaving in six hours, you've got six hours. If you don't fire that prosecutor, United States will not give you $1 Billion in Aid"* they said he didn't have the authority.  As he told it, he implicated Obama in the blackmail by saying, *"if you don't trust me call the president."*

While Biden's punch-line was that the prosecutor was fired before the delegation returned to the airport, for those Right-wing types who attacked Obama, the real punch-line was the fact that Barack Obama was ready to use Federal funds as part of a clearly stated and defined *Quid Pro Quo* blackmail a foreign government.  True Mafia tactics associated with Hunter Biden receiving millions of dollars in cash and other benefits.

What did Burisma Holdings get out of the deal?

Biden's action could trigger 18 U.S.C. Section 201 - Bribery of public officials and witnesses, but what he did was more like an act of extortion and might fall under 18 U.S.C. § 872.

Fast forward 20-months, to Wednesday, 25 September, and we have a National Review front-page headline which read, *"The Trump – Ukraine Transcript Contains Evidence of a Quid Pro Quo."*

Of course, there was no such evidence – unless they where referencing Biden's boastful confession.

The defense that has been offered for Biden is that the Mafia tactics were Administration Policy. Department of State witnesses have indicated Biden's *quid pro quo* extortion was a policy Trump inherited, therefore his impeachment is based on his failure to be blatant about it. An American President should not be engaged in an exchange of pleasantries with another head of state, nor should they negotiate points of shared interest – he should demand want he wants and become the global Mafia Don utilizing threats.

To be consistent, the 2025 inauguration should be staged so that World Leaders attend and kiss the POTUS' feet or ass.

When dealing with alleged impeachable offenses, the optics become as interesting as the spin. In 1998, when Bill Clinton was being impeached for Oral in the Oval – using perjury related to the definition of '*sexual relations*' being intercourse or any sexual act that triggers ejaculation – Joe Biden was on record saying:

*"Even if the President should be impeached, history is going to question whether or not this was just a partisan lynching, or whether or not it was something that in fact met the standard, the very high bar, that was set by the founders as to what constituted an impeachable offense."*

Twenty-on years later, President Trump stated:

*"So someday, if a Democrat becomes President and the Republicans win the House, even by a tiny margin, they can impeach the President, without due process or fairness or any legal rights. All Republicans must remember what they are witnessing here – a lynching. But we will WIN!"*

Naturally, because Trump used the term 'lynching', it served to invoke bipartisan criticism from all who needed Democratic voter support in the 2020 election. A couple of examples would be Maine's Republican Senator Susan Collins, who observed "*the President never should have made that comparison;*" Then there was California Senator Kamala Harris, a Democratic presidential candidate and the second African American woman ever elected to the Senate, who simply termed it "*disgraceful.*" The disgrace is found in rhetorical stretch linking racially motivated lynching of Blacks to what is a common term for a disregard for the law and any attempt at due process – ignoring all the whites hung by lynch mobs.

Thus, an act which was once a universal reality associated with irrational mob behavioral psychology is minimalized to reflect an intentional act of bigoted behavior; it is then minimalized more by ignoring the fact that their bigotry was not restricted to Africa Americans, but also extended to other ethnic and racial groups.

Here the differences couched in terms meant to incite mob reactions by invoking genetic identities seen as racial, but actually the differences are political – in political races, those distinctions are seen in the professional politician who gets rich pretending to serve the public interest while actually serving special interests with the deepest pockets, and the businessman who effectively eliminates the crooked middleman and exercises direct authority in accordance with the will of the people.

In terms of the use of 'lynching' in 1998, when the issue was raised in 2019, it revealed that multiple Democrats had called the Republican impeachment of Clinton a 'lynching'.

Speaking on the House floor, Rep. Charles Rangel (D-NY) has called the Clinton impeachment a *"lynch mob mentality, that says this man has to go."* But, as an African-American born in Harlem he was free to invoke lynching – he was shielded from the 'race card' Rep. Daniel K. Davis (also an African-American, D-NY) was free to play against Caucasian-American Trump on 21 October 2019. Also free to invoke the 'race card' was Rep. Gregory Meeks (African-American, D-NY).

In 1998, Rep. Jerrold Nadler (D-NY) invoked 'lynch mob' at least three times, but, 2018, Democrats wanted him to head the 'lynch mob' going after Trump – at least with Clinton, there was the sexual-relations 'perjury', with Trump, they have his invoking a 1998 'Mutual Legal Assistance in Criminal Matters' Treaty which Nadler supported. It seems comical that, on 13 September 1998, Nader had said, *"We shouldn't participate in a lynch mob against the president."* We now know, Nadler's comment to Newsday had a missing sub-text – which would read, 'unless it's our Democratic Swamp Denizen mob that is doing the lynching.'

On 18 September, five days after his first comment, Nadler told the South China Morning Post there was *"no evidence that the Republicans want to do anything other than organize a lynch mob."* Since the announcement of the November 2016 election results, we have seen the Swamp Denizens within the Democratic Party bending over backward to *"organize a lynch mob."*

On 12 September 1998, Rep. Jim McDermott (D-Wa), had showed the lynching to be the Democratic talking point which would actually describe what we have seen done with the way they have sought a basis to impeach Trump, *"This feels today like we're taking a step down the road to becoming a political lynch mob. Find the rope, find the tree and ask a bunch of questions later."*

Make is about race and you weaponize the *"lynch"* concept. You can do this because the modern masses are like those in *The Emperor's New Clothes* – they deny the evidence of their own eyes and refuse to use their brains to recognize the meaning behind the term.

The concept of "Lynching" is often said to derives its name from Captain William Lynch of Virginia and the 1811 use of "lynch law" to depict the methods of the 1780 *"Pittsylvania County alliance"* tribunal which was independent of the established legal system, and has been taken to mean *"a self-constituted court armed with no legal authority."* But, factually, the term comes from a Virginian judge named Charles Lynch, who imprisoned loyalists in the county jail under what was later referred to as *"Lynch's law"* – today we might term it *"Schiff's Law"* – which is defined as creating lies to justify judgement before the fact and outside the scope of law or any rational legal mode of conduct.

Looking to the Republicans, like Senator Mitch McConnell, who were among the Swamp Denizens forming the Clinton 'lynch mob', we see they are now very sensitive to use of the term, and, due to their actions in 1998/9, are hampered when it comes to formally dismiss or terminate any actions against Trump.

The Clinton Senate trial began on 7 January 1999 and was over on 12 February. Writing this in October 2019, and expecting any impeachment to be delayed until 2021, it would be weird for the Trump impeachment trial to last any longer than the 36-days of the Clinton event. But the survival of the Swamp Denizens is at stake, so, to ensure *"the most harm to the most people"*, they will doubtless drag things out as long as possible.

The Swamp Denizens rant about *"quid pro quo"*; we could also thing *"tit for tat"*; maybe even normal negotiation in which each party requires something – buying an item at the store is the same *"quid pro quo"* that the Denizens wish to call illegal. After all, you get a product (*quid*) in exchange (*pro*) give money (quo); isn't that the foundation of a Capitalist Society, and exactly what the Denizens assert to be illegal?

In the Talmud, the Hebrew phrase *yad rochetzet yad*, "one hand washes the other", gave rise to the colloquial Hebrew term *shmor li v'eshmor lecha* – "you protect me and I'll protect you" – which is what the 1998 treaty dealt with in terms of investigations into the very type of behavior now associated with Hunter Biden as a conduit to his father, 'Mutual Legal Assistance in Criminal Matters'; it was negotiated and signed by Democrat President Bill Clinton. The 2006 Secure Fence Act was supported by Senator Barack Obama and the funded section was completed by President Obama. Naturally, the Democratic Swamp Denizens want to label them immoral or illegal and bring them to an end.

Secret testimony taken in the basement of Congress, with only propaganda-driven 'leaks' that offer no means of verification or confirmation, so we cannot see a repeat of Schiff's rendition of his false representation of the Ukraine phone call being exposed.

The effort does feed a future ability to invoke impeachment against any president who has the nerve to negotiate with foreign governments or comply with a lawful Treaty.

'The Swamp Fights Back' (book 3 of this series) is being seen as reality, and the Swamp Denizens masquerading as Democrats are providing ammunition and to their Republican counterparts.

As Trump expressed it in one of his tweets: "*The Never Trumper Republicans, though on respirators with not many left, are in certain ways worse and more dangerous for our Country than the Do-Nothing Democrats. Watch out for them, they are human scum!*"

He could easily have pointed out their counterparts in the "*Bernie or Bust*" left-wing, but, where "*Never Trumper*" types want to crash the economy and reinstate what is euphemistically called "*The Deep State*", the "*Bernie or Bust*" are out to divide the Democratic vote and thereby assure victory for their counterparts.

Ah, the beauty of conspiracy theories to interject a level of thought and intelligence to explain the mass stupidity of those who see the Emperors New Clothes and then outdo themselves in the struggle describing how wonderful they are – or in this case, how awful Trump is and how really bad the economy has become under his guidance.

We saw a similar pattern of behavior among the Birthers as the debated flaws in a computer-generated birth certificate, while accepting as fact the idea a pregnant woman, with no passport, was able to travel from Hawaii to Kenya without leaving any trail as she first found a means of transportation that failed to record her existence, and then passed through various ports of entry with no record; gave birth – again with no record – and returned with no border or transportation records for either herself or her newborn infant.

Moreover, she did all that complicated criminal behavior so she could have a baby in Kenya and then falsify the idea that he was born in Hawaii.  Anywho believed that, and argued aspects of the birth certificate imperfections as proof of that belief, would readily accept a magnificently clothed naked emperor, or the impeachment lynching of a Constitutionally elected president.

When the elected occupant of the nation's Executive Office is being investigated, one would expect full transparency and that the methodology would strictly and stringently adhere to the ideal standards of *"legal due process."*  But instead, the world witnessed Adam Schiff conducting sealed closed-door hearings which denied even the faint appearance of *"due process,"* because intended to apply *"Lynch Law"* to his false rendition of what was said in a conversation for which we have a transcript.

More importantly, what was in complete compliance with the 1998 Treaty – we know that because the treaty states *the Central Authority shall be the Attorney General* and Trump had said, *"whatever you can do with the Attorney General would be great."*

The fact that the individual who boasted of his complicity in the corruption and the obstruction of an investigation was now a potential candidate for president would have any honest person seeking an investigation into the facts – if only to ensure that a criminal is not nominated for the American Presidency.

In terms of the possible candidates, while clearly, his ideas for improving the economic foundation of the nation are fantastic  and to be desired, it would be rather comical to see Bernie Sanders making trade demands of China – he cannot even get the Congress to consider policies he's advocated throughout his three decades in Congress.

In terms of Sanders inaction, on 1 March 2019, both he and Senator Elizabeth Warren were among eight members of Congress to sign a pledge drafted by the veterans advocacy group called *Common Defense* – which called for scaling back any U.S. military commitments overseas and bringing an end to what some termed "FOREVER WARS"; but that's exactly what Trump stated he was attempting to do in Syria, and both Warren and Sanders are on record praising President Trump for his decision to withdraw troops from Syria and Afghanistan.

On the campaign trail, it is only Hawaiian Congresswoman, and National Guard Major, Tulsi Gabbard who has been outspoken in terms of advocating for a more rational, less wasteful, more economically sound use of the military. And she can do so from the viewpoint of one who has twice served in modern combat zones defined by the war George W. Bush initiated with his desire to murder Saddam Hussein.

Of course, Draft Dodging Joe Biden is silent on the subject – unless you count the false Afghanistan visit war story he emphasized with the words: *"This is the God's truth. My word as a Biden."* A fact check of the story and its details concluded: *"In the space of three minutes, Biden got the time period, the location, the heroic act, the type of medal, the military branch and the rank of the recipient wrong, as well as his own role in the ceremony."*

The only accurate thing was Biden did visit Konar province – he claimed he did so as Vice President, but, at the time, in 2008, he was a Senator – accompanied by Senators Chuck Hagel and John F. Kerry. And as close as Biden came to actually addressing the horrors of war has been his use of the phrase, *"May God protect our troops."* He has never indicated he would protect the troops by pulling them out of the same type of idiotic war he dodged serving in.

As of October 2019, Biden was finally being seen as the fool he had always been, and Senator Warren began to take the lead. Bernie Sanders, had a heart attack, surgery, and was back on the campaign trail with the endorsement of AOC and The Squad. But since he is not a JPC and lacks many of the traits needed by a POTUS or world leader, his campaign remained both popular and a non-starter.

While the alignment of the candidates shifted, there were allegedly progressive organizations who told Pelosi, *"In place of this recess, we urge you to begin an aggressive hearing schedule, swiftly draft articles of impeachment, and vote to impeach Trump this fall."* If it was progressives pushing what became the Schiff farce, they were undermining the Democrats.

Historically, we have only three impeachment attempts to draw upon: two ended in acquittal, and one was prevented by the resignation of the guilty party before a formal vote could begin the formal impeachment.

Only two – Clinton and Nixon – occurred after codification of Stock Market behavior, as the Dow Jones Industrial Average, on 26 May 1896, by Charles Dow and Edward Jones.

The DJIA peaked just before the formal investigation into Richard Nixon and Watergate. Announcement of the investigation halted the upward trend, which then turned into a downward trend fed by the increasing certainty that Nixon would soon become the first POTUS in the nation's history to be removed from office. By the time Nixon Resigned, the DJIA had lost 45-percent of its statistical and monetary value.

When Bill Clinton was impeachment, the DJIA also peaked and began a downward journey which cost 22-percent of its value. In the case of Clinton, the Markets soon realized the impeachment for "perjury" hinged on a real-world definition of *"sexual relations"* – something that does not apply to *"Oral in the Oval"*, because it is a term used to describe actual intercourse of type his accusers engaged in with their mistresses.

Both instances show that financial markets will behave in a negative manner. It would be reasonable for members of Congress to believe the record-breaking Obama-Trump economic recovery would suddenly end and the financial market would lose about a fifth of its value on an impeachment voted. But that would require valid grounds for removal, and a Nixon model would reasonably see the financial market lose half its value. Thus impeachment is an attack on the economic wellbeing of the nation and all its Baby-Boomer retirees.

However, being shortsighted, many in Congress are focused on the expression, *"It's the Economy Stupid"* as if it meant that a recession or economic collapse would be blamed on Trump, and thus assure a Democratic victory to any nominated candidate.

However, in the era of BREXIT and the pressure imposed by early stages of Climate Migration in Europe, they were playing a game that depended on America retaining economic strength. As has been pointed out, the open borders opposition to Obama's Secure Fence Act and Trump's subsequent use of the term Wall to describe the competed project seemed to also be intended to create an economic crash and recession.

In either case, the economic consequences would extend across multiple presidential terms and create an advantage for Russia, China, and Iran – as well as any other nation which would see itself better off with America neutralized.

The problem that pro-Impeachment House members faced was one of establishing a valid basis. Since November 2016, they have labeled everything associated with the Trump name to be some form of an impeachable crime that warrants his removal.

The propagandists spread the rumor, subsequently blindly repeated by the media, that Trump asked for a "favor" that involved investigating Biden. But a reading of the conversation transcript shows the favor dealt with a private investigation of Russian hacking funded by the Democratic National Committee (DNC) in 2016 that involved the hacking of their server by two different Russian based entities.

As the transcript states, *"I would like you to do us a favor though because our country has been through a lot and Ukraine knows a lot about it. I would like you to find out what happened with this whole situation with Ukraine. They say CrowdStrike..."*

Curiously, on one level, Trump was asking Ukraine to utilize its contacts to resolve an issue affecting the DNC and the server security findings by the cybersecurity firm "CrowdStrike".

Referencing the "CrowdStrike" belief that the hackers had copied the full contents of the DNC server, Trump explained, *"The server, they say Ukraine has it."*

As cybersecurity expert Robert Johnson later explained to the media, *"It's possible to make copies of the physical server — forensically pristine copies. ... It's perfectly normal practice."* Johnson would know, he was the expert leading the investigation into the 2016 DNC hack.

In the context of FakeNews, Representative Mark Meadows observed in a tweet, *"Wow. The full Ukraine call transcript shows @realDonaldTrump asking Ukraine's President for a "favor," helping investigate 2016 election interference.  CNN cut the clip making it look like the 'favor' was about investigating Biden."*

Of course, soliciting help from a foreign government, or the act of blackmailing them with a possible refusal to provide the aid appropriated by Congress is a crime – but one that does not apply to a Democratic Vice President or, as noted, his President.  Thus Schiff and the House Democrats were determined to open a rather interesting *can of worms.*

As those worms emerge, they revealed a letter dated 4 May 2018 and signed by three Democratic Senators – Patrick Leahy, Robert Menendez, and Richard J Durbin.  The intended recipient was Ukrainian General Prosecutor Yuriy Lutsenko; its purpose was to solicit his cooperation with the Mueller investigation after rumors that his office engaged in *"efforts to impede cooperation with this important investigation."*

The letter references preventing *"special prosecutor Serhiy Horbatyuk from issuing subpoenas for evidence or interviewing witnesses in four open cases in Ukraine related to consulting work performed by Paul Manafort for former Ukrainian president Viktor Yanukovich and his political party."*

Based on the letter, both investigations were linked to *"the corrupt practices of the Yanukovich Administration."*  Both the investigations involved the time-frame and dealings Hunter Biden was connected to and the letter was written just three months after Bidens 23 January 2018 boast of how he blocked the investigation utilizing a withholding of a billion dollars in aid.

The Senate letter didn't explicitly threaten to withhold any concrete benefits, but it did solicit information in the form of the question: *"Did any individual from the Trump Administration, or anyone acting on its behalf, encourage Ukrainian government or law enforcement officials not to cooperate with the investigation by Special Counsel Robert Mueller?"*

Possibly encouraging non-cooperation versus Biden actively having the prosecutor fired.  Which is the greater crime?  And what connection did Trump have with Ukraine, apart from the *"meeting of Presidents Trump and Poroshenko on New York in 2017"* that was the final sentence and reference in the letter?  And why were the Senators interested in investigating normal White House operations or diplomatic meetings between Heads of State?

Regardless of any covert reasoning, the fact remains that these Senators were engaged in the very behavior they are now accusing Trump of – and they were doing so to undermine the American economy and contravene a lawful election.

In the context of Biden, Warren put her foot in it when she was asked, if her ethics plan allowed the son of a Vice President to serve on the board of a foreign company... her immediate response was "NO," but then she realized what she had said and replied, *"I don't know, I'd have to check my plan."*

It would be interesting to learn how her plan would handle her Vice President's child being hired into a high pay "do nothing" job, at a corrupt foreign firm associated with an ousted president, while her VP is directly engaged in U.S. efforts to support the new pro-Western government and its pledge to fight corruption.

In the case of Hunter Biden, the Russia-friendly president was ousted two months before he was 'hired' by a Russian political ally. In theory, this should have raised concerns and questions of the exact degree of protective influence that was being acquired.

But even four years later, there were no concerns by Swamp Denizens engaged in the same form of behavior through the letter inferring a withdrawal of support.  A year later, and true to form, Senator Chuck Schumer would continue to push to undermine the economy and nation.

Faced with the transcript reality, Schumer dismissed reality with these words: "*Simply to release the transcript is not going to come close to ending the need of the American public and the Congress to see what actually happened.*"

Curiously, this reflects the Biden statement: *"We choose unity over division. ... We choose truth over facts."*

Those protecting the senior old man from the consequences of his boasting are sowing division and ignoring the facts contained in the transcript in favor of their fantasy truth.  It's a fantasy related to that denounced by Greta – in this case, it's the Emperor's New Clothes all over again.  They determined that, because the Constitution worked as it was designed to work, Trump should be impeached; accordingly, the facts are ignored and their truth, the delightful beauty of clothes in which Trump is bedecked, all they see or describe.

Hawaii congresswoman, and long-shot 2020 presidential candidate, Tulsi Gabbard, demonstrated she possessed a level of superior intelligence that has been missing from American politics since Reaganomics and the Bush variation on Voodoo economics became the defining policy which gave birth to the 2007/8 Great Recession.

As she is wont to do, Gabbard broke with party leadership and, during a CNN interview, reiterated a long-standing position that *"impeachment would be terribly divisive"* adding it would *"further tear apart our already very divided country."* Because she is highly qualified to be president and has an unusual level of intelligence and moral conviction, the Swamp Denizens among the Democratic leadership had made a concerted effort to hamper her campaign and keep her from the Debate Stage – something that was scheduled to change with Debate Four in on 17 October 2019.

As this is being written, the debate is three weeks away and the current problem is that posited by a former top aide to past Democratic Senate majority leader Harry Reid, a man named Jim Manley who observed that the impeachment hearings were being defined by *"Members have a tendency to spend too much time talking and not enough time focusing on the questioning."*

Gabbard was not hesitant in insisting that, *"It's important that Donald Trump is defeated,"* and showed military confidence by adding, *"I believe I can defeat him in 2020. But it's the voters who need to make that choice, unequivocally."*

When it comes to the voters, many were observing that the Impeachment might be the best thing for Trump's reelection. As already pointed out, the Ukraine flap has served to highlight the criminality associated with Biden's misuse of his political office.

While when it comes to public opinion versus their actual actions, polls are notoriously unreliable, but, as our only available unit of measure, they do need to be considered. And polls taken as the Swamp Denizens initiated their farce established there was no real support for impeachment and intense division along partisan lines. Roughly three-quarters of Democrats, along with a third of independents, comprised the third of the population supporting the proceedings. The timing of the poll was such that their opinion was based upon the intentional misrepresentation and lie put forth – as part of his committee's official record – the Chairman of the House

Permanent Select Committee on Intelligence, Adam Schiff, said, without actually seeing the transcript, it

> *"reads like a classic organized crime shakedown. Shorn of its rambling character and in not so many words, this is the essence of what the president communicates. We've been very good to your country, very good. No other country has done as much as we have, but you know what, I don't see much reciprocity here. I hear what you want. I have a favor I want from you, though. And I'm going to say this only seven times, so you better listen good. I want you to make up dirt on my political opponent understand the loss of it on this and on that."*

When called out for his demonstrative lies, Schiff claimed he was only doing a "parody" of the inferred transcript content. This is not the first time Schiff lied to the American People or his fellow Congressmen. During the Mueller investigation, he asserted he had evidence – beyond circumstantial – of collusion.

In one interview, on ABC's 'This Week,' Schiff stated, *"I use that word very carefully because I also distinguish time and time again between collusion, that is acts of corruption that may or may not be criminal, and proof of a criminal conspiracy. And that is a distinction that Bob Mueller made within the first few pages of his report. In fact, every act that I've pointed to as evidence of collusion has now been borne out by the report."*

Of course, as we know from the Mueller testimony, there was absolutely no evidence of collusion – Mueller covered himself by asserting the President still had to prove innocence ... effectively saying the standard or burden of proof is "guilty until proved innocent." The Mueller standard, while at odds with that of the criminal justice system, creates a problem for Schiff, whose false claim to have irrefutable evidence of collusion resulted in the March 2019 calls for him to resign his position as chairman.

At the time, Schiff sought to deflect matters by referring to the campaign period offer of opposition research data to Trump's son (at a time when Hillary was paying a related source for similar data) and said, *"My colleagues might think it's OK that when that was offered to the son of the president, who had a pivotal role in the campaign, that the son did not call the FBI, he did not adamantly refuse that foreign help — no, instead that son said he would 'love' the help with the Russians."*

But, Vice President Biden's son was being paid by a corrupt Ukrainian firm, and traveling to China with his father, where he again received funds – in the 2018 Peter Schweizer book, "Secret Empires," it alleges, *"Hunter Biden's firm scored a $1.5 billion deal with a subsidiary of the Chinese government's Bank of China."*

The Mueller "Guilty until you prove you are innocence" is a litmus test for those advocating Trump-Russia Collusion – it is also worth noting that collusion is not a crime, it is simply supporting the side you prefer would win; if it also worth noting that the Russians worked hard to alter the votes in California and that with all their efforts Hillary won a landslide victory, as she did wherever hackers were established to be active.

Of course, the media and "FakeNews" distortions are also coming into play. With the release of the actual transcript, it was self-evident that media outlets omitted a 540-word section of the conversation for the express purpose of making it appear as if the "favor" Trump was asking for was an investigation of former vice president Joe Biden and his son Hunter's illegal dealings with the corrupt Ukrainian energy company. This is the omitted portion:

*"I would like you to do us a favor, though, because our country has been through a lot and Ukraine knows a lot about it. I would like you to find out what happened with this whole situation with Ukraine, they say Crowdstrike... I guess you have one of your wealthy people... the server, they say Ukraine has it. There are a lot of things that went on the whole situation. I think you're surrounding yourself with some of the same people. I would like to have the Attorney General call you and your people and I would like you to get to the bottom of it. As you said yesterday, that whole nonsense ended with a very poor performance by a man named Robert Mueller, an incompetent performance, but they say a lot of it started with Ukraine. Whatever you can do, it's very important that you do it if that's possible."*

Consider this sentence from a 1999 "Letter of Transmittal' from the White House to the Senate, and the party identified in the underlined portions in both:

*Article 2 provides for the establishment of Central Authorities and defines Central Authorities for purposes of the Treaty. For the United States, the Central Authority shall be the Attorney*

*General* or a person designated by the Attorney *General.*

The item being transmitted and summarized is a properly ratified treaty between the United States and Ukraine. While we could quote the treaty, the fact that the Attorney General is to handle the requested matter is without dispute. That Trump would term it a *"favor"* only indicates the matter has not yet been determined to warrant formal charges. Naturally, if the intent is to *prevent* disruption of the election process, any investigation would be secured until there were clear grounds for formal criminal or political action against Russia or other parties.

As we can clearly see, the actual transcript shows Trump's focus was help with an investigation into meddling in the 2016 election — that is, Trump was seeking to fill gaps appearing in the Mueller investigation {dubbed *"a very poor performance"*}, along with information on Russian hacking of the DNC servers which had been established by *Crowdstrike*a.

A comical aspect of Mueller's investigation and the period involving Biden is the indictment of Former Obama White House counsel Gregory Craig for perjury relative to Ukraine in the same time-frame that involves Hunter Biden.

However, the "Whistleblower" distorted the content of the call and then used it to undermine the Biden campaign, by making it seem Biden was the target of the investigation – which was being conducted in lawful compliance with the Clinton Era Treaty.

The distortion included charges that Trump was, as Biden had, using funding as leverage – subsequently it was established Ukraine authorities weren't made aware that the assistance being delayed/reviewed until more than one month after the call. Thus there was no leverage and the events were unrelated – other than Trump awaiting European actions to see if the nominal funds were necessary.

The fact that Trump was pushing the investigation taken on by the Democrats could have a major effect on those aware of the apparent dishonesty and hypocrisy among Left-wing Swamp Denizens or, as I call them, Reagan-Democrats. That hypocrisy is, as has been pointed out, clearly evident in Chuck Schumer and his opposition to the "Wall" which is the improved *2006 Secure Fence Act* co-sponsored along with Senators Barack Obama and Hillary Clinton.

Polls also show a third of the nation is firmly in President Trump's camp, and view the two-and-a-half years of searching for grounds to impeach as evidence of a deep state coup d'état, that calls into question the very legitimacy of our electoral system. It is clear to them, the "deep state" or Swamp Denizens are fighting back against a POTUS who promised to "drain the swamp."

Meanwhile, the Swamp Denizen activists appear to be looking forward to being rewarded for their persistent efforts to overturn the results of an election they don't like. But, as Gabbard noted, in November 2020 voters will be deciding for themselves whether or not they want to keep Trump in the Oval Office, or if they wish to have a Joe Biden, or the progressive economics of an  Elizabeth Warren or Bernie Sanders – progressive policies which have not been fully thought out and which, in the absence of clear border control policies, could prove destructive to the nation.

Trump's technique is to attack those he wants as opponents – those he knows will be easily defeated at the finish line. When we see him giving nicknames to individuals, we can be sure they have a fatal flaw that someone will expose well before he needs to expose it. Trump's allegations against Joe Biden have coincided with the boost to Elizabeth Warren. Or, as Quinnipiac University Polling Analyst Tim Malloy described it:

*"After trailing Biden by double digits since March in the race for the Democratic nomination, Warren catches Biden. We now have a race with two candidates at the top of the field, and they're leaving the rest of the pack behind. There's a lot of talk about Biden's son, that Biden stopped the prosecution and a lot of people want to find out about that so whatever you can do with the Attorney General would be great. Biden went around bragging that he stopped the prosecution so if you can look into it... It sounds horrible to me."*

Warren had a choice and chance, then flubbed it. She said the son of her Vice President should not be sitting on the board of a foreign firm; implicitly family members should not be in the pay of foreign entities. But she couldn't hold to her own  judgment, she needed to consult some imaginary plan that might contain the issue, saying, *"I don't know, I'd have to check my plan."*

More important, Warren is in a deep pickle with the Wall Street crowd. In September she started playing-up the fact she had not held the typical big fundraiser events and was going for small donors.  The problem with that is Wall Street had turned their back on her and the big-money fundraiser would yield very little.

As it was reported, Warren's impeachment stupidity turned off Wall Street, because they know damage impeachment can do.  They now know that, in addition to her other ill-conceived ideas on economics, she's backing her recession prediction in ways that make it a self-fulfilling prophecy. Warren doesn't care – she has no interest in maintaining the Obama Recovery; as with those who promote the worst versions of socialist programs, she's under the delusion that the recession would negatively impact Trump's shot at reelection.

In fact, like so many others, she's alienating Democrats who understand economics.  As one Wall Street executive phrased it, *"You're in a box because you're a Democrat and you're thinking, 'I want to help the party, but she's going to hurt me, so I'm going to help President Trump."*  Adding that the Wall Street Democrats are warning the party: *'We'll sit out, or back Trump, if you nominate Elizabeth Warren."*

Given that Bernie Sanders is not a POTUS Cousin, were he to be the nominee, and win, the nation will have shattered about four centuries of established leadership structure; simultaneously it introduces the very conflicts the emoluments clause is designed to prevent.

Bernie Sanders' brother and nephew have made careers as elected United Kingdom government officials.  That means they are not just on the board of some politically connected firm, they are insiders – decision making and influencing political members of a foreign government.  Phrased another way, they are the very essence of the Emoluments Clause {Article 1, Section 9, Clause 8}.

*No Title of Nobility shall be granted by the United States: And no Person holding any Office of Profit or Trust under them, shall, without the Consent of the Congress, accept of any present, Emolument, Office, or Title, of any kind whatever, from any King, Prince, or foreign State.*

For Bernie Sanders, his family constitutes the foreign state and representatives of its Queen and nobility.  He cannot place them in trust or divest of his interest.  More important, the fact they immediate blood relatives means they can enjoy unrecorded, unreported, undocumented private meetings – meetings that are in fact with individuals who have sworn allegiance to Queen and Country (the UK).  If you want to yell at President Trump when he has private diplomatic meetings with his foreign counterparts, how much more valid would it be to attack Sanders for talks with his own family – who may, or may not, express views that are in the best interest of the Crown or the British Green Party?

Granted, Lawrence Sanders is still an American citizen and, for the first time since 1968, voted in the 2016 election.  But, he is still a representative of a foreign government, and would trigger actions by those who could not openly attack a Jewish POTUS any more than they could attack Obama for being black – thus we had the Birther Kenya nonsense.

But Trump knows how to play the game and instinctively positions himself.  As a result, when, without reviewing any of the evidence, House Speaker Nancy Pelosi reversed herself and moved forward with impeachment, the next day a Gallup Poll showed she was attacking Trump at a time when his approval rating 3-points higher than Obama at the same point in his administration.

But, since impeachment is the issue, it's worth noting that Trump was a point behind Clinton – who was impeached for Oral in the Oval, and only because he was returning a budget surplus to the treasury.  Trump was 4-points behind Reagan – who gave us Iran Contra, with no impeachment, and created record budget deficits and initiated the runaway National Debt growth that has defined Republican Administrations.

To avoid impeachment, Trump must do things that are at least as criminal as Biden's Mafia tactics which covertly undermine other nations.  Only then would the Reagan-Democrats be happy.  As is, Trump has been repositioning American trade, promoting growth in the Stock Market, and improving on Obama's Fence while also continuing  Obama's tough border control policies.

On 27 September, the U.N. General Assembly, heard Sergei Lavrov blame the countries that declared themselves winners of the Cold War for challenges facing the world, and the fragmentation of the international community. However, since November 2016, it was as if he was describing the ongoing response to Trump's election: *"When it is advantageous, the right of the peoples to self-determination has significance.  And when it is not, it is declared 'illegal'."*

By calling it 'illegal', AOC affirmed her position advocating the elimination of the Electoral College – opposing the wisdom of the Founding Fathers and "checks and balances" representation.

On 1 December, Elizabeth Warren formally came out against the Founding Fathers and in favor of the most populous state controlling the nation. "My goal is to get elected—but I plan to be the last American president to be elected by the Electoral College. I want my second term to be elected by direct vote."

In the face of the call for impeachment, Tulsi Gabbard was one of less than a dozen Democrats who opposed the destructive political nonsense, and, even as the evidence was being ignored by Pelosi, Gabbard showed her intelligence and dedication to the country by stating: *"I think when you step outside of the bubble here in Washington and you get to where most folks are ... I think most people reading through that transcript are not going to find that extremely compelling cause to throw out a president that won an election in 2016. And instead what I think most people will see is, 'Hey, this is another move by Democrats to get rid of Donald Trump,' further deepening the already hyper-partisan divides that we have in this country."*

Major Gabbard was also very clear in asserting, *"Donald Trump is corrupt, he is unfit to serve our country as president, he is unqualified to serve our country as commander in chief ..."*

Naturally, Gabbard avoids specifics, because she is echoing the November 2016 propaganda for impeachment. Given, based on the known facts, that Trump called for an investigation of Joe Biden, a POTUS Biden would face impeachment if just one foreign dollar went into the family. And Biden's record as Vice President is clear as to the millions which have already gone to his family or granted anything China. We have Biden bragging about interfering in the Ukraine judicial system at a time when Viktor Shokin was investigating Burisma, the energy company paying Hunter Biden a no-show do-nothing $50,000 a month.

Ignoring what Biden had boasted of doing, House Speaker Nancy Pelosi pointed to Trump, saying, *"A president of the United States would withhold military assistance paid for by taxpayers to shake down the leader of another country unless he did him a political favor - that is so, so clear."*

On 28 September, while she was traveling the country on the

taxpayer dime, Pelosi spoke of the impeachment investigation with a massive IF-statement: *"If the facts are persuasive to the American people, they may be to some Republicans."*

Of course, she could not forecast how long it may take the House to complete impeachment proceedings, saying, *"It will take as long as the Intelligence Committee needs to follow all the facts."* And with those words, basically declared the matter would drag out for as long as possible, then result in the conclusion that no viable action. In this instance, given that she spent most of her life in Washington, living off the taxpayers, the matter is one of Trump having adhered to a Clinton era Treaty ratified by a Congress she was a member of.

The idea of dragging it out is one of convincing the public of the validity of their futile actions. At first, they will seek to carry things into the Christmas shopping season, when voters would tire of hearing about it. Or, Pelosi might just assume BREXIT would trigger a recession to distract voters, allowing things to pass while leaving the subliminal memory of the need to remove Trump for the voting booth. The Swamp Denizens are both working towards, and counting on, a recession happening.

For those pushing agendas that have not been thought out, but which are deemed to carry a socialist objective, recessions are good. Governments get overthrown during recessions, the New Deal was passed after four or five years of a Great Depression – people fail to realize its programs were being promoted for nearly a century. The idea of National or Universal Health was promoted by Teddy Roosevelt in 1912 and has roots dating back nearly two centuries – unless we count the biblical "Good Samaritan" which would have the roots going back two millennia.

Impeachment or Open Borders brings on a Recession – so the goal is to cheer them on. The impeachment assures the Stock Market falls – based on Clinton – 22%. Ant chance of a conviction in the Senate and half the value of retirement portfolios vanishes before it even reaches the Senate floor.

And, of course, there is a 'witch-hunt' beauty to the process in which Pelosi avoided a vote and sent the matter to a closed-door series of hearing headed by Adam Schiff who, as we already know, lied about having conclusive evidence of a Trump-Russia collusion and, after Mueller concluded there was no evidence, lied about the contents of the Ukraine Transcript.

As that process moved forward, the nation was treated to the October Debate in which Major Tulsi Gabbard was cutoff and denied equal time against Warren.  But she had time to declare:

*"I don't see deplorables, I see fellow Americans worthy of respect even when we disagree strongly. I will restore a WH w/ compassion & respect for all regardless of race, religion, orientation, gender or political affiliation."*

During the Debate, Gabbard also stated, *"The New York Times and CNN have also smeared veterans like myself for calling for an end to this regime change war [in Syria]. Just two days ago, The New York Times put out an article saying that I'm a Russian asset and an Assad apologist, and all these different smears."*

The mention of "deplorables" was an obvious reference to the insulting Hillary Clinton comment which justified dismissing more than half the American voters.  Of course, the media ignored the dig – they weren't going to give Gabbard free publicity – still, it wasn't lost on Hillary.  In 2016, Tulsi exposed the incompetence that was Hillary Clinton's positions on everything a POTUS would need to know how to handle.  Now, avoiding specific mention of  Tulsi, Hillary responded by retasking the attacks of Trump in the context of the Times article Tulsi had referred to:

*"They are also going to do third party again.  I'm not making any predictions, but I think they've got their eye on somebody who is currently in the Democratic primary and are grooming her to be the third party candidate.  She is a favorite of the Russians.  They have a bunch of sites and bots and ways of supporting her so far. That's assuming Jill Stein will give it up, which she might not because she is also a Russian asset.  They know they can't win without a third-party candidate, and so I do not know who it is going to be but I can guarantee you they will have a vigorous third-party challenge in the key states that they most need it."*

By spouting Russian conspiracy theories about a Combat Veteran – one who had first-hand on-the-ground experience with the 19-year conflict – and, by so doing, proved that POTUS Trump was evidence the Electoral College had performed properly.  Bill was a good POTUS, but Hillary was proving herself a nutcase who could not accept her loss or the reality that, throughout its history, America has only elected JPCs.

Tulsi responded with a Twitter triplex:

*"Great! Thank you @HillaryClinton. You, the queen of warmongers, embodiment of corruption, and personification of the rot that has sickened the Democratic Party for so long, have finally come out from behind the curtain. From the day I announced my candidacy, there has been a concerted campaign to destroy my reputation. We wondered who was behind it and why.*

*"Now we know — it was always you, through your proxies and powerful allies in the corporate media and war machine, afraid of the threat I pose. It's now clear that this primary is between you and me. Don't cowardly hide behind your proxies. Join the race directly."*

It is curious. The media, and social media, happily attacked Trump for "bone spurs" and called him a draft dodger, and now they are attacking a woman who, after 9-11, not only volunteered for military service but served twice in combat zones and earned the rank of Major. But they are quiet about the draft-dodging Joe Biden and the Conscious Objector Bernie Sanders. Does Ukraine matter?

Does it matter that Hunter Biden, was the lawyer retained by business executive Gabriel Popoviciu in 2015? Or that it was because Hunter's father was vice president and helped fend off the Romanian criminal charges being pursued by the anti-corruption prosecutors. Or that Hunter was placed on the Board of Directors of a Ukraine company also being investigated by anti-corruption investigators – and that daddy has publically boasted he got the investigating prosecutors fired by threatening to withhold aid ... and implicating President Obama as supporting that threat.

In 2016, Popoviciu was convicted on charges related to a northern Bucharest land deal. But, by then Papa Joe's influence had ended because his term in office was coming to an end. That loss of authority and power was a direct result of the death of Beau Biden and the 21 October 2015 announcement that daddy would not be seeking the Democratic presidential nomination in 2016. Thus, Joe Biden formally declares the basis for Hunter's position and the safety accorded Popoviciu was at an end – it was safe to convict Popoviciu.

In Ukraine, the loss of the prosecutor brought an end to the investigation. That the new anti-corruption administration will revise it, and implicate Hunter Biden, is a logical reason for Papa Joseph Robinette Biden Jr. to seek the 2020 Presidential nomination, maybe become president, quash the investigation, or demonstrate sufficient residual power to shield Hunter.

Doesn't matter, Schiff is doing that shielding by yelling it is the campaign announcement, and not corrupt events during the Obama Administration, which are at the heart of an investigation into those events – as coordinated through the *Attorney General* in accordance with the 1998 *'Mutual Legal Assistance in Criminal Matters'* Treaty. It's an investigate Adam Schiff wants to quash for his own political, and/or possibly person, gain.

# CHAPTER TWELVE – Joseph Biden

***"If the facts are against you, argue the law.***
***If the law is against you, argue the facts.***
***If the law and the facts are against you,***
***pound the table and yell like hell."***

In June 2019, former Vice President Joe Biden stated a basic truth: *"Here's the deal: we all know, and I don't think this is hyperbole, we all know in our gut this election is the most important election we've ever engaged in — and not just because I'm running."*

Gee, it's important because Biden is running? And Trump is the one who is supposed to have the ego.

Then there is the Obama problem which includes persistent criticism of Biden's campaign from Obama's inner circle and the lingering questions over why Obama failed to endorse his former vice president – which were matched by reports of Obama making derisive and discouraging comments about his candidacy.

Consistent with a political career that began in 1972, Biden stated: *"Eight years of Donald Trump will fundamentally change who we are in profound ways. ... With Trump gone, you're going to begin to see things change. Because these folks know better. They know this isn't what they're supposed to be doing."*

Biden clearly expressed an undeniable truth, eight years of Trump would mean the Right-wing Swamp Denizens were gone, and their Left-wing counterparts probably were too. We are also seeing changes – America has stopped outsourcing to China and American firms in China are being treated with more respect. If we look at *"this isn't what they're supposed to be doing,"* there is a semantic issue that underlies the word *"this"* – is he speaking of the current system he said will change, or the changing process, or the eventual change result? It's the semantics of politics.

We know Biden's history, the media has documented it and then pushed it to the back pages where they can honestly say they reported it, but know few will read it.

We have fake news. The historical record shows that Biden blackmailed the Ukraine President into terminating a prosecutor: *"I'm leaving in six hours, you've got six hours. If you don't fire that* *prosecutor, United States will not give you $1 Billion in Aid. ... If you don't trust me, call the president."*

These words are the definition of an irrefutable example of a criminal *"quid pro quo."* They were uttered in 2014, shortly after Hunter Biden was appointed to the Board of Directors of Burisma – a Ukrainian natural gas firm being investigated for corruption – and, concurrent with Trump attending the 48th World Economic Forum Annual Meeting in Switzerland, on 23 January 2018, Joe Biden was speaking at the Council on Foreign Affairs (CFR) where he boasted of his role in forcing the firing of the key prosecutor.

On 29 October 2019, an article by Davey Alba, *"Debunking 4 Viral Rumors About the Bidens and Ukraine,"* was published in The New York Times, in which it was stated, *"Mr. Biden received payments that reached up to $50,000 per month."*

The C-SPAN video of the Biden confession was accompanied by a caption: *"Former Vice President Joe Biden confesses to being in charge of Ukraine for the Obama Administration, and withholding $1 billion in loan guarantees from the USA to force Ukraine to fire prosecutor who was looking into the company that Hunter Biden was receiving $83,000+ PER MONTH from"*

So we have a "minor" reporting discrepancy of $33,000 per month in Hunter's no-show job salary. The Times article tells us Viktor Shokin, Ukraine's prosecutor general, was the one fired and that his successor cleared Burisma and its oligarch owner, Mykola Zlochevsky, of any wrongdoing. What we are not told is that the new Ukranian President – the one Trump spoke with – terminated a major portion of the prosecutor general's office staff for legal incompetence (inability to pass a basic law exam) and corruption.

As we read the article, we find that the basis for debunking the matter is that there is no evidence – even though the facts show there could be no evidence because of both the incompetence and corruption associated with those who replaced the fired prosecutor.

In 2019, the World witnessed America going through what was a highly questionable phase in its history – a breakdown of its mental and intellectual credibility, combined with what is best seen as a disregard for "the Rule of Law."

World Leaders see is the United States seeking to impeach a President for invoking a valid 20-year-old treaty when a former Vice President publicly brags of interfering with the internal affairs of a nation – at a time when it is fighting for its survival after Russia invades its territory – and makes it clear that the tactics he used were stereotypical Mafia Tactics.

Biden's statement in the C-SPAN video was declared "false" by Snopes "fact-checkers", which provided this verbatim quote:

*"And I went over, I guess, the 12th, 13th time to Kyiv. And I was supposed to announce that there was another billion-dollar loan guarantee. ... I had gotten a commitment from Poroshenko and from Yatsenyuk that they would take action against the state prosecutor. And they didn't.*

*"So they said they had — they were walking out to a press conference. I said, nah, I'm not going to — or, we're not going to give you the billion dollars. They said, you have no authority. You're not the president. The president said — I said, call him. I said, I'm telling you, you're not getting the billion dollars. I said, you're not getting the billion. I'm going to be leaving here in, I think it was about six hours. I looked at them and said: I'm leaving in six hours. If the prosecutor is not fired, you're not getting the money. Well, son of a bitch. (Laughter.) He got fired. And they put in place someone who was solid at the time."*

In Mafia parlance or phraseology, "solid" means obedient to the Mafia Don in this context, by implication, either Biden or Obama. However, there is no factual basis to assert or believe that Obama, an expert in Constitutional law, would in any way condone the illegal conduct of Biden.

When Snopes alleged it fact-checked Biden's C-SPAN brag, it asserted they were those of the Administration *"filtered up from officials at the U.S. Embassy in Kiev."* Because it belongs to the Administration, the responsibility is that of Barack Obama and not Joseph Biden.

The article also stated Hunter was hired two months after the probe into Burisma Holdings was initiated – indicating the motivation for the hiring was separate from the corruption, rather than a defensive action that was triggered on by the investigation, which then motivated Biden's blackmailing Ukraine officials on the part of the Obama Administration.

The defense of Biden was acceptance of the facts the Obama administration blackmailed Ukrainian officials, but: *"That's not to say the former vice president's 2018 commentary at the Council on Foreign Relations meeting was worded well."*

Inherent in the article, through a reference to the Trump conversation and tone, was that asking a "favor" can be considered a crime, but outright blackmail is acceptable when initiated at the Embassy, *"according to a person with direct knowledge of the situation."*

If we look at Schiff, we see two statements, which reflect a *quid pro quo* and coercion?

- *If you don't fire that prosecutor, United States will not give you $1 Billion in Aid.*

- *I would like you to do us a favor though because our country has been through a lot and Ukraine knows a lot about it.  I would like you to find out what happened with this whole situation with Ukraine,"*

Seems like the second is asking for an investigation of the first. If that's the problem, then we can assert that those seeking an investigation into the quid pro quo are guilty of a crime – which infers Adam Schiff's desire to investigate Trump is a criminal act that warrants his removal from office.

In terms of the timeline, the $1 Billion Biden used as a basis for the bribery/blackmail was appropriated on 27 March 2014 for the express purpose of being Ukraine aid.  This aid fell under what is termed "a sovereign loan guarantee" – In the Constitution this is Article IV, Section 1, *"the full faith and credit"* clause in which no POTUS or VP has the right to contradict or subvert.

Moving forward to the Trump-Ukraine phone call period, we first note the new Ukraine President was elected in April, and, on 18 JUNE 2019 The Department of Defense {DOD} announced a plan to provide $250 million to Ukraine in security cooperation funds for additional training, equipment, and advisory efforts to build the capacity of Ukraine's armed forces.

These funds were from the DOD budget providing the funds is S.3159, JUNE 28, 2018, entitled: *"Making appropriations for the Department of Defense for the fiscal year ending September 30, 2019, and for other purposes."*  Within that budget Ukraine is only mentioned three times:

*SEC. 8098 (b) items (2) The armed forces of the Russian*

*Federation have withdrawn from Crimea, other than armed forces present on military bases subject to agreements in force between the Government of the Russian Federation and the Government of **Ukraine**; and (3) Agents of the Russian Federation have ceased taking active measures to destabilize the control of the Government of **Ukraine** over eastern **Ukraine**.*

No money was specifically allocated to Ukraine, within the budget, and the right to provide the money and military assistance was granted under H.R.5859, the "Ukraine Freedom Support Act of 2014" which was signed by Barack Obama on 18 December 2014. Nothing in that legislation authorizes mandating that any Ukraine officials be fired. However, there was a request for FY 2019 ESDF funding to support Ukraine's fight against corruption – dated 12 February 2018, which predated Ukraine's election, but followed Biden's C-SPAN confession of his corrupt Mafia-style activities.

Concurrent with Ukraine's election of March & April 2019, on 11 March 2019, the Department of State provided congress with a rustication for its FY 2020 request which included *"Ukraine's National Anti-Corruption Bureau and Special Anti-Corruption Prosecutor's Office."*

Politically, a formal anti-corruption statement by the newly elected Ukraine President would certainly help bolster approval of the requested dedicated funds. Such a statement would normally be requested via back-channels or through unofficial means – such as the American President's personal attorney, Rudy Giuliani using his existing professional or personal connections to negotiate the wording.

Looking at the phone call on 25 July 2019: *"The other thing, There's a lot of talk about Biden's son, that Biden stopped the prosecution and a lot of people want to find out about that so whatever you can do with the Attorney General would be great. ... Biden went around bragging that he stopped the prosecution so if you can look into it ... It sounds horrible to me."*

There is a clear reference to Joe Biden public bragging about his Mafia-style actions as recorded and documented by C-SPAN – which comports with the facts as commented on by Trump, who has a legal obligation to request the Ukraine both investigate and document any findings with the Attorney General as outlined in the

*'Mutual Legal Assistance in Criminal Matters'* treaty.

And again, were Ukraine to investigate Biden's bragging, it would show that they were honest in their desire to address all possible evidence of corruption and provide further support for the funds requested by the Department of State.

In November, Nancy Pelosi said, *"The facts are uncontested – that the President abused his power for his own personal, political benefit, at the expense of our national security interests."* But what political benefit would Trump attain by investigating a public confession – with the investigator results handed directly to the Attorney General?

Ukraine Minister of Foreign Affairs Vadym Prystaiko told Reuters, *"Ambassador Sondland did not tell us, and certainly did not tell me, about a connection between the assistance and the investigations. You should ask him. I have never seen a direct relationship between investigations and security assistance."*

We have a very real problem in that the alleged victim of the abuse by Trump saw no abuse. But Adam Schiff and Nancy Pelosi see a problem in asking the victim of Biden's self-confessed crime for supporting evidence which, if Burisma Holdings corruption was as serious as is documented, could reveal further corruption which the Congress has said should be addressed.

We also know, from the transcript of the 25 July phone call, Biden bragged about committing an impeachable crime of bribery against the previous Ukraine President:

*"The other thing, There's a lot of talk about Biden's son, that Biden stopped the prosecution and a lot of people want to find out about that so whatever you can do with the Attorney General would be great. Biden went around bragging that he stopped the prosecution so if you ·can look into it ... It sounds horrible to me."*

Curiously, Biden is considered a viable candidate or political opponent. And is true, even though he confessed to impeachable crimes. What Congressional member would defend, as Schiff has done, someone who openly and freely boasted his confession to a Mafia tactic High Crime as Vice President and then consider him to be a viable presidential applicant? That is unless they too are Mafia-types.

Moreover, why is it a crime to have Ukraine investigate the related underlying corruption?

On 4 December 2019, in giving impeachment hearing legal testimony, Constitutional law Professor Jonathan Turley pointed out that Schiff violated the law – declaring the *"facts don't matter."*

If we look at the call, we see the new Ukraine President was going to appoint, in September, an honest Persecutor General. But we also see an interesting comment about the US Ambassador:

*"... it would be very helpful for the investigation to make sure that we administer justice in our country with regard to the Ambassador to the United States from Ukraine as far as I recall her name was* Yovanovitch. *It was great that you were the first one. who told me that she was a bad ambassador because I agree·with you 100%. Her attitude towards me was far from the best as she admired the previous President and she was on his side. She would not accept me as a new President well enough."*

The reference is to Ambassador Marie Yovanovitch who was in office between 29 August 2016 – 20 May 2019 and was removed two months prior to the call.

But, we need a context for Trump's requested "favor." Foe that, we can look at a 2017 research paper by Emilio J. Iasiello, the abstract for which says:

*"After a series of military reforms resulting from the 2008 conflict with Georgia, Russia used information warfare operations more effectively in Crimea. Russia's continued refinement of its information operations may keep it ahead of the United States."* {Innovations in Warfare & Strategy,

{Russia's Improved Information Operations:

{From Georgia to Crimea

While the focus is on what was Soviet Georgia and Crimea, the methodology goes to Mueller's investigation and how Russia has been interfering with the American political system. In the first two paragraphs, the author references Georgia in 2008, and states, *"Russia adjusted its information confrontation strategy six years later against Ukraine, quickly and bloodlessly reclaiming Crimea and keeping potentially intervening countries at bay."*

Apparently, Russia adjusted its techniques to play within the

American system – probably being the active force behind the calls for impeachment which began 9 November 2016 and were tailored in a way that allowed them to fit either Trump or Clinton.

If we need an analogy, why not consider Russia the fraudster tailor in The Emperor's New Clothes, and the masses as those who supported Hillary Clinton.  As Iasiello says and documents, "*Russia has been long credited with having formidable information warfare capabilities. ... The broad nature of these activities views offensive information campaigns more as influencing agents than as destructive actions, though the two are not mutually exclusive. Simply put, the information space lends information resources, including "weapons" or other informational means, to affect both internal and external audiences through tailored messaging, disinformation, and propaganda campaigns.*"

As a Democrat and former County Chairman, I see what has the appearance of a dual problem.  California voters – the few who honor the law – have the moral obligation to remove Schiff based on the very standard he established.  And because the debunking of Biden's actions involved Federal Administrative Policy, Biden's implicating Obama in the *quid pro quo* blackmail requires that the administration – though no longer in power – be investigated so that we Democrats can remain proud of Obama accomplishments.

There is also an issue of bribery – not of Trump, but rather Joe Biden.  Were unjustified payments to Hunter Biden intended to launder bribery payments to his father?

It should be obvious to all but the most dim-witted among citizens that the easiest way to "launder" any criminal payments is to make them look legal in the context of a family member – the red flag is that the payments are not "normal."  For Hunter Biden, this means enormous payments for non-work – as distinguished from payment in the event services are needed (a lawyer might be "on retainer", meaning they are paid a small amount on a regularly scheduled basis to assure availability if needed).

As we know, one of the more popular assertions has been a violation of the Emoluments Clause, so bribery would be among the assertions aimed at Trump, but intended to deflect attention away from the unearned millions transferred to the Biden family.

Of course, if the DNC nominates Joseph Robinette Biden Jr. as its candidate for the 2020 election, they are declaring support for someone who blackmails foreign Presidents – and brags about it while laughing at its success.

As noted, Biden also utilizes the services of his son, Hunter Biden, who serves in the role of a *Patronage Hire* – Hunter was not loath to state as much in an October 2019 interview: *"I gave a hook to some very unethical people to act in illegal ways to try to do some harm to my father. That's where I made the mistake, ... I don't think that there's a lot of things that would have happened in my life if my last name wasn't Biden."*

Because his name is Biden, Papa Joe need not take bribes, he need only direct them to his son, who then reports the income and effectively launders it.  Is there any benefit to Papa Joe?  Not really – other than having millions in bribes legally laundered and passed on to his heir.  As previously noted in this series, Frederick  Trump engaged in a legal version of this during the final days of Rent Control, when he created a construction that was owned by his children – making the children independently wealthy.

We see lots of people "defending " Papa Joe and denying the reality of the voluntary confession delivered on and recorded by C-Span.  But those "defenders" know that Biden is taking the wind from the sails of the Democratic candidates – he's siphoning off the contributions which would otherwise give Senator Warren or Tulsi Gabbard a financial base for the 2020 election.

By occupying media time and attention, the Biden support has the effect of distracting the media from honest politicians who, on a level playing field, could defeat Trump.

But the idea is to keep Trump in power.

Thus we see him being charged with that which Biden freely admitted to – so an impeachment would yield Senate acquittal based on the fact Trump had followed and adhered to his Oath of Office to support the Constitution and Laws of the United States.  Specifically, when a politician confessed to the abuse of his office, Trump was obligated to have the Attorney General investigate.

As the crime confessed to was committed in the Ukraine and involved firing of a Ukraine Prosecutor General, the matter fell under the 1998 Treaty for sharing information on criminal finding,  it mandatory to ask the Ukraine President who was investigating corruption in that time related period to share information with the Attorney General – as required by the Treaty.

By attacking Trump, Adam Schiff ensured he could inflict the maximum harm on the Democratic candidates.  But why harm his own party?  Is it that he opposes Medicare For All, opposes free College Educations, opposes the Green New Deal,  or any platform issues that do not comply with what were once Reagan programs – open fenceless borders and lower taxes on the wealthy – many of whom are based in California?

The question was, who was he talking about?

"Uncle Joe" was promoting bipartisan behavior at a point in history when the Democrats had turned on their own hard-fought agenda – their Fence, which Ronald Reagan had denounced in 1980 and followed up on with a program that saw a steady rise in southern border crossings that only ended with the 2006 Secure Fence Act which was promoted by Senators Barack Obama and Hillary Clinton as part of a bipartisan response to events following 9/11.

With the Obama Administration, Republicans opposed all things Democratic; with Trump, the Democratic response to the election was to first complain about the Constitution and Electoral College and then to yell for impeachment – even before Trump had been sworn in.  California had long supported Reagan, Pelosi has always been for open borders and voted against the bipartisan 2006 Secure Fence Act, while Biden voted for it, but is now against it – because he needs the support of California.

On 8 November 2019, The Huffington Post reported that the Schiff investigation had deterred Ukraine President Zelensky from investigating the possibility of a Biden connection to the corruption that has plagued the Ukraine government for decades.  The spin allows for further revelations about Hunter Biden related profits from his father's office and also opens the door to further attacks on Trump that are aimed at disrupting the 2020 election.

It should be noted, the 6th Amendment of the Constitution gives defendants the right to "a speedy and public trial," and that legal experts hold that this applies to the impeachment of any government officer – including the President. Under Schiff, House Democrats are trying Trump in secret, while  denying him the right to a public proceeding, proper representation, and all normally provided rights

Impeachment is predicated on the definition of High Crime or misdemeanor.  Google "High Crime Legal Definition" and there are numerous possibilities.

The Merriam-Webster Legal Dictionary yields: "*a crime of infamous nature contrary to public morality but not technically constituting a felony; specifically: an offense that the U.S. Senate deems to constitute an adequate ground for removal of the president, vice president, or any civil officer as a person unfit to hold public office and deserving of impeachment.*"

As noted, Joseph Biden freely confessed to blackmailing the head of the Ukraine government, while serving as Vice President. That confession was documented by C-Span on 23 January 2018.

This creates an obvious problem.

If Blackmail or a "*quid pro quo*" involving Federal funds is a high crime, than Biden confessed to one while in office and the Oath of Office requires the President to enforce American Law – in doing so, the first step is to investigate in accordance with the law and any relevant treaties, such as the 1998 Criminal Investigation Treaty with Ukraine, which is where the crime was committed.

Obstructing the investigation would seem to constitute some form of "Obstruction of Justice" – which is also a crime; one being committed by the House of Representatives utilizing impeachment as the weapon or means of obstruction.

Under civil law, Bribing, extorting, or coercing an Executive to terminate the employment of an underling would be deemed to be a crime.  When done by members of the Department of State — it would be a crime.  It remains a crime when done by the Chief Executive or his Vice President.

Adam Schiff has said the bar for a "High Crime" is very low – simply asking for "*a favor*" without the other party being aware that funds are being withheld pending performance constitutes the level of qualification.  With the bar that low, Biden easily cleared it with the facts he presented and therefore must be prosecuted.

Since Joe Biden cleared the bar of illegal conduct, President Trump is obligated to investigate the crime and acquire whatever facts are made available to the Attorney General under the terms of the 1998 Treaty.

On multiple occasions, Adam Schiff lied about the existence of evidence of Trump-Russian collusion necessary for the Mueller investigation.  Schiff then entered a false recitation of the Ukraine phone call into the Congressional Record – he would have gotten away with it if Trump had not unclassified and released the valid transcript.  In October 2019, Schiff then obstructing a criminal investigation stemming from a public admission, by former Vice President Biden, dealing with a commission of a High Crime during Biden's time in office.

Were America a nation of laws, the public would be reading about Schiff's removal from office.  This statement should be considered in the context of Senator Alan Stuart Franken resigning over an incident when Leeann Tweeden cited an incident during a 2006 USO tour when Franken is said to have *"forcibly kissed her while they rehearsed a skit together."*  At the time, Franken was a professional comedian and the incident was part of a routine being tried.  If kissing during a skit rehearsal requires resignation from Congressional Office than Schiff lies and misrepresentation of facts should too.

Biden confessed to blackmailing the President of Ukraine to fire his Prosecutor General — that would, in civilian life, be a crime … it, therefore, MUST be a high crime.

The President is obligated, by his Oath of Office, to enforce the laws — which includes a former VP confessing to a High Crime which would warrant investigation of the confession and to see how far that corrupt act penetrated the Deep-State establishment.

Some have raised an issue of Ukraine funds being delayed in February 2019.  But the corrupt Ukrainian government was still in power, and a two-round system Ukrainian presidential election was held on 31 March and 21 April.  Therefore, the Department of State had no way of knowing if they were going to be funding an honest or corrupt administration.

We hear from the *"Never Trump"* group how stupid Trump is, which means he couldn't make the connection to the funding of corruption that falls under the Department of State purview.

Alternatively, given level of intelligent that exceeds that seen among the *"Never Trump"* crowd, we need not assume that Trump demonstrated enough intelligence to pick the right time to run, the ability to outsmart the professional Republican candidates and win the nomination, plus a lifetime of business experience which would see the logic of withholding funds from thieves or corrupt oligarchs – who controlled Ukraine since the Soviet Union collapsed.

The majority of Democrats would certainly appreciate the wisdom of withholding funds from corrupt governments; paying such funds has traditionally been a mainstay Republican policy.

Volodymyr Zelensky received 73.22% of the vote by running on an anti-corruption platform. Embassy and Department of State officials would allowed over a month from the inauguration on 20 May for the new President to settle in and verify his intent to keep his campaign promises. Trump's call of congratulations was made on 25 July 2019, and the funds were released delivered a few weeks later.

As of November 2019, Ukraine authorities were still trying to root out the corrupt or incompetent elements within the office of the Prosecutor General, there was no "quid pro quo" of a type Schiff alleges. However, if we look at Schiff, we see a man who read a false transcript into the Congressional Record, and during the Mueller, investigation repeatedly lied about having seen evidence of collusion with Russia. His failure to provide Mueller with that evidence constitutes either obstruction of justice or impeding a Congressional investigation.

We still have unanswered questions posited by Trump:

- *"Why did Hunter Biden get a special business deal in Ukraine while his father Joe Biden was Vice President?*

- *"Why did Hunter Biden get a special deal in China?"*

Trump provided a truism: *"The media can't answer those questions, and neither can Joe!"* But the reality is, the media can answer the questions – they just prefer not to. Impeachment is blood in the water, and the media functions on the axiom, *"If it bleeds it leads."*

On 11 September 1932, New York Times Magazine quoted future President Franklin Delano Roosevelt {FDR} saying:

*"The Presidency is not merely an administrative office. That's the least of it. It is more than an engineering job, efficient or inefficient. It is pre-eminently a place of moral leadership. All our great Presidents were leaders of thought at times when certain historic ideas in the life of the nation had to be clarified."*

While being interviewed in June, Candace Owens, founder of Blexit {BlackExit}, stated: *"I think Joe Biden probably has the shadiest history of all the candidates running when it comes to race — for somebody that authored the three-strikes bill — to pretend that he's somehow a hero for black America is a joke."*

We should note that the Blexit movement seeks to awaken African Americans to the fact the Democratic Party might be failing the Black Community and that its current agenda has detrimental effects.

Back in 1972, Biden's winning technique was summarized by News Journal political reporter Curtis Wilkie with the words: *"He's Irish, for god's sake. He's full of blarney if you will, he always has been. He's a bullshit artist."* And we have the problem that Biden never evolved beyond bullshit, but he added an Italian Mafia-type element to his repertoire.

As stereotypical as that might seem, Wilkie revealed Biden to be the type of person many claim Donald Trump to be – with the difference that Biden is a professional politician who, in a 1974 Kittey Kelley interview, bragged, *"I am proud to be a politician. There is no other walk of life which can do more good for mankind than politics. It influences everything that happens to the American people."*

He then leaned over his desk, shook his finger at her, saying: *"And, whether you like it or not, young lady, us cruddy politicians can take away that First Amendment of yours if we want to."*

Biden declared an ability to nullify: *"Congress shall make no law respecting an establishment of religion, or prohibiting the free exercise thereof; or abridging the freedom of speech, or of the press; or the right of the people peaceably to assemble, and to petition the Government for a redress of grievances."*

# CHAPTER THIRTEEN – 19 & 57

**"If you impeach a president,
if you make a high crime & misdemeanor
out of going to the courts,
it is an abuse of power.
It's your abuse of power.
You're doing precisely what you're criticizing the
president for doing."
~ Jonathan Turley, Constitutional Scholar**

Pay attention to the words and reality.  On 10 December, the twin articles of impeachment were announced with the pre-vote hearing scheduled to begin two days later – everything hinges on the actions of Joseph R Biden and Trump's reaction to them.

At the same time, the public was informed by MSN:  *"Bernie Sanders regained second place in a Monmouth nationwide Democratic primary poll, pushing Elizabeth Warren down to third place.  Sanders secured 21% support in the poll ..., slightly behind former Vice President Joe Biden, who has 26%.  Warren had 17% support and Pete Buttigieg had 8% support. - Washington Examiner."*  Interestingly, as a POTUS Cousin, Buttigieg is viable.

The title of chapter 5 in book one of this series is *"Emperor's Wardrobe"* – it opens with the words *"The Emperor's New Clothes is a classic tale of how people will ignore the evidence of their own eyes, ignore reality, rather than face the condemnation of others too fearful of public opinion to address reality."*

Those words were published on 8 April 2017; it has taken until 11 December 2019 for their meaning to be made evident in the halls of Congress.  To deflect from their obvious foolishness, within 30-minutes of the reading of the impeachment charges, the world heard Speaker Pelosi praise and attempt to take credit for a revised NAFTA trade agreement, known as USMCA, which she opposed and sat on for nearly a year.

The magnificent wardrobe the world was to praise was that which described the actions the presumptive Democratic nominee, Joseph Robinette Biden Jr., bragged of committing when he used Federal appropriations as leverage in a bold act of extortion against

Ukraine authorities; the goal was to have a corruption prosecutor fired within a clearly defined six-hour timeframe.

Then add the fact that Congress has accused Trump of doing a minor variation on what Biden boasted he had done – possibly at Obama's direction; it becomes interesting that the House defends Biden as a viable candidate worthy of the Presidential Office and yet attacks Trump for enforcing the law and a related treaty.

Let us forget that nonsense and focus on the ridiculous idea that House Judiciary Committee Chairman Jerrold Lewis 'Jerry' Nadler asserts claims: *"The president is a continuing threat to that Constitution and to our democracy."*

This is the same Nadler who, on 10 December 1998, told the Judiciary Committee:

*"Benjamin Franklin called impeachment, 'a substitute for assassination.'"*

Should we now assume his goal is to assassinate Trump?

On day two of his hearings, Nadler stated: *"We invited the president to participate in this hearing, … and to present evidence that might explain the charges against him. President Trump chose not to show."* Of course, he neglected to state that there were no clearly fixed and defined charges – that the alleged offenses continually changed until a point where only two allegations were made: 1. Abuse of Power because Trump asked *"the Government of Ukraine to publicly announce investigations"*.

Of course, the U.S. Congress had appropriated about $125 million for those investigations and any such announcement would serve to validate they would be done. And, in accordance with the 1998/9 treaty, and since Joe Biden had bragged of using extortion against Ukraine officials, Trump was charged with requesting any relevant findings be turned over to the Attorney general – as per the treaty requirements.

Interestingly, Biden had explicitly boasted that he was going to withhold or nullify a Billion Dollars in appropriations unless his directives were followed within six-hours. In that same context, Nadler alleged – without any such admission or documentation to support the assertion – that Trump had conditioned the release of $391 million on the announcement of the investigations.

The second charge was "Obstruction of Congress". But they

had no problem holding hearings or calling witnesses who then established they had no direct evidence of wrongdoing. At best, they could assert hearsay opinions. The alleged obstruction was a challenge to the legal basis for several subpoenas that infringed on Executive Privilege or Executive authority and the failure of the House committees to adhere to the law and Constitution by having SCOTUS rule on the validity of those subpoenas.

In an ideal Impeachment World, in 2020 history will see the first actual conviction and removal of a sitting American President based on his enforcing both law and treaty. To which, there is the added crime of allegedly wanting a public assurance that the funds appropriated by Congress would be spent for which they are being provided and were intended.

Compounding the hypocrisy of a House that condones Biden boasting of extortion, but condemns Trump for enforcing a treaty, we have the issue of candidate ages. The current life expectancy for an average American in 2019 was 78.87 years. Donald Trump is 73, both former Vice President Joseph R. Biden and former New York City Mayor Mike Bloomberg are 77, Senator Bernie Sanders 78 and recovering from a heart attack, while Senator Elizabeth Warren is only 70 and the only one of them who could reasonably be expected to run again in 2024.

On Thursday, 12 December, Biden went on record saying, if he were elected in 2020, he would run again for re-election in 2024 – when he would be 83-years-old. Granted, based on his parents, Biden could live long enough to serve two terms. But based on the behavior and memory loss that has been documented during the campaign for the nomination, if his impeachment based on his C-SPAN confession failed, he would likely be removed based on the determination that he was senile and unable to fulfill the duties of the Presidential Office.

Of course, were Bernie Sanders elected, since he's 14 months older than Biden and has already had a heart attack, age and health would invoke a family history that has only he and his baby brother living past age-60.

Including assassinations, America has seen eight POTUS die in office – meaning, even if they were young, there's an 18% chance they'd die in office, with about an 8% chance it would be of natural causes.

In that fictional universe, hard evidence will emerge to affirm a real crime – not just idiots yelling Trump is a crook, since, if he was, that crooked activity could be used to impeach.  There is no basis to assert the Constitution requires the crime be committed while in office.  The argument is that a "High Crime" is any crime that serves to undermine the public trust or ability of the people to rely on the honesty of their leaders.

As a matter of history, it was in 1386 that King's Chancellor, Michael de la Pole, 1st Earl of Suffolk provided the first case that involved high crimes and misdemeanors committed against the crown – a broken promise and failure to pay a ransom.  We might well see a parallel in Biden threatening to brake America's promise of aid by withholding it.

With Biden there are questions, but we'll save enumerating them for our final chapter.  For now, Carl Sandburg gave us a guide to how impeachment trials are conducted: *"If the facts are against you, argue the law.  If the law is against you, argue the facts.  If the law and the facts are against you, pound the table and yell like hell."*  Well, we don't pound the table, we simply say the evidence or non-existent facts are overwhelming or exceptionally compelling  – as Nancy Pelosi phrased it, *"I've never seen evidence so clear."*

We need to wonder if Pelosi saw Biden's C-SPAN confession.  Or if she has ever heard the words of Marcus Aurelius quoted on page 430 in my January 2017 book, *Jonathon's POTUS Cousins:*

*"Whenever you are about to find fault with someone, ask yourself the following question: What fault of mine most nearly resembles the one I am about to criticize?"*

Going into the impeachment hearings, the popular mantra was eminent recession came to an end – breaking with tradition – the impeachment resulted in the DJIA achieving a record 28,290 high and, on Friday the 13th, closing at a record 28,123.

Five days earlier, on Sunday, December 8, 2019, an OAN Newsroom interview in which *"Former Prosecutor General Viktor Shokin spoke to OAN about Joe Biden's direct role in getting his office to stop investigating his son Hunter."*  In that interview, the Prosecutor Biden told On America News {OAN} that his office had been preparing to question Hunter Biden regarding various money laundering activities which traced directly to Burisma Holdings.

In his statement, Prosecutor  Shokin said Ukraine President

Petro Poroshenko had been pressured by Biden into asking him to drop the investigation. In the months that followed, corruption investigations continually led directly back to Burisma and Biden increased pressure of Poroshenko to shut down Shokin's team. As Biden threatened termination of a Billion Dollars in aid, President Poroshenko called Shokin and said: *"you are a patriot and we need this aid"* and that the ceasing of Burisma assets had pushed Biden over the edge. When directly asked, Shokin responded that Biden was the sole driving force protecting Burisma.

Biden then initiated a campaign slandering Shokin – against whom there have never been any charges of corruption. Biden was using the classic defame the victim and blame the victim – a tactic well known to the #MeToo movement which opposes its use when applied to women exposed to sexual harassment, but, apparently, acceptable if utilized by Joseph Biden for the benefit of both his son and corrupt foreign firms.

More important, Shokin revealed there are transcripts of Biden's telephone conversations with Poroshenko which provide evidence of Biden's illegal influence foreign officials to *"protect his son Hunter and shield illegal money laundering activities."* In this context, there is also a twelve-page sworn affidavit before the Austrian Courts.

At the time of the initial investigations, the focus was on the founder of Burisma, Mykola Zlochevsky, the former minister of ecology and natural resources of Ukraine – it appears that he was the one who appointed Hunter Biden to the Board of Directors *"in order to protect himself."*

As with Pelosi's *"evidence so clear"* assertion, the only claim that refutes Shokin is that of the Biden Campaign calling Shokin discredited – where his discredation is exclusively from Biden and his supplicants. Apparently, the impeachment, which has been the goal since the 9 November 2016 announcement of election results, serves to discourage Ukraine corruption investigators' compliance with the 1998/9 criminal investigation treaty – which serves the purpose of suppressing the Biden-Poroshenko transcripts.

Moreover, an article by THE HILL on 26 September 2019, raises the specter of:

*"Hundreds of pages of never-released memos and documents — many from inside the American team helping Burisma to stave*

*off its legal troubles — conflict with Biden's narrative. And they raise the troubling prospect that U.S. officials may have painted a false picture in Ukraine that helped ease Burisma's legal troubles and stop prosecutors' plans to interview Hunter Biden during the 2016 U.S. presidential election."*

The article's author: "*John Solomon is an award-winning investigative journalist whose work over the years has exposed U.S. and FBI intelligence failures before the Sept. 11 attacks, federal scientists' misuse of foster children and veterans in drug experiments, and numerous cases of political corruption.*"

Thus we can say that this is not "Fakenews" – but credible investigative journalism like that which exposed Watergate and so brought down Richard Nixon.  Where it to continue, this form of investigative journalism, and if the existence of credible evidence keeps emerging, in 2020, any vote for Joseph R. Biden becomes, in reality, a vote for his Vice President to be the POTUS.

And this brings us to the title of this chapter and the words in Jonathon's POTUS Cousins which "*spoke to cycles: the 49-year OMER; the 19-year Metonic; the Stonehenge eclipse period of 56 to 57 years.  These natural cycles are used in ancient prophecy; they can be considered a form of superstitious nonsense or a scientifically significant companion to evolution.*"

The 19-year Metonic cycle is named for a Greek, Meton of Athens, who utilized it in 432BCE – but, long before that it was the basis for both the Hebrew and Chinese calendars, and incorporated into the structure of Stonehenge, whose fifty-six stones create fifty-seven spaces.  Because of a nesting effect, as with the biblical which often equates days to years, we can view 19-years of 12-months as twelve 19-year cycles and see the coincidence of the 228 years that have passed between the first American election in 1788 and 2016.

Coincidently, that period also equates to 57 of our four-year election cycles.  And, therefore, making the first Trump term a start of a new American era – the last one having ended with George Washington's 10th cousin, Barack Obama marking an evolution of the nation from one of slavery to having a Black man in the Oval.

It befits the era that we should have a trade war with China and see such a focus on Anti-Semitism, while the First Daughter is an Orthodox Jewess, and the first Jewish member of a First Family, promoting women's rights among nations that have long histories of opposing such rights. This creates a symbolic link to the Jewish concept of *Tikun Olam* – the point where the righteous will 'repair of the world'; a time when the swamp is drained and idolatry will be disposed of.

The modern calendar was created when a Scythian Monk reset the Hebrew calendar to one at its 198th-Metonic node. For some reason, the 107th node was selected as a symbolic marker for the age when the population decline we now associated with the death of Baby-Boomers was to combine with mass extinctions we associate with Climate Change and decrease all life by a third.

For those who believe in mystic powers, that node is 2033 – Hebrew year 5795 – in terms of American transformation the year could be 2035, but both are controlled by the 2032 election.

If there is to be a war, the President elected in 2032 must be experienced in military leadership and decision making. But, that is for the future – a dozen years after the decisive election that will be determined on 3 November 2020. Will America elect Joe Biden, a man who boasted of committing a High Crime while in the office of the Vice President. Or will we see Donald John Trump elected after surviving the impeachment which followed the symbolically significant release of the Committee Majority report, outlining the basis for impeachment, on 7 December 2019 – Pearl Harbor Day.

Some, those who are pushing recession fears, believe that the economy is in a bubble, when, in fact, the economy is at the end of a generational demographic cycle. The current three-generation cycle began in 1945, with the birth of the first Baby-Boomer. Traditionally, as affirmed by a December article published in *Scientific Reports*, each generation is 19-years and falls in the context of the ancient warning: *"the sins of the parents pass unto the third or fourth generation"* – we are, therefore, looking at the periods 1945 to 1964 to 1983 to 2002 to 2021. Consider those periods as economic periods or eras. Does it work?

The first of the Baby-Boomer generation was officially born in 1945 and will be 76-years-old in 2021 – they are comfortably bracketed by America's 78-life expectancy or the period from 1944 to 2022. Coincidently, for those who didn't notice, that same 78-year period separates 1941 and 2019.

Commonly, the Baby-Boom Generation consists of all those born between 1945 and 1964. In the context of the expression, "sins" does not actually infer a negative, rather it is a characteristic which is undesirable and will take about 57-years to vanish from the social norm. This means we would see the change in the first phase of the next 57-year cycle – after 2002 and before 2021.

In 1945, racism was an issue; anti-miscegenation laws – marriage based racial segregation – was deemed the norm but, by 2019, interracial couples and relationships were commonly presented in the entertainment media and product commercials commonly featured mixed-race couples. Hallmark Chanel had run commercials – inciting outrage among bigots – featuring a same-sex marriage.

Even while reproductive generations change – we hear that women are having children later in life – the 19-year cycle holds. And, because it defines changes in human thinking or culture, it also controls economics. This reality was observed by a Russian economist named Nikolai Kondratiev who, in 1925, published his observations in a book entitled *The Major Economic Cycles*. His observation is now known as the *Kondratiev wave or K-Wave* and is the basis for studies into long economic cycles.

Kondratiev observed three phases – expansion, stagnation, recession – which I associate with a 19-year pattern which defines the universe and is found in the 56-upright stones of Stonehenge; the 57th stone becomes the first stone defining the start of the new cycle. This was seen in the book *"Genesis of Genesis"* where ages or dates connected to a patriarch are used to define eras, with a common pattern of Hebrew Calendar dates that are, if significant, divisible by 19.

What does this have to do with Trump, the 2020 election or any aspect of this book series?

Beginning in 2019, the media was continuously reporting on the idea that this or that action by Trump was going to cause a recession. In Britain, in 2016, the people voted for BREXIT – by 2019, the Britain-European Union divorce was triggering a British recession that threatened to bring down Europe's economy and, if America were tied to it, bring down America as well.

The landslide re-election of Boris Johnson's Conservatives affirmed the divorce commitment. Comically, Johnson had been referred to as the British Trump and produced a resounding victory for the Conservatives – making BREXIT unstoppable.

As the record shows, upon assuming Presidential authority,

Trump immediately initiated a series of policies that were aimed at disengaging America from Europe, China, and any other economy that might fall victim to a BREXIT collapse – while also setting things up to allow for favorable trade deals with an independent Britain.

We've noted the cycles, and that *"the actions of the parents pass unto the third or fourth generation"* – and it's rally actions, not sins, but people tend to be more enraptured by negatives and, in ancient times, needed to be warned to avoid the negatives.

Look at the eras 1945 to 1964 where 1945 to 1960 is seen as a period of phenomenal economic growth. Kennedy was elected and three years later assassinated; Vietnam became a war Hippies had no use – they wanted the age of Peace, Love, and Rock-n-Roll.

The era between 1964 and 1983 began in 1965 with inflation edging up, unemployment at 1.4-percent, and economic growth of 9-percent, as the Baby-boomers entered the workforce and pushed unemployment to 3.8-percent  – in 2019, with the Boomers exiting the workforce at the rate they had entered it, that number is at 3.7-percent. This phase was one that saw real inflation and had leaders who traded Social Security for debt and military growth.

Then we went into the era dominated by Reagan-Bush, and the National Debt soared out of control with what we might see as a McCarthyism mindset taking hold and allowing to sins of that era to be reflected in the third political generation. As a result, we see ourselves with the fourth era 2002 to 2021 being defined by war. As with McCarthyism, we have the Russians defining everything, as we talk of anti-Semitism, Climate Change, and all the little sins that were in the shadows, or monsters in the closet, in 1945.

Now, at the dawn of the next cycle, which parental line will we follow – or will we begin anew? Our choices are basic: 1964 to 1983, the age of Hippies crushed by Reagan Conservatives, with the impeachment that yielded a resignation; 1983 to 2002, the age of economic disaster and debt, when a POTUS could produce budget surpluses and be impeached for Oral in the Oval; 2002 to 2021, a return to the age of both low inflation and high employment when, once again, the goal is to impeach economic success because of the audacity to seek to get information on a former Vice President who boasted of abusing his authority and engaging in extortion using taxpayer funds.

The heading of this chapter focuses on traditional cycles of the type that have manifested themselves in many things over the millennial eras since the time of Stonehenge.  But, in the world of economics, there are other cycles to consider – when we speak of recessions, many economists will point to the inverted yield curve, when interest rates on long-term loans are lower than those on short-term loans.  Analysts will also tell you there is a 11-year cycle for recessions, therefore also for inverted yields.

On 2 October 2019, Forbes published an article entitled "Inverted Yield Curve Suggesting Recession Around The Corner?", which posited the theme as a question: "How successful has the difference between the 10-Year Treasury rate and 2-Year Treasury rate (T10Y2Y) been in predicting a recession?"

Readers were then informed, "*The inverted yield curve has consistently predicted a recession each of the 5 times in the last 5 decades.*"  But, further reading reveals the inversion precedes what is termed a "robust" S&P 500 which, eventually, comes to an end and results in a recessionary cycle.  Which simply means, when the short-term (up to three months) interest rates are higher than the long-term (3-7 year) rates there is a likelihood of a recession that is reflected in the higher demand for immediate capital to fund an immediate investment need.

At some point after the short-term acceleration, there will be a recession – "*a period of temporary economic decline during which trade and industrial activity are reduced.*"  We could look at this in terms of something we can all recognize – the Holiday Shopping season when purchases drive-up store sales and appear on credit cards, only to see store-sales fall during the period when the cards are being paid off.

In June 2007, the yield curve inverted and in December the recession began.  In 2019, yield numbers for August revealed the inversion; so, if the House Impeachment is conducted on a proper schedule, the recession should occur concurrently with the Senate Impeachment Trial.

That pattern, which can be seen in the relevant charts, tells us the recession cycle is not dependent on the Administrations in the Oval.  Something happens in the debt market which manifests in intersecting cycles whose intensity is under the control of the government or political power structure.

And if we look at the Trump administration, he's doing something that has disrupted the cycles – the 2007-2009 Great recession should have resulted in a 2018-2020 recession, and we see that Swamp Denizens are making a last-ditch effort to force the recession to occur concurrent with an impeachment – in part, we can say they are doing it because their efforts to impeach, which it has been shown during the 17 December hearing, to have begun in days leading up to the 2017 inauguration.  In the past, any effort to impeach resulted in a Stock Market decline; with Trump we see the markets brush it aside to create record highs.

Which explains why the media and Democrats are pushing the idea that a recession is looming.  They want it to happen.  More importantly, they want the economy to crash.  They want an end to the Obama-Trump economic expansion; they want the nation to be flooded with undocumented immigrants who will go onto welfare and be counted in the 2020 census so they can have non-voter bodies expanding their powers in the House of Representatives.

If we look to Europe, any no-deal BREXIT could trigger the recession that could also end the Obama-Trump economy.  But the Swamp Denizens cannot rely on Europe to bring down America – not with Trump improving upon Obama's programs; improving upon NAFTA with USMCA; repatriating industries outsourced to China; improving upon the 2006 Secure Fence Act structure so it will serve when the anticipated Climate Change Migration begins; as Trump suggested, that "Wall" could serve as a platform for solar collectors that help fight climate change and reduce American need for fossil fuels – making the transformation the oil-rich Saudis have already begun.

If the European Union goes into recession, China will still be linked to the United States and that reality provides Trump with the necessary negotiating leverage to bring about a *"face-saving"* end to the *'Trade War'* – which happened, on schedule, when *"Phase One"* of the negotiation was finalized in December 2019 and China agreed to purchase $200 Billion in US Trade goods over the next two years, including $50 Billion in agriculture products.  The result is projected to trigger an additional 2-percent growth in the American economy and prevent the recession the Swamp Denizens want so dearly to cause.

Prior to a *"Phase One"* deal, the record for agricultural sales was the $26 Billion achieved by Obama in 2012. Farmers hurt by the extremes in heat and rain that accompanied the 21-month trade warm had experienced bankruptcies at a rate that was 24-percent above 2018; ideally, *"Phase One"* will aid in making marginal farms profitable and allow them to transition to the new Climate Change demands for improved farming methods – known as Controlled-environment agriculture, which produces yields of pesticide-free, high-end that are up to 20 times that of produced by conventional farms of the land area, using renewable energy resources.

Throughout the era of the American Baby-Boomers, there has been one industry that has continually supported the Balance of Payments that defines the international balance of trade – that has been agriculture.

Traditionally, agricultural production has been tied to the climate and weather patterns – global warming is pushing things northward and increasing the intensity of storms. For America, it can mean benefit or harm based upon how it addresses an issue that is supposed to reach a point of no return by 2030 when most Climate Agreements are speaking in terms of 2050 or the end of the century.

With a population equal to a sixth of global humanity, China needs America and is looking to the vast emptiness of Russia for its nutritional needs. For centuries it has relied on pork for meat, but that means importing a product detrimental to the environment – China lacks the arable land to meet its dietary needs.

China ranks fourth behind in arable land – behind India, United States, and Russia, in that order. Where the population of India is 1.35 billion to China's 1.4 billion, while India has 50% more arable land. But America also has 50% more land, with a third of the population of either India or China. Therein lies the key to the Trade Wars and the Climate Change future – unlike China, 30% of India is at a latitude that will be most affected by global warming. But with good management, India can adapt, but not China.

Warren and Sanders seem aware of the ramifications that are associated with some aspects of Climate Change. Trump can be viewed as addressing them from a business angle – you cannot overrun the nation with Climate Change Migrants, you need to take steps that will allow their orderly integration into the culture and economy.

Biden has said he'd accept two million a year but has no idea where they would live or how they can be processed so as to quickly become productive members of an aging society.  Nor has Biden indicated he has any grasp on the cost of the educational to local communities – sixty-percent of those at the border are children.

We have our generational cycles and a pattern that brought America to a critical turning-point in its history – to a time when a President is impeached for asking for facts, from an investigation American Taxpayers are funding, that pertain to a former Vice President bragging that, while in office, functioning in an official capacity, he brazenly committed what *every Democratic* member of the House of Representatives agrees is a High Crime.  As one news report, linked to the C-SPAN brag-video, stated: *"Joe Biden Forced Ukraine to Fire Prosecutor for Aid Money"* – which is abuse of power, extortion, bribery, coercion, and we need not ask about personal gain resulting from firing a lawyer and replacing him with a "solid" corrupt ex-felon with no law degree.

Cycles, *'The Sins of The Fathers'*, a quatrain that began with Tricky Dick Nixon as Vice President and America breaking its word to the people of Vietnam – a promise that, after helping America in the War against Japan, they would be free of European colonial occupation and be allowed to chose the governmental system they favored.

Over the next two quatrains, a broken promise became an Asian war America lost – with its end marked by America embassy personnel being airlifted from their embassy roof.

It was 23 April 1975, when President Gerald Ford declared the Vietnam War *"finished as far as America is concerned,"* and on 30 April *Operation Frequent Wind* became the largest evacuation of its kind in history.  And because the Administration which gave us Vice President Richard Nixon reneged on a promise of political freedom America made to the Vietnamese people.

As a related aside, my cousin, Dr. Jeffery Simon – who spent his non-professorial career as a NATO and Presidential advisor – in 1968, made the point that, if we simply gave the Vietnamese the money we were spending to kill them, per capita, they would be the third richest nation in world and have no reason to be Communist.

But the first era of our generational quatrain was the time of *"the red scare"* and saw a war between North and South in a nation divided by the victors in the second world war.  It is a war that, nearly

65-years later is technically still being fought.  Nine years after cessation of combat there was the assassination of a young President Kennedy and escalation of the war resulting from our broken promise.

The second era saw the loss and was marked by Tricky Dick resigning because of and being pardoned, rather than prosecuted, for his numerous and very real crimes.  It ended with the election of a "Red Scare" era b-actor, who had spied on his associates in the entertainment industry on McCarthy's behalf, for the FBI to the Oval and initiated an era of militarism matched by runaway National Debt.  Looking at the damage done by excessive taxes in Britain, the b-actor accepted the analysis of the Laffer Curve and instituted a downward adjustment to America's tax code.

The third era saw an impeachment attempt brought against a philandering President who brought the debt under control and achieved years of budget surpluses.  This economic success inferred that the larger adjustments, combined with a rational approach to spending, might actually have worked.

This third era concluded with a President who tossed away rational budgeting, returned to downward larger adjustments, and returned the nation to deficits and runaway debt, while he initiated a 19-year war – rather than hold his oil business partner's brother accountable for the World Trade Center mass murder –then closed the era with a Great Recession.

The fourth era saw America's first African-American POTUS – whose father was African, as opposed to just having a claim to that ancestral connection.  It also saw an African-Jewish-America actress become a British Dutchess and Princess.

As of this writing, we are entering the final year of the fourth quatrain.  We again have deficits, but in the context of record low inflation, levels of unemployment that have not been this low since the first quatrain, growing incomes with record-high employment and stock market levels.  So, naturally, the President is facing impeachment because he asked for any relevant information behind a former Vice President's brag of committing a HIGH CRIME while in office -- information that is part of a corruption investigation American Taxpayers are helping to fund.

The parties at war in the first era are now talking of peace and cooperation; trade treaties are being renegotiated, with outsourced manufacturing being repatriated, and the candidates for the 2020 election are saying we went too far in the Laffer Curve adjustment -- that taxes on the wealthy must be increased; that, because of past inflation, the income subject to Social Security withholding is now far below its funding needs, and removing the cap would correct for the Laffer Curve errors without harming the economy or having a detrimental effect on the purchasing power and income of Americans on any level of the economic ladder.

On the contrary, it could lower costs by eliminating known or established healthcare system waste and allow Medicare-for-all at a time when the majority of Americans, the Baby-Boomers, are already covered by Medicare.

Given the chapter mentions "19 & 57", let's take a second to look at that 57. Obvious it is three times 19. But is there something else?

We are talking about impeachment – which is supposed to be the Constitutional removal from office. But, as we see with Trump, it's a purely irrational political act removal which opens the door to thinking just in terms of removal of a POTUS.

Assassination is a very effective means of removal, and we know John Fitzgerald Kennedy was killed on 22 November 1963 – which, three weeks after the 2020 election, will be 57-years ago. In that time, we had the Kennedy assassination, an attempt on the life of Ronald Reagan, the impeachment of Nixon, Clinton, and Trump.

Then there was a little-noticed event on 10 June 2008, when Congressmen Dennis Kucinich and Robert Wexler introduced 35 articles of impeachment, which the House then voted 251 to 166 to refer the resolution to the Judiciary Committee, where the effort to remove George W Bush received no further action.

In 57-years Americans engaged in six attempts to remove its elected President. Only Twice successfully. That means roughly every 9.5 years – or twice every Metonic cycle – Americans want to change or alter the outcome of an election without an election.

As we have seen, we are at the beginning of a new cycle – is there any better way to mark it, other than nominating and electing someone whose impeachment would be a slam dunk?

According to Peter Schweizer, author of "Secret Empires, *"President Trump would be negligent if he did not bring this matter,*

*Biden, up. If the V.P. of the U.S. is self-enriching & engaged in criminal behavior, at a minimum corrupt behavior, it ought to be looked at."*

When better to look at Biden's confessed High Crime than after he becomes the Democratic nominee and is elected President?

If we honestly examine all of the Committee assertions, it becomes rather easy to see they have built an ironclad case against Joseph Robinette Biden, Jr. We have his 2018 confession and the fact that Hunter was hired by a man who was the subject of various criminal investigations.

We know that Yuriy Vitaliyovych Lutsenko – the man Biden claimed was "solid" – was charged with abuse of office and forgery in 2010; then in 2012 was sentenced to four years in jail for abuse of office and embezzlement. We also know he's an engineer and not a lawyer – which raises the issue of how he could be a credible Prosecutor General. It was an office he held from 12 May 2016 to 29 August 2019.

Lutsenko replaced Attorney Viktor Mykolayovych Shokin, who served from 10 February 2015 to 29 March 2016. He replaced General Prosecutor Viktor Pshonka and was unable to properly prosecute cases initiated by Pehonka when it was discovered that related criminal orders and casework had vanished.

Within six-months of Shokin's appointment, there was an attempt to assassinate him. As we know from Biden's confession, the Obama administration withheld $1 Billion in loan guarantees to leverage a firing of Shokin, who, unlike his successor, has never been prosecuted for or convicted of criminal behavior.

It's been reported that the Office of the Prosecutor General has conducted 15 investigations on Burisma's owner Zlochevsky.

There are no obvious 19s in the Ukraine. But, why distract from the facts and get a bit weird – noting that the finial Democratic Debate for the Year of the House Impeachment was on 12/19/19 and followed a Vote of Impeachment on 12/18/19 that Pelosi shelved on 12/19/19.

But that was seven months before the scheduled Democratic Nominating Convention 12+7=19 and we have our three 19s – which should please the mystics, conspiracy theorists, and even evangelicals seeking a Second Coming.

# CHAPTER FOURTEEN – Consider

**"Why, then, 'tis none to you, for there is nothing either good or bad, but thinking makes it so. To me, it is a prison. Well, then it isn't one to you since nothing is really good or bad in itself—it's all what a person thinks about it."**

**~ Shakespeare: Hamlet: Act 2 Scene 2**

Thinking does make it so. That's the premise or essence of *"The Emperor's New Clothes."* If you want people to think your smart, you do that which is said to show that you are smart – you see magical threads from which, supposedly, the Emperor's clothes are woven.

Under Article 1 Section 3 of the Constitution: *"Judgment in Cases of Impeachment shall not extend further than to removal from Office, and disqualification to hold and enjoy any Office of honor, Trust or Profit under the United States: but the Party convicted shall nevertheless be liable and subject to Indictment, Trial, Judgment and Punishment, according to Law."*

We note the final sentence indicates that impeachment does not fall under the rules governing double jeopardy, we also know that the standards are somewhat different – impeachment determines the qualification to hold an *"Office of honor, Trust or Profit under the United States."* Thus, laws worded in a way as to be domestic can be applied to foreign or non-domestic circumstances for impeachment. A pattern of dishonorable behavior knows no borders.

In judging Trump's actions concerning Ukraine and Joseph Biden, it behooves us to ask certain primary questions regarding the C-SPAN documented bragging referred to in the phone call. These questions are fundamental to the rights and authority of the United States and those individuals elected to its highest offices – that of the President and vice president – and are independent of whether they are exercised for the good of the nation or personal gain.

The fundamental issue is whether these powers exist or if their assertion is an abuse of American authority as a superpower or an abuse of power vested in the High office.

In that context – while allowing that there are times of national emergency and special unique circumstances which might allow for a temporary or special case caveat modifying any of the following -- we must ask which, if any, of the following questions can be answered in the affirmative:

1. Does the United States have the authority of approval over individuals employed by foreign governments?

2. Does the United States have the right to force the termination of employment of key foreign officials -- specifically those having no direct relevance to the health, welfare, safety or security of America?

3. Does the office of the Vice President carry with it the authority to unilaterally withhold or nullify the use of taxpayer funds lawfully approved by Congress and the President?

4. Does the office of the Vice President have the unilateral authority to use taxpayer funds for bribery, coercion, or extortion at home or abroad?

5. Can the President delicate a unilateral authority to use taxpayer funds for bribery, coercion, or extortion at home or abroad to the Vice President?

6. Is the authority to use taxpayer funds for bribery, coercion, or extortion at home or abroad vested in the Constitutional or legal powers of the office of President of the United States?

7. Given that the Congress has the sole authority to appropriate and place terms and conditions on the use of taxpayer money, does the President or Vice President have the unilateral right or authority to arbitrarily change those terms and conditions to suit their professional, political, or personal needs and desires?

8. Given, Congress has the sole authority to appropriate and place terms and conditions on the use of taxpayer money, does the President or Vice President have the unilateral right or authority to use of leverage those funds for personal or family gain or benefit?

If, as a general rule, none of the above can be answered in the affirmative, would an affirmative behavior constitute a HIGH CRIME or illegal act under the Constitution and laws of the United States?

As an example, if you say we can utilize extortion to remove foreign officials who are generally disliked, can we then exercise that power to remove Delegates to the United Nations?  We can then do this with any nation that opposes us and our allies.

In terms of Criminal Statutes, the actions of Joseph R Biden which were freely confessed to in January 2018, and publicly bragged about, violate numerous laws that carry prison sentences of up to 20-years in a federal Penitentiary. As stated, the burden of proof for the criminal convention is necessary for an impeachment conviction – which is why the Founding Fathers allowed for subsequent criminal prosecution.

Since the affirmative is a crime, as well as breach of authority, and abuse of power, does the President and/or Office of the Attorney General have the right and obligation to investigate those who openly admit to committing the related crime, breach of authority, or abuse of power?

Does the President and/or Office of the Attorney General have the authority of legal obligation to determine any underlying facts before initiating or asking Congress to initiate any judicial authority warranted?

If the answers are affirmative, it follows the President and/or Attorney General are within their rights to invoke such laws or, if the matter is international, it follows the President has both the legal and Constitutional obligation to invoke the terms of such relevant treaties as might be necessary to obtain the relevant underlying facts and details.

Given the sworn Presidential obligation to uphold the laws of the land, would it not be obstruction of justice for any individual or elected official, or co-equal Branch of Government to oppose and/or hamper the gathering of the facts, or use an arbitrary legal process to attempt to remove the President and/or Attorney General from office based on their efforts to comply with the law and obtain the facts?

Consider Biden's bragging of having Viktor Shokin fired and replaced by the "solid" Yuriy Vitaliyovych Lutsenko, who held the office from 12 May 2016 to 29 August 2019; during that time, *"the National Anti-Corruption Bureau informed the United States Department of State that Lutsenko had both thwarted Ukraine's investigation into Kilimnik and allowed Kilimnik to leave Ukraine for Russia."* {Waas, Murray (8 October 2019). "Ukraine Continued: How a Crucial Witness Escaped".}

Konstantin V. Kilimnik has been identified as *"a person of interest in the 2017 Special Counsel investigation into Russian interference in the 2016 United States elections,"* and *"is believed by CNN and The New York Times to be 'Person A' listed in court documents filed by the Special Counsel against Manafort."*

Interestingly, Biden is boasted of affecting the installing of a "solid" Prosecutor who arranged for a known Russian intelligence operative to escape to Russian and evade prosecution in Ukraine.  It is also important that the "solid" Lutsenko lacks the basic credentials associated with a Chief Prosecutor or American Attorney General – Lutsenko never went to law school and had no knowledge of the laws he was supposedly prosecuting.  Moreover, as we know, he was a convicted felon who, before replacing Shokin, served four years on a felony conviction.

Viktor Shokin graduated from Yaroslav Mudryi National Law University and was aggressively prosecuting Burisma and ceasing its money-laundering related assets.  It was claimed Shokin blocked prosecution of some major cases – which happened after discovering his predecessor's files had vanished.  Meaning the evidence needed conviction was missing and needed to be massed anew.

When former Vice President Biden bragged about his Ukraine role – allegedly on behalf of the Obama Administration and with the full and unqualified support of President Barack Hussein Obama – he was confessing to a violation of multiple statutes – including, not limited to 18 U.S.C. § 201 - "Bribery of public officials and witnesses":

In 2012, President Obama signed  § 201 into law;  Chapter 11 - Bribery, Graft, and Conflicts of Interest would apply directly to the January 2018 bragging about using Federal credit assurance to effect the firing of Prosecutor Shokin; it would also apply to the context of Hunter Biden serving on the board of Burisma from April 2014 to April 2019 – leaving the firm a year after his father bragged about extorting the firing of the Prosecutor General and a few days before his father announced the start of his 2020 Presidential campaign.

Burisma Holdings is a Cyprus based energy company owned by Ukrainian oligarch Mykola Zlochevsky, and through Burisma Holdings he is the owner of Sunrise Energy Resources, a Delaware Corporation – and in 2016 they added the director of the Counterterrorism Center of the Central Intelligence Agency Joseph Cofer Black to its Board of Directors.

In 2012 Ukrainian Prosecutor General Pshonka had instituted an investigation into Zlochevzky's involvement in money laundering, tax evasion, and corruption during 2010-2012; in 2014 Zlochevzky fled charges of unlawful self-enrichment and legalization of funds which saw the courts impound $23 million of British held assets. These were released for lack of evidence around the time the  Biden forced the removal of Ukrainian prosecutor general Shokin – who was then replaced by the "solid" convicted felon.

Subsequent efforts to prosecute for embezzlement and other Ukraine related crimes have proved fruitless because Zlochevzky's whereabouts are unknown.  It is worth noting that, concurrent with the 2010 charges against Zlochevzky, Prosecutor Pshonka filed abuse of office and forgery charges against Biden's "Solid" replacement for Shokin – who served 14-months before being sentenced to 4-years and soon after release becoming Biden's "Solid Prosecutor General".

In terms of Biden's January 2018 boastful bragging confession of his 2016 crimes, as we saw, there are numerous Federal Criminal statutes that can be applied and then tried in the courts.  There are still more for impeachment purposes – Impeachment is the qualification for a position of trust, not a criminal prosecution.

Foreign Corrupt Practice Act - 15 U.S.C. § 78 (FCPA) makes it illegal to bribe a foreign government official. With some rather minor limitations, anyone can be prosecuted under it.  In the case of Biden, the use of a Billion dollars in taxpayer money to coerce, bribe or extort action from Ukraine's President more than meets the standard.  The statute does not allow for "migrating circumstances" such as not liking or getting along with someone.  Nor does it excuse criminal behavior because other criminals or governments approve such actions.

The only issues are that it be (1) willful (2) makes a payment, offer, or promise of anything of value (3) to a foreign official, foreign political party or party official, or candidate for foreign political office (4) to influence any official act or decision, induce unlawful action, or secure any improper advantage. There are questions of corrupt intent and advancing third party business interests which would then involve Burisma which had been under some level of sustained or varied Ukraine and international investigation since 2010.

However, the element of intent is irrelevant for impeachment; the criminal trial would consider it and a guilty verdict carries results in a maximum of 5-years' imprisonment and a fine of $100,000. That $100,000 is comical because it is what Hunter Biden was being paid by MBNA, in 2005, when his father was pushing legislation to prevent them from losing money as they forced their cardholder into bankruptcy – a Senate role earning Joe Biden the title, "The Senator from MBNA." It also establishes a pattern where the political actions of the father enrich the son.

Having voted on and passed two Articles of Impeachment on 12/18/19, and then adjourned for the Holidays, when they return, the House could, on 7 January 2020, pass a resolution – referred to as a "Sense of the House" – stating they are aware of the employment history for Hunter Biden and it does not introduce and conflicts with the offices held by his father. This would eliminate Hunter from any impeachment discussions relevant to the 2018 boastful confession.

Let's forget Hunter and just look at what Biden said he had the "authority". We presented part of the quote on page 154, here's a bit more:

> *"So they said they had—they were walking out to a press conference. I said, Nah, I'm not going to—or, we're not going to give you the billion dollars. They said you have no authority. You're not the president. The president said—I said, call him.*
>
> *(Laughter)*
>
> *"I said I'm telling you, you're not getting the billion dollars. I said, you're not getting the billion."*

Biden is declaring he, apparently with the backing of Obama, would terminate the billion dollars. However, neither he nor Obama had the authority to do that – it was a violation of *The Impoundment Control Act of 1974.*

On the other hand, memos show, 91 minutes after his Ukraine call Trump authorized a delay (not cancellation) of aid funds. What we saw Biden threaten to do was blatantly illegal, but what Trump did was, under the same law, perfectly legal. If Trump intended not to pay the appropriated funds, he would have had to notify Congress and ask for their approval. However, under the law, Trump could delay funds for "*45 Session Days*," unless the appropriation was to expire within that period, in that case, unless Congress authorized otherwise, release of the funds is mandatory.

What this means is that Biden either knowingly lied or boasted of violating the 1974 law; it also means our trio – Pelosi, Nadler, Schiff – knowingly misrepresented facts to the American people when they complained about Trump withholding funds. The 1974 Law explicitly authorizes the executive branch to withhold appropriated funds for up to nine calendar weeks.

A Trump-era legal opinion from the Government Accountability Office in 2018 holds that if the President proposes a rescission, he or she must make the affected funds available to be prudently obligated before the funds expire, even if the 45-day clock is still running. Thus, Trump obtained the appropriate legal opinion before taking action. Trump is scrupulous in his obedience to the law, something which we can assert cannot be said of Joseph Biden, based on the following:

In terms of the various laws, which do not warrant the intense space need to properly discuss their applicability at this time, readers are invited to review:

Hobbs Act Extortion and Robbery (18 U.S.C. § 1951)

18 U.S. Code CHAPTER 41—EXTORTION AND THREATS

§ 871 through § 880 inclusive and selectively identify applicable sections their current knowledge would indicate could apply to an impeachment hearing. 18 U.S. Code § 878. Threats and extortion against foreign officials, official guests, or internationally protected persons. Article § 880, Receiving the proceeds of extortion, could be seen as representing the salary Hunter received or proceeds derived through later payments to corporations in which he had an ownership or partnership interest.

Readers might also want to consider the issue connected with the assertion of 14,000 Ukraine deaths and the number of deaths that would have occurred if the Billi9on in loan guarantees had been canceled – as Joe Biden explicitly stated he had threatened. This would, for impeachment, relate to 18 U.S. Code § 1116 - Manslaughter of foreign officials, and specifically (4)(B) *"any other representative, officer, employee, or agent of the United States Government, a foreign government, or international organization who at the time and place concerned is entitled pursuant to international law to special protection against attack upon his person, freedom, or dignity, and any member of his family then forming part of his household."*

The impeachment vote of 18 December revealed only three wise Democrats – two voted *Nay* with one candidate Tulsi Gabbard, voting *Present.* As she explained it:

*"My 'present' vote was an active protest against the zero-sum game the two opposing political sides have trapped America in. My vote and campaign is about freeing our country from this damaging mindset so we can work side-by-side to usher in a*

*bright future for all #StandWithTulsi"*

She also tweeted a play on Abraham Lincoln's famous quote:

*"A house divided cannot stand.  And today we are divided. Fragmentation and polarity are ripping our country apart. Today, I come before you to make a stand for the center, to appeal to all of you to bridge our differences and stand up for the American people. #StandWithTulsi"*

She also set forth her promise to the nation, one which the Swamp Denizens will prevent her from acting upon until she takes office in 2025 and/or 2029:

*"As president, I'll invest the trillions wasted on regime change wars, new cold war and nuclear arms race into winning the 'wars' at home — fighting for quality affordable healthcare, environmental protection, and increasing the quality of life for all Americans. #StandWithTulsi"*

For now, the Swamp Denizens will block a nomination of Tulsi Gabbard, though they would be wise to offer her the position as Vice President on the 2020 ticket.

As we know, Hillary Clinton has worked to undermine Tulsi's campaign to remove the only militarily experienced rational individual from the nomination process.

At the same time, the impeachment process has been an effort to protect and promote Joe Biden – this is consistent with the fact that, after successfully getting the partisan vote on the Articles, House Speaker Nancy Pelosi proved unwilling to confirm if or when the approved articles would be transferred to the Senate – saying: *"We'll make a decision... as we go along.  We'll see what the process will be on the Senate side."*  A position indicating she needed assurance that there will be a Kangaroo Court – one devoid of facts and reality.

Or, as Trump Tweeted, *"Nancy Pelosi is looking for a Quid Pro Quo with the Senate.  Why aren't we Impeaching her?"*

For Senate Majority Leader Mitch McConnell, the view was a bit different.  McConnell does not believe it is the job of the Senate to find evidence the House Hearings showed did not exist and/or failed to present.  His view was basic:

*"We have this fascinating situation where, following House Democrats' rush to impeachment, following weeks of pronouncements about the urgency of this situation, the*

*prosecutors have now developed cold feet. We'll continue to see how this develops, and whether the House Democrats ever work up the courage to take their accusations to trial.*

*I continue to believe that the unanimous bipartisan precedent that was good enough for President Clinton ought to be good enough for this president, too. Fair is fair."*

Comically, the basis or focus of the House vote, Joe Biden, the man they are defending and consider a viable opponent to Trump has, in the 12/19 debate, stated without hesitation that he would put an immediate end to a hundred thousand jobs rather than allow them to naturally phase out the way Trump is doing with the coal industry.

Thus we have an economic boast and assertion by Biden if he were President he promises to crash the economy and place hundreds of thousands on unemployment and welfare – an action that instigates a GREAT DEPRESSION.

Biden has already indicated he wants to destroy local economies by saying he would allow two million illiterate migrants into the nation every year – so the welfare roles would swell and, since 60% of them are children, communities would be burdened with $27 Billion a year in education costs to be supported by increased property taxes.

What the world has witnessed is the House – the California and New York City elitist delegation who loved Hillary Clinton – engaging in a Machiavellian impeachment.

It would be funny to see Pelosi, Schiff, Nadler, and other swamp denizens supporting Biden as impeachment moves forward. There is only a limited period in which American voters will marvel at magical threads and praise THE EMPEROR'S NEW CLOTHES.

There is a point in time when even the most dim-witted of them must choose between a President who has overseen what has become the longest economic expansion if American history and a candidate whose every proposal is designed to crash the economy and expand welfare.

However, we are seeing from the unjustified mindless hate and defense of those, like Biden, who blatantly flaunt their violations of Federal Laws in the name of "Policy", that there are lessons for America to learn – lessons which prevent those advocating policies which Bernie Sanders would approve – one is: *"Never look down on someone...unless you are helping them up."* If we look at the deeds and not the words, we see that Donald John Trump helps people up.

A FAIR and impartial jury would dismiss the impeachment of Trump immediately — allowing the Democrats a shot at winning the White House.  Pelosi fair means ensuring a loss in November 2020, but a win for California & NYC (which both realize the greatest gains from tax cuts).  On the other hand, Republican control of Congress and the Oval Office helps the NYC & California elite...and Pelosi retires laughing at the wealth she keeps in her pocket...while frustrating the efforts of Elizabeth Warren and Bernie Sanders Progressives.

There is also the issue of the "stolen election" that has caused many to denounce the Electoral College system which gave us Bush43 and Donald Trump – as well as multiple other Presidents.

As shown here, the non-California vote totals show the popular vote, on a national basis, went to Trump:

TRUMP

| | |
|---|---|
| National Vote: | 62,984,828 |
| California Vote: | 4,483,810 |
| **Net Real National Vote:** | **58,501,018** |
| New York Vote | 2,819,534 |
| **Net Real National Vote:** | **55,681,484** |

CLINTON

| | |
|---|---|
| National Vote: | 65,853,514 |
| California Vote: | 8,753,788 |
| **Net Real National Vote:** | **57,099,726 {-1,401,292}** |
| New York Vote: | 4,556,124 |
| **Net Real National Vote:** | **47,987,478 {-7,694,006}** |

Removing New York and California – those pushing the lies associated with the impeachment – Trump had received **7,694,006 more votes** than Clinton.  That means, outside of the two states pushing impeachment, trump received 16% more votes than Clinton. In propaganda terms, 20 percent of the nation's newsroom employees live in these same two states plus Washington DC which has three Electoral College votes and, therefore, is only significant as a tie-breaker.

Consider, the last time New York voted Republican was Ronald Reagan in 1984. And, its 29 electoral votes are the third-largest in the nation and tied it with Florida.  Barack Obama won New York in 2012 by 28.1 percentage points and Florida by 0.9% points; Trump took Florida by 1.2% points.

Factually, across the nation, Trump won the National Vote.

Exclude California's 55 Electoral College votes and Trump won by 304:172 – delete New York and the ratio is 304:143, which is better than 2:1, and means that the race wasn't even close.

Now, we note those who are taking the lead on attacking Trump, with Adam Schiff lying about the facts;  Schiff is a native New Yorker who represents California; Nancy Pelosi is a native of Maryland who represents California; Chuck Schumer and Jerry Nadler are from and represent New York.

Thus, two states, interconnected through their representatives, seem to be behind an attempt to overthrow the 2016 election.  These states are pushing to admit millions of migrants – who would settle in those states – actually creating a form of legal gerrymandering aimed at replacing "trees" with non-citizen human bodies with a minority identification. Apart from gaining representation based on the census, they would acquire millions of dollars in Federal Public Assistance or funds in the form of SNAP, LIHEAP, and benefits that would build their foundational economy and lower the tax burden on Hollywood or Silicon Valley elite in California and related elite in NYC.

Native New Yorker Alexandria Ocasio-Cortez, who invokes race as part of her anti-democracy argument, said: "*Due to severe racial disparities in certain states, the Electoral College effectively weighs white voters over voters of color, as opposed to a 'one person, one vote' system where all our votes are counted equally.*"

AOC called the Electoral Collage a "*scam,*" but if it is a "*scam,*" than the Senate is clearly a massive ongoing one.  For a state like New York, "*voters of color*" are more fractional than slaves prior to the 1870 Constitutional Amendment which made them into citizens and whole citizens in the census.

Naturally, if the "'*one person, one vote' system*" were to be implemented, it means the elimination of the Senate and the basis for all "*checks and balances.*"

Think about "*one person one vote*" applied to the Senate. AOC endorsed Senator Bernie Sanders, who represents Vermont (Population: 627,180), its neighbor,  New Hampshire (Population:

1,356,458) has twice the population, meaning they enjoy half the Senate representation; California (Population 39,536,653) renders Sanders voters 63 times as powerful as either Dianne Feinstein or Kamala Harris. But, Wyoming (Population 577,737) Republicans Mike Enzi and John Barrasso are more powerful than Sanders.

Where are the minority voters AOC is so concerned about? Are they in New Mexico (Population 2,095,000) – maybe she was thinking of Colorado (Population 5,696,000)?

In a speech given on 23 October, Trump told his audience: *"And we're building a wall on the border of New Mexico and we're building a wall in Colorado, we're building a beautiful wall, a big one that really works that you can't get over, you can't get under and we're building a wall in Texas. We're not building a wall in Kansas but they get the benefit of the walls we just mentioned."*

Of course, the mention of landlocked Colorado resulted in a range of twitter attacks on Trump's apparent lack of geographic knowledge. But, in terms AOC might understand, 9.8 percent of Colorado residents are foreign-born; of those, about 40.8 percent are from Mexico and 12.3 percent are from other Latin American regions.

It would seem that the state is seeking to gain sanctuary status; in an effort to do so, it passed *Protect Colorado Residents From Federal Government Overreach act* HB19-1124 – were it to accept the 2 million migrants Biden asserted America could accept annually, within 3-years its population would double without adding a single voter. It should then be entitled to more than the current seven Congressional Representatives – and it would gain billions in Federal public assistance money.

In terms of foreign-born populations, California (27.0%) and New York (22.6%) have the most, and would likely attract more. But California has a homeless problem that is being complicated by the wildfires associated with Climate Change.

National Guard Major, Democratic member of Congress and Presidential candidate, Tulsi Gabbard has said:

*"Americans are sick of hearing from politicians that we can't afford clean water, upgraded infrastructure, healthcare, education, etc. I'm running for president to end regime change wars/the new cold war/arms race and redirect our country's resources to caring for our people."*

Have we seen anything from Pelosi, Nadler, or Schiff which indicates they care for people?  Does Biden wanting to terminate the livelihood of a hundred Thousand Americans show he cares for them?

Impeachment and using illegal migrants to gerrymander districts is far more fun than being concerned about the health and welfare of American Citizens.

Had Trump made a clear link between appropriated funds and the "favor," there might have been grounds for asserting bribery, As we saw with Biden's confession, the link was clear and carried with it a time-clock for performance.

With Trump, Ukrainian officials were unaware the money had been appropriated and made available for release.  Other funds were flowing freely – including funds designated for the investigations at the heart of the "favor."

Accordingly, Trump was, as stated in the transcript, had only asked that any findings which cited the name Biden be directed to the Attorney General, the reason for that request was Biden's confession of a High Crime or, as phrased by Adam Schiff, an illegal *quid pro quo* that constituted a crime under a statuary definitions of extortion, bribery, or coercion of foreign officials.

Because American taxpayers are funding Ukraine corruption investigations, and because Biden's brag conformed to the statuary crime of extortion, Trump was simply asking for the background information on a freely confessed crime.  Therefore Congress – the Democrats supporting the Biden candidacy – had, on 18 December 2019 voted to impeach a President for enforcing the law and seeking documents American taxpayers had paid to have generated.

Normally an election can be reduced to party bias versus choice between the lesser of two evils.  In November 2020, voters will get to express their opinion with regard to a corrupt Congress attacking a President who enforces the law.  They might even get the opportunity to vote in support of a candidate who brags about violating Federal Law.

Only three Democrats – Minnesota Rep. Collin C. Peterson, New Jersey Rep. Jeff Van Drew, and Presidential Candidate Hawaii Rep. Tulsi Gabbard, stood up for the nation and Federal law; Gabbard later stating: *"Fragmentation and polarity are ripping our country apart.  My vote today is a vote for much-needed reconciliation and hope that together we can heal our country."*

Maine Rep. Jared Golden split his vote based on the idea that Trump might have abused his Presidential power – qualifying that vote by saying: *"But while the president's resistance toward our investigative efforts has been frustrating, it has not yet, in my view, reached the threshold of 'high crime or misdemeanor' that the Constitution demands."*

Jared won his seat in 2018 through the use of ranked-choice voting and because his incumbent opponent proved to be sufficiently incompetent to be a "lesser of evils" election in a Republican district.

In asking for "a favor" on behalf of the Citizens of the United States, as opposed to initiating a formal investigation based on the freely given confession of guilt by Joseph Biden, Trump made the decision to obtain the facts quietly and thus avoid embarrassing the implicated co-defendant, Barack Obama – who Biden said approved a violation of a criminal statute Obama had signed into law in 2012.

As was revealed during the hearings, Adam Schiff had caused the matter to become public by coaching the whistleblower and then promoting a created document as the basis for the impeachment they had been seeking to bring since 9 November 2016.

There is a reality, the actions of Biden cannot be escaped and they are being defended by Pelosi, Nadler, and Schiff – along with multiple others who have no regard for the Rule of Law.

Biden had, by implicating Obama – whose name Biden had forgotten in other contexts, to the point where he used "my boss" in references where Obama's name would have been more proper – Biden had asserted a Constitutional scholar and Harvard Law honors graduate had signed a law and then intentionally violated it several years later.  And had done so for the purpose of replacing an attorney with a corrupt politician who had just been released from prison.

If Biden continues to be the Democratic frontrunner, there is little doubt that, in November 2020, voters will get to chose between the man impeached for enforcing American law and one who boasted of violating it.

The alternatives are not that pleasant or easy to choose among. Bernie Sanders is intelligent and, for decades, has shown his strong desire to honor the moral obligation we have to each other and this planet which is our home.  For all her faults, his protegee, AOC shows the basic traits which will further the moral cause – though she does need an education on the Electoral College and its relationship to the

Senate, and through them, to the Balance of Powers necessary for a true Representative Democracy.

Unfortunately, Bernie is old, is not a POTUS Cousin descended from the five sisters and has had a heart attack – which means voters would really be voting based upon his choice for Vice President.

Elizabeth Warren is an expert on Bankruptcy law. Both she and her current husband are POTUS Cousins – while little is known of him, it is even possible her first husband was also a POTUS Cousin. In the traditional world, this is very important and highly significant.

The mention of Bankruptcy law infers a knowledge of finance that has not yet been evident in her presentations, but could be of value in continuing what is now the longest economic expansion in American history – it has even broken the eleven-year recession cycle which has defined economic cycles since Charles Dow and statistician Edward Jones created the Dow Jones Industrial Average (DJIA) on 26 May 1896. If there is no American Recession before 2021, the Obama-Trump recovery and expansion will have made history.

In both game and economic theory, there is the mathematical representation of a situation where the gains and losses for the various participants exactly balance so that both sides actually gain – just in very different ways. For Trump, it was called *"The Art of the Deal"*, and he profited by having someone else write it.

The wealthy are being attacked, and, via Trump Impeachment have attacked back – then their Congress adjoined for the two weeks in which the nation celebrates Chanukah, Christmas, and the New Year.

There is an Ashkenazi Jewish tradition involving the giving of money, *gelt,* on Chanukah; this teaches the children about the mitzvah of "righteousness" and "uprightness" known as *tzedakah* – what non-Jews call charity."

For a Christian, this would be obedience to the law: *"Do not do to your neighbor what you would not have done to you,"* or the Golden Rule, *"Do unto others what you would have others do until you."* Biden's Ukraine extortion and regime change are America's way of declaring its desire to have a  foreign power change its government – meddle in its elections.

Having wealth can be self-serving, or the government can say it hates those with money. The founding fathers originally said that those with tangible property and wealth would pay the costs associated with the running of the government.  When America became "service-based," the basic idea that the landed gentry should support those that defend their wealth was amended to become the Income Tax.

We hear calls to provide free college educations.  The rich might avail themselves of it – and the selfish resent that – but for the rich, if their children have high enough SAT scores, they will happily pay the cost of Harvard, Yale, Princeton, or any other top-notch private school – and still not begrudge America's children educational opportunity to improve themselves and the nation through the publically financed system.  Don't the rich also send their children to public and private elementary schools?

For the rare person who understands the structure of the Bible and the Thirteen Tribes – twelve with land-based inheritance and the one responsible for the administration of the nation and territories – notice that the Merchant Tribe was charged with supporting the Scholars and their families.

To challenge free college is to further insult the Bible – a book which tells you to wash when dirty, to eat healthily, and gives us the moral code our culture and society is built upon.  Many today would be surprised at the number of "modern" ideas that are actually part of the 613 laws in the Hebrew doctrine which Christ and Peter advocated.  But, that link is lost because the medieval Christian Church opposed the Biblical laws.

Going into 2020, we need Free College Education available to all citizens; we need free medical care available to all citizens; we need to feed the poor and house the homeless; certainly, *tzedakah* infers we have the option of expanding these to all who are in the nation legally.

Climate Change is going to send millions of poor and homeless to our borders.  We have an obligation, consistent with *tzedakah*, to establish a means of processing them and granting them legal entry – we have no such obligation to those criminals who enter illegally.

As a nation of laws, we have dual rights one is to demand those laws be respected by foreigners; the other is to not structure those laws so as to harm those truly in need of immediate assistance.

We end here, going into Chanukah, Christmas, and a 2020 New Year when American choices will define America's future for the 21st century – or, maybe, just until 2050, when a Third of Life has died.

9 781672 476911